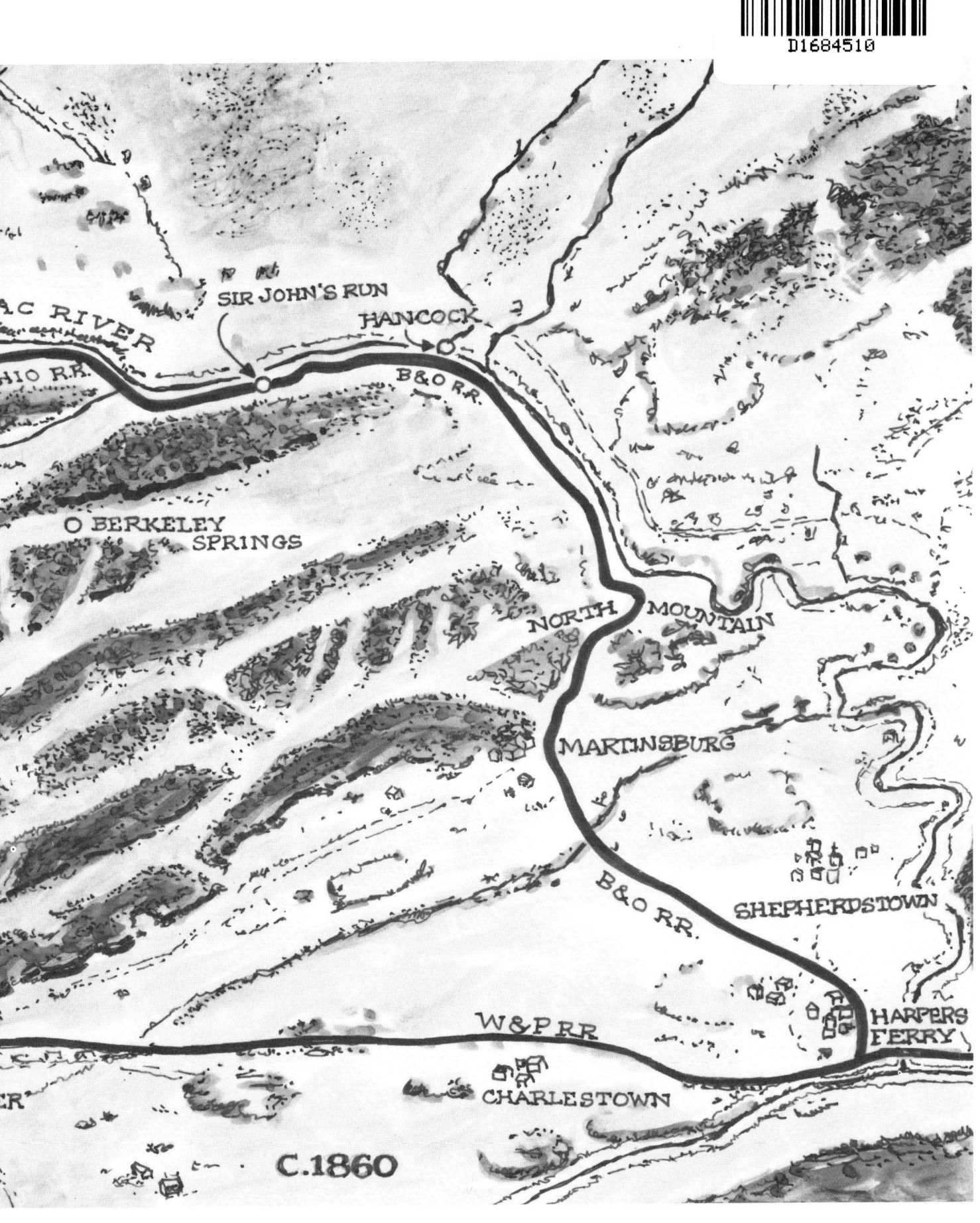

EAST END

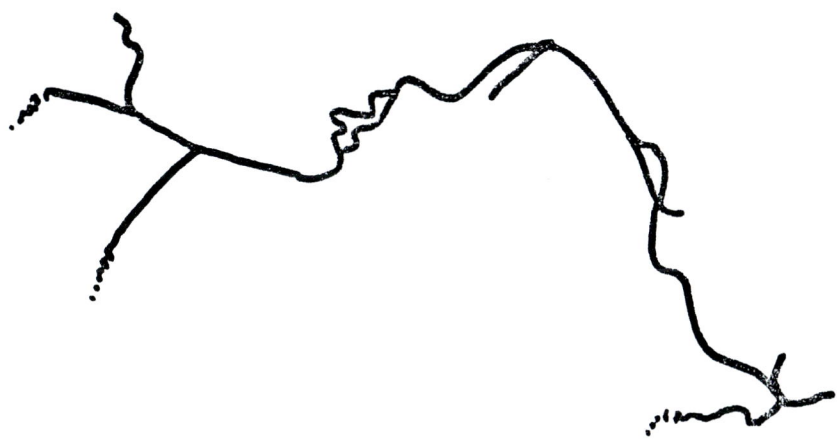

Harpers Ferry to Cumberland 1842-1992

by Jeffrey R. Hollis
and
Charles S. Roberts

COPYRIGHT © 1992 BARNARD, ROBERTS AND CO., INC.
Manufactured in the United States of America

FIRST EDITION October 1992

All Worldwide rights reserved. No part of this book may be reproduced in any manner without permission in writing, except in the case of critical reviews.

Published by
BARNARD, ROBERTS AND CO., INC.
305 Gun Road
P.O. Box 7344
Baltimore MD 21227
(410) 247-2242

Library of Congress Catalog Card No. 92-72990
ISBN 0-934118-19-1

FRONTISPIECE: Led by Alco FA 837, a westbounder crosses over at Orleans Road to take the Magnolia Cutoff to Cumberland in the early 1950s. The smoke from the lead unit hints that the Alcos were not one of B&O's best buys. *B&O Museum.*

COVER: Looking east from the distant signal at Sir Johns Run c. 1950, a set of FTs and a Big Six keep traffic moving on the East End. Almost certainly a posed publicity photograph, this view nonetheless accurately suggests that a lot of trains used this piece of railroad in a day.

CREDITS: Lack of credits indicate that the subject came from the cameras or collections of the authors. "B&OHS" acknowledges material from the archives and collections of The Baltimore and Ohio Railroad Historical Society, P.O. Box 13578, Baltimore MD 21203. Memberships in the Society are available at modest cost.

*This book is dedicated to the memory of
Miss Barbara Jean Hopkins, who graduated
from Frostburg State College in 1976 with a degree
in History and was the first woman engineer to
be killed in the Service of the Company at
Orleans Road on 12 February 1980.*

*She was at the throttle of a westbound
manifest train, where she was supposed to be,
doing what she was supposed to be doing, when the
accident occurred and she joined the lamentably
long Honor Roll of those who fell while
faithfully performing their duty.*

*But for this twist of fate,
she may well have been the
author of this book.*

ONE HUNDRED AND FIFTY YEARS

In the formative stages of development, book projects acquire code names that rarely survive to publication ... for example, *Impossible Challenge* was "Odyssey" and *West End* "Three Seasons." The code for *East End* was "East End" and the co-authors were in complete agreement at the beginning that this would *not* be the name of the book.

Fifty-two titles were considered and rejected before final selection was decided. A few finalists were *Neck of the Bottle* (which survived as a subhead), *Quart into Pint, Neck, Chokepoint, Throat, Artery, Flood, Funnel, Floodtide, Deluge, Lifeline* and *Link*. We will spare the reader our selections related to the digestive tract save for *Constipation*.

The discarded titles reflect the essence of this legendary stretch of railroad and the theme of the work ... the East End of the Cumberland Division became the focal point of the entire Baltimore and Ohio Railroad as it was deluged with floods of traffic, floods of water, floods of tears and floods of blood.

It was not until the second decade of this century that B&O finally managed to efficiently handle the traffic outpouring, almost three quarters of a century after the line was opened from Harpers Ferry to Cumberland in 1842. The other floods will be treated throughout the work, but at this point co-author Roberts would like to relate that the late Julian Barnard and he conducted a mini-debate some years ago about the impact of the Civil War on B&O's fortunes. Barney felt that the war was a decisive setback for B&O and Roberts felt that it was merely used an an excuse. Today, having just completed the Civil War chapter, Roberts concedes that Barney might have been right after all.

On one subject there can be no debate ... the railroad revolutionized America. A few simple numbers graphically illustrate the impact of the railroad on society. By 1853, it cost about fifteen dollars to move a ton of freight one mile on a turnpike ... on a railroad, between one and two dollars. While it cost less than fifty cents to do the same on a river or canal, waterways seldom flow where traffic flows and are rarely all-season arteries.

The East End is regarded as being the most scenic on B&O lines with some justice. Less remarked are the place names along this historic line of road. They range from the lyrical to the ludicrous and laughable ... Shenandoah, Skeetersville, Springhouse Curve, Old House Curve, Rattling Bridge, Dry Run Creek, Sleepy Creek, Grasshopper Hollow, Red Rock, Wet Rock, Pear Orchard Curve, Turkey Foot Curve, Doe Gully, Magnolia, Paw Paw, Long Girl Curve (B&O has at least another one of these on the Old Main Line near Baltimore), Brick House Curve and Mexico Farm.

Certainly the authors agree, and hope the readers will concur, that the best of all official B&O place names is just west of Paw Paw ... Old Bird Shit Hollow.

There is some limit to what can be wrong with a railroad with names like these.

Charles S. Roberts
20 July 1992

TABLE OF CONTENTS

1	Opening the Floodgates	8
	An Eastern Gold Rush	17
2	Harpers Ferry	19
	Winchester and Potomac	35
3	Into the Valley	41
4	Martinsburg	54
	Cumbo	73
5	Back to the Potomac	78
	Cherry Run	82
6	The Funnel	92
7	The Magnolia Cutoff	109
8	Easy Passage	138
9	Cumberland	151
10	The Uncivil Civil War	175
	Employee Timetables	184
11	Color Pictorial	193
12	Operations	209
	Form 6	213
13	Reflections	218
	Bibliography	221
	Index	222

Chapter 1

Opening the Floodgates

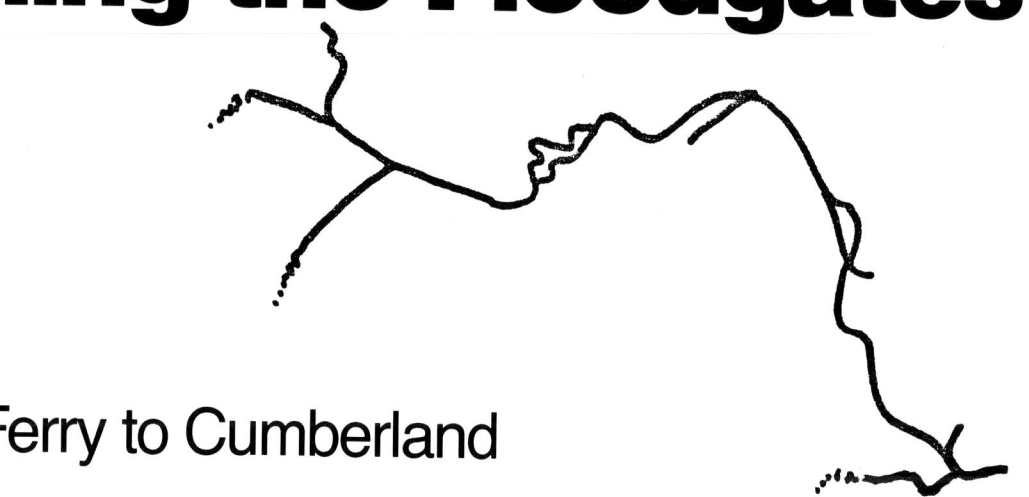

Harpers Ferry to Cumberland

The Baltimore and Ohio Rail Road Company reached the east bank of the Potomac River at Harpers Ferry, Virginia, on 1 December 1834 with a sigh of exhaustion, in a state of *de facto* insolvency and hundreds of miles from its goal of the Ohio River. Worse, the railroad from that point to Baltimore was "a wreck" and that was putting it kindly.

Thus the Mother of Railroads in the United States was seven years from conception and, in the event, eighteen years from delivery. The pregnancy was proving to be a very hard one, indeed.

The Mother in this analogy, of course, was in reality the seductive State of Maryland in league with the City of Baltimore and well aware that she was heavy with child and in bare feet. The Fathers . . . that intrepid band of gay cavaliers who first met at the home of George Brown in Baltimore on 12 February 1827 . . . were convinced that they had sired a monster and no doubt were thrashing about pointing fingers and drafting denials of paternity as men are wont to do after the rapture of creation has passed and the invoice for child support is presented for payment.

As most fathers do after contemplating the temptations of flight to foreign shores, B&O's band of brothers decided to brace themselves to their duty and soldier on.

The task was formidable. They had learned in seven tumultuous years that railroads were capital intensive *and* labor intensive *and* cyclical *and* subject to the laws of financial gravity when heavily leveraged. While it was also true that railroads were inherently very profitable, those profits had an inexorable tendency to disappear in the maelstrom of essential technological improvement, vast expenditures for new construction and interest on a mountain of debt.

And in 1834, the sources of vitally needed capital . . . to some extent, British investors . . . were awash in railroad securities, in the throes of financial panic and in no mood to spare a farthing to bail out a bunch of adventurers who had fathered children beyond their capacity to pay. In a version of "let them eat cake," the capitalists adopted an attitude of "let them eat their own children if they're so hungry."

How did B&O get into this predicament?

The story really begins in prehistory. As man's society evolved from subsistence in tiny enclaves, it became necessary to reach out into neighboring territories to acquire food for survival and raw materials to feed a slowly growing manufacturing base. Mother nature is perverse if nothing else and managed to distribute these essential resources in greatest abundance ever more distant from where man wanted to use them. Hence, systems of transportation had to be created.

The development of Maryland turned out to be quite typical. From the earliest days of coloniza-

OPENING THE FLOODGATES

tion, her bounty was exported by water. As the frontier moved ever westward, systems of land transportation became essential.

In 1704, the first "modern" highway act was passed. Roads were to be cleared and well grubbed, fitted for travel, twenty feet wide with good substantial bridges. Most of these remained local in character.

By 1770, twenty ferries had been established on the Potomac River from Maryland to Virginia. Inland trade was on the upswing. A road had been established from Baltimore to Frederick and agricultural lands began to pour their harvest eastward to port. Produce, wheat, and other grains were in demand for export and Maryland was proficient at supplying these items.

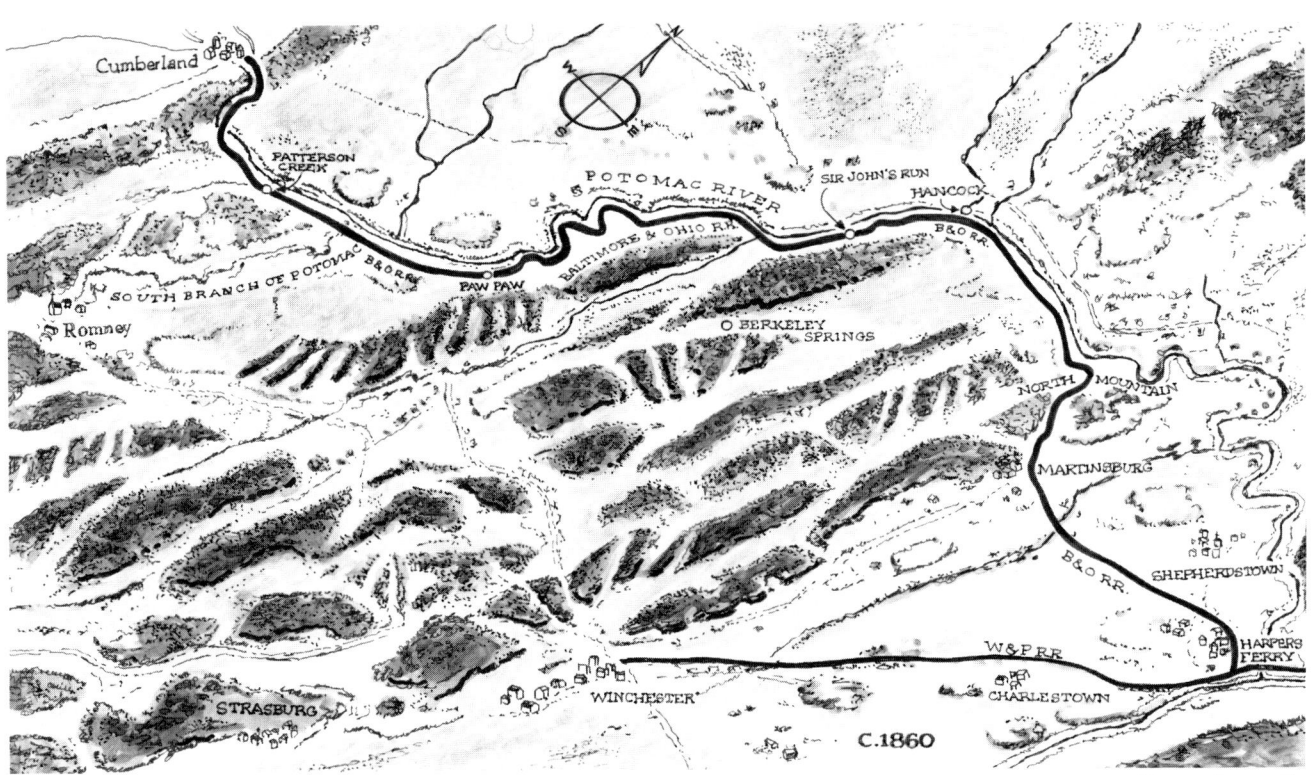

Warren Somerville

WHILE AN ARTISTIC impression rather than a precise map, this overview of the East End as built provides a splendid perception of the subdivision as a whole as well as the contiguous terrain. Climbing out of the Potomac River declension on a modest grade, the line enters the lovely Shenandoah Valley and crosses to Martinsburg. En route to that town, the mild Nine Mile Grade is topped. West of Martinsburg, B&O opted to cut through a gap in North Mountain rather than take the long way around, a decision sensible enough at the time but the source of future problems. West of North Mountain, the Potomac Valley is rejoined and the railroad clings to the south shore almost all the way to Cumberland. Again, the grades are gentle but the route serpentine ... particularly the famous "Loops of the Potomac" east of Paw Paw. The Winchester and Potomac Railroad leaves its connection with the B&O at Harpers Ferry and also crosses the lush Shenandoah Valley to Winchester. The whole area is fertile and rich in resources, providing B&O with profitable traffic to this day. The hints of future trouble are vague. River line railroads are very nice, but subject to floods and the Potomac River would prove to be a very bad actor in this regard. That the subdivision would also be subject to floods of eastbound traffic would turn those minor grades into major chokepoints. And that sylvan Shenandoah Valley would prove to be a major battlefield in the Civil War, with Union and Confederate forces sloshing back and forth up and down the valley and regarding the railroad as a major strategic target. For the convenience of the reader, this map is enlarged and reproduced as the front end paper ... other more detailed maps of the subdivision appear on the back end paper.

Baltimore had emerged as a substantial seaport city, vying with Philadelphia for second place behind New York City. It was the only Mid-Atlantic seaport not effectively blockaded by the British during the Revolution and profited immensely from war trade and traffic with Central and South America.

After the Revolution, Maryland held out that the "Old Northwest," which was to become Ohio, Indiana, and Illinois, should be placed in the hands of the young national government which would hold it until three or four states could be formed. This position was taken to prevent a dispute between Virginia, Pennsylvania and Maryland as to which one would be fortunate enough to obtain this land for its own settlement. Maryland declined to sign the Articles of Confederation until this issue was settled and in 1781 the others acquiesced.

In 1787 an ordinance was passed obligating the Federal Government to build a road across the mountains to the new territory, this at the insistence of Virginia. Ironically, the path chosen ran through Maryland. This road became part of the National Road, later US Route 40. The road followed part of the old Nemacolin Indian Path, which had been widened into a crude military road during the French and Indian War.

In 1802 Congress began appropriating money for the National Road, to start at Cumberland and run to "somewhere in Ohio." Selecting Cumberland as the eastern terminal was a wise move on the part of Congress as it avoided the feud which would have surely erupted between Baltimore and Philadelphia had either one or the other been selected. Also, the farther west the road started, the less money the Federal Government had to cough up.

Having promised to build a privately financed turnpike to Cumberland, and, already having a good road system partially in place, Maryland was elated that Baltimore would be assured a leading East Coast position of economic power.

Construction began in 1811 and was completed to Wheeling in 1818. Western produce immediately flooded eastward toward Baltimore. In 1838, the National Road reached Vandalia, Illinois.

During the construction west of Cumberland, a private turnpike was constructed from Baltimore to Boonsboro near Hagerstown, leaving a gap from there to Cumberland. As time wore on, it was apparent that no one was going to step forward and build the missing link, so Maryland created a powerful club.

It seems that Maryland's banks were regulated and that their charters were all up for renewal in 1816. Maryland was quick to spread the word: ante up toward the worthy cause of building a turnpike from Hagerstown to Cumberland or risk your charter being allowed to expire! Banks contributing to this extortionary tactic would be graced with their charters being renewed until 1835. Direct, effective, and probably unconstitutional, the ultimatum resulted in the highways being surveyed in 1815 and completed in 1821 at a cost of $500,000. With a little more coercion, the banks who contributed to the final segment, Boonsboro to Hagerstown, had their charters renewed until 1845. By 1824 this had also been accomplished and the road was the first in the country to have used Scotsman John McAdam's revolutionary new paving system.

The banks earned 20% on their investment for several decades, and when earnings plummeted to 3% in 1870 and major repairs were needed, the banks abandoned the road and folded the road company. By that time, charters did not need renewal and the railroad was king.

In its heyday, the road was traversed by coaches with eight to ten passengers and boasted inns every twenty miles or so. A trip from Baltimore to Wheeling was accomplished in a few days. An 1827 traveler noted passing 235 wagons in 35 miles, generally large and heavily loaded. In the early days, it was not uncommon to wait five days for a vacancy on a stagecoach.

With roads established, the nation became enamoured with the canal, and indeed it paid off for New York City, which forged ahead in trade with completion of the Erie Canal in 1825. Maryland was quick to come to the aid of the old Potomac Canal, later the Chesapeake and Ohio Canal, from Georgetown in Washington D.C. with grandiose plans of reaching Pittsburg. Baltimore soon saw that it stood to gain little from a canal to which it would have to build an access branch "somewhere west of Frederick." Without such a connector, freight would flow from Western Maryland to Georgetown, making Washington a rival port! Realizing that the expenditure for the enterprise would not be worth the minimal gain, Baltimore knew it had to come up with a new idea.

That new idea, of course, was the Baltimore and Ohio Rail Road Company.

Pioneering the nation's railroad history, the B&O was chartered on 27 February 1827.

Railways or tramways had existed in England since the 1600s. The steam locomotive was just being perfected. America, for example, had a tramway in 1826, near Boston, to carry granite a few miles. As perhaps the first garden railroader, John Stevens of New Jersey had been advocating railroads since 1812 and had built one in his own backyard. New York had approved the charter of a railway line between Albany and Schenectady two months before the B&O charter, but it was not built until later and then only as a shortline as an attempt at competition with the Erie Canal.

American transportation was on the eve of changing the nation forever. A farmer in Wheeling who had received one dollar for his flour which sold on the Baltimore docks for five dollars, four of which were cost of transport over the National Road, would soon receive four dollars, the B&O's share being one dollar!

From its inception, the goal of the B&O was the Ohio River at Wheeling by way of Pittsburg. But the mid-1830s money crunch caused B&O more than financial heartburn.

During the pause at Harpers Ferry, the B&O charter in Virginia had expired. Construction west of Harpers Ferry was blocked until the charter could be renewed and the political landscape had changed.

Virginia, wanting the benefits of the B&O, reissued the charter with the stipulation that the B&O must remain in Virginia from Harpers Ferry to a point within five miles of Cumberland.

In considering routing of the line west of Harpers Ferry, numerous routes were studied, some of which excluded Virginia. When the final die was cast, and the prospect of battling the C&O Canal for every inch of Maryland shoreline was contemplated, Virginia won, and the B&O proceeded westward.

To review the surveys considered for the B&O's routing, one could surmise that the railroad chose the present path almost as a last resort.

Surveys made in the spring of 1836 considered Harpers Ferry to the North Mountain barrier on the Maryland shore of the Potomac, then on to Cumberland in the same fashion. In August of 1836, the survey from Harpers Ferry to North Mountain was complete and the North Mountain-Cumberland segment was compiled by July 1837. A means of avoiding further conflict with the C&O Canal was considered by building the line from Weverton, just east of Harpers Ferry, through Pleasant Valley to Boonsboro and Hagerstown.

To further confuse the issue, a route from Harpers Ferry westward on the Maryland side of the Potomac to Antietam Creek was explored, as was using Little Catoctin Creek through Middletown Valley and across South Mountain by a tunnel to Boonsboro, then to Hagerstown. Routes involving the mouth of Antietam Creek included an aqueduct to avoid the canal. The Pleasant Valley grade was 1.0%.

From the narrows at North Mountain to three miles above Hancock, the route was favorable in Maryland with no canal conflict and this segment led planners to raise the question, "Why cross the river to avoid the canal?"

West of Hancock to the mouth of Fifteen Mile Creek, the C&O Canal again would cause trouble as there were narrows in the river valley between these points. The only solutions were to avoid the canal by two or more river crossings. Thought was also given to the valleys drained by Fifteen Mile and Town Creeks.

From Old Town to Cumberland, the railroad had a choice of either side of the river alternatively . . . until Virginia's ultimatum was made.

During the ensuing time, the Virginia surveys were held up by illness and no real progress was made until April 1837. The first Virginia route surveyed was begun at Harpers Ferry and followed the river until Antietam Creek where it crossed the river and joined the earlier Maryland surveys. Close on the heels of this survey was one which proceeded westbound from Harpers Ferry to Elk Run, Tuscarora, and Tulisses Branch Creeks, passing near Martinsburg and reentering the Potomac River Valley at North Mountain narrows.

It is likely that the most desirable Virginia route was one of utilizing the tracks of the Winchester and Potomac to Halltown where the B&O could then build west to Elk Run and rejoin the aforementioned survey to Martinsburg. This is well borne out by the alignment of the original Harpers Ferry bridge, which was built at an angle aimed directly at the W&P. Not only did the B&O see the easier way west, but also envisioned the W&P as a future deep south route.

EAST END

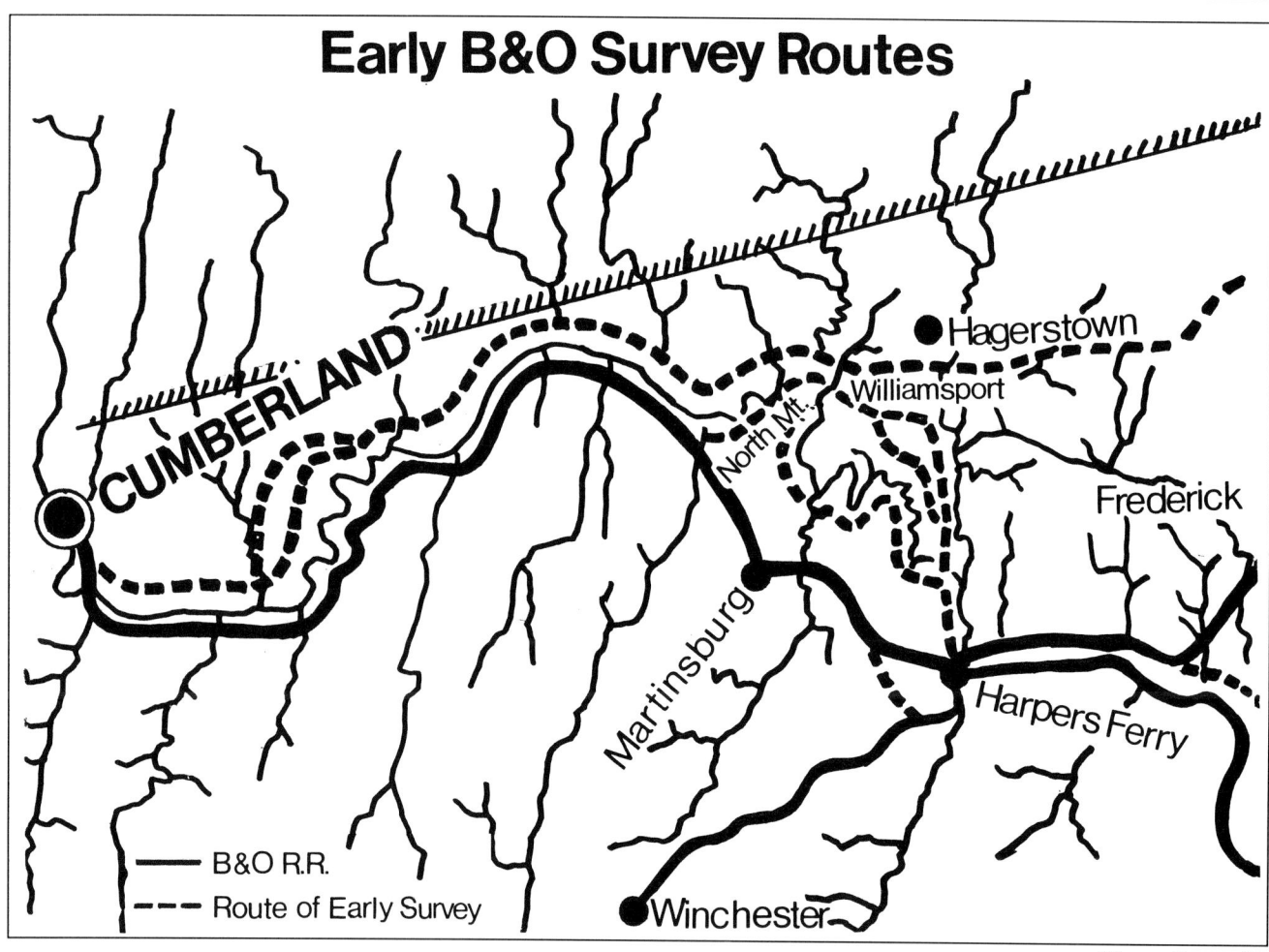

Early B&O Survey Routes

— B&O R.R.
--- Route of Early Survey

Warren Somerville

COMMENTATORS AND HISTORIANS, particularly in recent years, have eviscerated B&O management for all their mistakes and miscues in the early days. Whatever the merits of such arguments, B&O cannot be accused of sparing efforts in surveying possible routes to the Ohio. This map, taken from a rendering done circa 1914, shows all the routes considered before the final decision was taken for the building of the East End. Each route was exhaustively surveyed and analyzed in minute detail and voluminous reports. The desire to bleed traffic from the turnpikes extending east from the National Road, the necessity of dodging around the C&O Canal, the prospects of on-line traffic potential, grades, curves, length, terrain and engineering problems were all weighed in a manner that would please a modern MBA. As all too often in B&O history, politics determined the final route as detailed in this chapter. Yet it appears now as well as at the time, the route of the East End was a wise as well as forced selection and the problems that would develop operationally on the East End would have been even worse on the other routes considered. Of course, we are showing only the East End alternatives ... the entire rendering details all the various routes considered from Baltimore to Wheeling and the reader can be assured that no plausible route was ignored. Early planning may have produced a feeding ground for surveyors, but the thoroughness of B&O management's search for alternatives cannot be faulted.

With the July 1837 lapse of the Virginia charter and its five-year amended extension in 1838, the choice was clear. Virginia had played its hand well. The final route avoided complications with the C&O Canal and B&O had to come to terms with Virginia so it could reach the Ohio River through the western reaches of that state.

B&O had bridged the Potomac at Harpers Ferry by the Fall of 1836 and met the W&P straight on. For some obscure reason, the W&P refused to allow B&O to use its line to Halltown ... B&O had no alternative but to negotiate with the Federal government to use the land of the United States Arsenal. Even there, land space was at a premium and B&O had to build its bridge practically hanging over the river and with a very sharp curve.

That the B&O east of Harpers Ferry was in deplorable condition was caused by many factors, not the least of which was the necessity to evolve wholly new technological answers to a vast array of problems. To an astonishing degree, the B&O guessed right on a lot of issues . . . when they were wrong, however, there was nothing for it but to rebuild or replace. For example, iron straps on solid "ties" sounded good in theory but were bad in practice.

Perhaps B&O's largest initial error was to look to the world's first true railroad, the Stockton and Darlington in Great Britain, for guidance. The British opted to build a super railroad from the beginning and poured resources into the infrastructure, as it would be called today. The B&O emulated this approach from Baltimore to Harpers Ferry, investing mounds of money and, worse, months and years of *time*. No revenues are coming in from a railroad that is not finished and the longer it takes to finish it, the longer the wait for income.

Now poised for a lunge to Cumberland, B&O faced reality. No more "stone railroad." B&O did not have the money *or* the time. *Quick and cheap* was the only way to go. Later, when money was flowing in rather than out, the line could be improved and expanded. To some extent, this method was trading a long term disadvantage for a short range advantage, a philosophy disdained by most students of business and history. B&O's new approach was more primitive . . . "one way we *know* we are going to die—the other way we have a *chance*."

And the building of the East End, with as much liberality as a latterday observer can muster, was slapdash.

Wooden bridges and wooden ties . . . forget stone. No nicely seasoned wood, either . . . cut wood nearby and use it green. Use iron U rail . . . the cheapest available. Never mind lining tunnels . . . we'll get to that later. Stations and depots? Grab the cheapest wood available and cobble up a shed. Wherever possible, go around rather than through.

And *hurry*! Don't do it tomorrow . . . do it yesterday. Money for contractors? Promise them anything, but give them scrip. Virginia wants us to stay in Virginia? How much money are they going to kick in? Sheriff at the door? The check is in the mail. Need cars and power? Run them twice as fast and that will double the supply. Maryland out of money? Print wallpaper.

If necessity is the mother of invention, then desperation is the spur to achievement. It worked. Not well, but it worked. It took B&O seven years and a king's ransom to go 81 miles from Baltimore to Harpers Ferry. It took three years and $3,623,606 to span the 97 miles from Harpers Ferry to Cumberland. Martinsburg was reached in May of 1842 and Hancock in June of that year . . . Cumberland was attained in November 1842.

The siting of the railroad was really rather good, as B&O had learned that cheating on this aspect of construction was false economy. In the Annual Report for 1841, it was reported that no grade on the first 30 miles exceeded .7% and on the last 67 miles .5%. Most curves were little less than a mile in radius . . . a few one thousand or so feet, but on light grades. Only three tunnels were needed and two of those were short . . . one 90 foot long bore near Harpers Ferry, another 250 feet long at Paw Paw. A 1200 foot tunnel at Doe Gully was the longest and while it would prove to be a source of trouble in the future, it got the job done for many years.

Passing sidings were approximately one-quarter mile long and spaced every seven or eight miles with a water station at each.

The rise westward was mellow and generally did not face eastbound tonnage. From 287 feet above sea level at Harpers Ferry to 463 feet at Martinsburg, 540 feet at North Mountain and only 648 feet at Cumberland and stretched over almost one hundred miles, the grades were modest. The dip from North Mountain to Cherry Run was only 136 feet. The total climb from Harpers Ferry to Cumberland was only 361 feet. Although this was not a constant gradual grade, the whole line was a cakewalk compared to what B&O would face when the mountains had to be crossed west of Cumberland . . . or, for that matter, had already faced crossing Parr's Ridge east of Harpers Ferry.

The miracle of railroad transportation became evident when traffic began to flow. Freight between Baltimore and Cumberland took only fifteen hours . . . passengers but ten. On the turnpikes time was measured in days. And it was cheap . . . by rail tariffs were measured in pennies, by turnpike in dollars. And even at those rates, B&O made money. The Annual Report for 1846 showed a gross profit on revenues of 48% . . . that is to say, after the transportation cost of carrying the freight and passengers was deducted, B&O was keeping almost half of revenues. This relationship was not unique to B&O. In the early years, almost

EAST END

all railroads were enjoying lush profits of this magnitude and it is the basic reason why capital, ever greedy, poured into railroad securities. This was as close as one could come to counterfeiting without risking a jail sentence. The intermittent financial panics were really fits of fear on the part of investors suddenly having nightmares that it was all too good to be true.

Of course, over time it *was* too good to be true . . . competition and rate wars reduced those gross profits to the point that today a railroad earning twenty cents on the dollar is regarded as being very well managed, lucky, or both.

Another aspect of railroad operations became apparent when the East End was built and that was "divisionalization," for want of a better word. The railroad was getting too long to base operations just in Baltimore, so it was necessary to create a new maintenance and crew facility . . . in this case, Martinsburg was chosen.

Of course, there is no free lunch. Quickee construction means quickee maintenance problems. Seasoned ties might last six to eight years, but green ones only three or so. The longer term solution to the tie problem was treatment and, as will be seen, B&O built a tie plant at Green Spring for just that purpose.

By 1847, B&O noted that the "considerable multiplication of wooden bridges" were decaying, a process worsened by ever increasing weight of power and trains. Covering them for protection from the weather helped a little, but increased the fire hazard. And those green wood depots were falling apart.

But at least B&O had some money coming in to finance what turned out to be an ever increasing problem of maintenance, improvement and expansion. The stone railroad approach did not work . . . the speedy method did. It is significant to note that when B&O made its final lunge to Wheeling from Cumberland the rush-rush method was used with only a few refinements. So the departure from Harpers Ferry proved to be the end of one era and the beginning of another. B&O saved the baby.

However, fertile B&O was soon blessed with another pregnancy. By the mid-1840s, after B&O had reached Cumberland and was poised for a leap to Pittsburg, Pennsylvania had become a "railroad fever" state.

B&O's northern neighbor had managed to divide itself into two rival regions . . . the eastern, or Philadelphia, faction wanting all western trade to flow to that city and the western, or Pittsburg, faction convinced that their interests would best be served by allying itself with the B&O and not caring whether Philadelphia lived or died.

B&O's original Pennsylvania charter, while extended once, had expired and was up for renewal. The fight in the state capital of Harrisburg was ferocious and the final vote a near-run thing, but the upshot was that the B&O and their western friends lost. The Pennsylvania Railroad was chartered 13 April 1846 and would soon become B&O's most deadly enemy . . . for starters, B&O could not touch Pennsylvania in their quest for the Ohio.

In the end, of course, B&O reached Wheeling on New Year's Day 1853 by building the fabled West End. They still longed for Pittsburg and, after a long and tangled battle, managed to reach that city in 1871, breaching PRR's wall. And B&O also built a more direct line to the lower midwest by way of Grafton to Parkersburg in 1857.

With the opening of so many lines and the growth in overall traffic spurred by the availability of cheap, swift transportation, an avalanche of tonnage descended upon Cumberland from several directions and had to be squeezed through the East End, which rapidly became B&O's "Neck of the Bottle."

And then there was coal.

The children in the streets knew there was a lot of coal west of Cumberland. As odd as it seems today, B&O was hesitant to tap this tonnage in the early years and with good reason.

By the early 1840s, coal was rapidly becoming the fuel of choice along the eastern seaboard. But anthracite was king. And almost all the deposits of this "hard" or "stone" coal were to be found in eastern Pennsylvania. Railroads like the Reading and a network of canals were inundating the market with this mineral . . . even B&O specified anthracite as the fuel to be used in early steam locomotives. The coal west of Cumberland was bituminous, or "soft." Could soft coal displace hard coal or even get a share of the market? Could B&O haul soft coal at a profit while keeping its rates low enough to make the final cost to the user competitive?

These were valid questions . . . as late as 1851 B&O was reporting to its stockholders that "Cumberland coal must be brought into competition with anthracite before any substantial increase in

OPENING THE FLOODGATES

consumption can be expected."

The answer, of course, was "yes" and by the late 1850s the flood of traffic descending upon the East End reached Biblical proportions. The flood of traffic was to become unrelenting and the East End became B&O's throat.

It should be noted that the ton miles pushed through the East End were higher than any other section of the B&O throughout its long independent history *and* the Chessie System era *and* the

COMMODITIES TRANSPORTED EASTWARDLY
on the Main Stem to Baltimore

ARTICLES TRANSPORTED	1832 Tons	1833 Tons	1834 Tons	1835 Tons	1836 Tons	1837 Tons	1838 Tons	1839 Tons	1840 Tons
FLOUR	136,936 bbls. 12,610	169,957 bbls. 16,390	182,211½ bbls. 17,630	268,162 bbls. 25,862	174,643 bbls. 16,845	113,870 bbls. 11,569	142,512½ bbls. 15,391	264,033½ bbls. 23,516	392,449½ bbls. 42,383
Tobacco	 174	631 hhds. 351	801 hhds. 312	2,309 hhds. 898	2,377 hhds. 913	2,328 hhds. 908	1,468 hhds. 624	861 hhds. 368	2,115 hhds. 900
Grain	353	280	523	1,500	2,348	1,848	11,106	1,263	2,004
Meal, etc.	512	1,056	741	2,463	2,349	2,660	1,920	1,429	2,373
Provisions	29	289	161	53	354	737	647	451	414
LIVESTOCK	....	51	23	46	71	16	834	427	432
Whiskey	66	69	130	208	244	295	413	468	492
Granite, lime, soap and limestone	8,332	13,343	10,592	8,026	9,269	10,031	7,812	4,121	5,218
Iron	1,574	1,143	1,548	2,523	3,796	4,883	3,269	5,006	3,030
Iron Ore	....	....	....	....	....	....	....	....	....
Lard and Butter	....	....	....	....	....	....	....	....	....
COAL	....	....	....	....	....	....	....	....	....
Firewood	....	....	....	....	....	....	....	....	....
Leather	....	....	....	....	....	....	....	....	....
Bark	....	....	....	....	....	....	....	....	....
Fire Brick	....	....	....	....	....	....	....	....	....
Miscellaneous	5,766	4,194	4,562	5,400	4,616	7,799	3,647	2,803	3,257
TOTAL TONS	29,446	37,166	36,192	46,979	40,805	40,696	45,663	44,852	60,503

ARTICLES TRANSPORTED	1841 Tons	1842 Tons	1843 Tons	1844 Tons	1845 Tons	1846 Tons	1847 Tons	1848 Tons	1849 Tons	1850 Tons
FLOUR	255,618 bbls. 27,642	233,536 bbls. 25,233	266,146½ bbls. 28,744	241,550 bbls. 26,066	235,602½ bbls. 25,446	413,776½ bbls. 44,586	579,870½ bbls. 62,599	416,110½ bbls. 44,717	469,261 bbls. 50,007	508,127 bbls. 54,636
Tobacco	1,367 hhds. 572	1,884 hhds. 769	3,456 hhds. 1,510	3,598 hhds. 1,517	6,670½ hhds. 2,885	5,539 hhds. 2,344	4,130 hhds. 1,700	5,582 hhds. 2,322	4,496 hhds. 1,761	2,217 hhds. 876
Grain	166	255	2,508	1,878	1,923	1,172	6,693	1,475	3,347	818
Meal, etc.	1,012	885	1,001	1,102	1,370	1,394	1,967	1,593	1,532	1,408
Provisions	502	201	2,870	2,403	2,352	3,192	3,824	4,705	3,808	2,121
LIVESTOCK	671	326	1,219	4,669	5,172	4,382	8,204	12,713	18,991	14,863
Whiskey	395	26	566	733	730	547	700	1,111	1,078	807
Granite, lime, soap and limestone	4,225	3,399	2,597	4,501	5,644	5,205	6,030	6,081	4,358	5,409
Iron	1,024	1,389	2,485	3,552	4,810	7,543	8,855	7,326	6,722	7,556
Iron Ore	....	....	....	....	....	....	....	....	3,123	2,470
Lard & Butter	....	....	476	780	1,206	1,661	1,489	1,752	1,767	987
COAL	....	....	4,964	5,687	16,021	18,394	50,259	66,289	71,699	132,534
Firewood	....	....	....	....	....	....	....	....	91	88
Leather	....	....	....	....	....	....	....	....	696	956
Bark	....	....	....	....	....	....	....	....	1,169	559
Fire Brick	....	....	....	....	....	....	....	....	1,508	962
Miscellaneous	4,273	4,133	3,694	4,219	3,502	4,250	6,146	7,861	3,353	3,288
TOTAL TONS	40,482	36,616	52,634	57,107	71,061	94,670	158,446	157,405	175,610	230,338

THERE ARE THREE KINDS of liars ... liars, damn liars and statistics. Yet, buried in the above abstracts from B&O's 1850 Annual Report, some significant truths emerged over the span of years. First, the tonnage was so overwhelmingly eastbound that B&O did not even bother to report westward tonnage in detail ... reference was made, however, to the need for planning and power to facilitate the return of empty cars. Second, a key element in extending the railroad to Cumberland was to siphon traffic from the National Road, yet the inference from these figures suggests that the loot was something less than expected. Third, whiskey shipments soared after Cumberland was reached, which has to be counted as a socially productive development.

Fourth, flour remained the mainstay of railroad revenues during the first nineteen years of B&O's existence. And then there was coal. The movement of coal, which would prove to be the backbone of B&O operations and inundate the East End, got off to a very slow start ... when the flood started, however, the increases were almost geometric. By 1850, the East End was becoming very, very busy without regard to the increases in traffic which would result from the opening of the railroad to Wheeling. Note the jump in Livestock shipments. No reference to manure disposal has been found nor any hard evidence to support the arguments of skeptics that this substance was used in Annual Reports in any great quantity.

EAST END

CSX system era until just the last few years when the Cincinnati-Deshler line pulled slightly ahead because of a number of changes affecting that territory. And that includes *all* the railroads that became part of Chessie and CSX... not just B&O.

It was remarked in the 1891 Annual Report as to just how heavy the traffic flood had become: "The large increase in tonnage within the past ten years, and the lack of a commensurate increase of side or third track facilities, demands the attention of those interested in the Company, and in order to meet the growth of traffic, and to properly grasp the existing traffic situation, it will be absolutely necessary to increase our side track facilities for the purpose of passing trains, especially between Cumberland and Baltimore. *A moment's thought, and a glance at a map of this road, will show that the portion of the road extending from Cumberland to Locust Point is in fact its main artery.*"

"It is fed by and must supply to the other portions of the system, the greater part of car movement, and that portion of the road is, and must naturally be the most crowded. Portions of the road beyond Cumberland, may within their environments, move with profit and least expense to the company, a large amount of traffic; yet, if upon its reception at Cumberland, the facilities for its further movement are inadequate, the gain which has been made upon the one part, has been lost upon the other; and in order to maintain good service throughout the entire system, it is absolutely necessary that its main highway shall be so arranged, with regard to facilities, as to enable it to receive and dispatch promptly, the aggregate tonnage and car movement offered to it by the various avenues with which it is connected."

Various improvements were introduced over the years to try to alleviate the bottleneck which had developed. In 1891, a block system was being developed and the quote of the day was "where it is most important, it should be first applied"... thus work was concentrated from Washington Junction (Point of Rocks) to Cumberland. By 1892, a complete block system, telegraph offices, and semaphores were installed and in operation.

Three position manual block signals and an interlocking system for switches and signals, developed by Frank P. J. Pattenall, were installed. Mr. Pattenall had developed this system in England before coming to America to be employed as B&O's signal engineer. Color position lights were being installed as early as 1928. Pattenall died on 11 January of that year, but his signal system worked on, allowing three tracks to serve as four where a track could be directionally controlled by signal indication.

Telegraph lines were experimented with in 1844 on the Baltimore-Washington line and were extended to all points soon after.

By 1857, the telegraph on the B&O was deemed "indispensable" with 27 offices being located every 14 miles between Baltimore and Wheeling, a total of 380 miles. In 1906, locations included Harpers Ferry, Engle, Shenandoah Junction, Hobbs, Opequon, Martinsburg, Fawver, Hedgesville (Cumbo), North Mountain, Cherry Run, Miller, Sleepy Creek, Hancock, Sir Johns Run, Great Cacapon, Orleans Road, Hansrote, Baird, Magnolia, Paw Paw, Okonoko, Green Spring, Patterson Creek, North Branch, Evitts Creek, Virginia Lane and Cumberland.

The early 1900s would see a series of well-known improvements such as the Cherry Run and Potomac Valley Railroad lowgrade line, the Patterson Creek Cutoff and the Magnolia Cutoff, which would see B&O through the heaviest traffic which was yet to come.

Density was the greatest between Patterson Creek and Cherry Run, where all traffic MUST pass. Eastbound from the Patterson Creek Cutoff and Cumberland to Cherry Run, where the first diversion of traffic is made to the Western Maryland Railroad, the four lines into Cumberland as well as the P Creek diversions all come together in the "neck of the bottle."

In this 57 miles of railroad, the eastbound grade was .1% in the direction of ruling traffic. The westbound grade was .4% with empty traffic allowing for a balance of power operations.

The next eastbound diversion after Cherry Run is Cumbo and Martinsburg where the Cumberland Valley Railroad (PRR) interchanges. Farther east, the Norfolk and Western Railroad's Hagerstown-Roanoke line connects at Shenandoah Junction.

The East End was single track as built. By 1850, with the West End to Wheeling under construction, double tracking began. From then until the middle of the second decade of this century, the story was one of constant additions of trackage to handle the flood.

By then, the maximum trackage the East End would boast was in place. Two tracks Harpers Ferry to Engle, three Engle to Shenandoah Junction, four Shenandoah Junction to Hobbs, three Hobbs to Martinsburg, three Martinsburg to Hancock (including the CR&PV), four Hancock to Sir Johns Run, three Sir Johns Run to Orleans Road, four Orleans Road to Okonoko (including the Magnolia Cutoff) three Okonoko to Patterson Creek (two from there on the cutoff to McKenzie), two Patterson Creek to North Branch, three North Branch to Evitts Creek and the entrance to Cumberland yards. The story of these and other improvements will be told in chapters to come. By World War I, B&O finally was able to handle the torrent of traffic with efficiency and dispatch . . . almost three quarters of a century after the line was open to Cumberland and the flood started.

This book is a history of the East End . . . in effect a tour through time and space. In reality, East End is simply a name the authors chose to delineate what was actually a section of railroad that had a hodgepodge of names throughout its life.

The railroad from Baltimore to Martinsburg was the "first division" and from there ultimately to Piedmont the "second division." Around the turn of the century it became the Cumberland Division from Weverton (just west of Brunswick and east of Harpers Ferry) . . . shortly thereafter it was the East End subdivision. That boundary was moved to Harpers Ferry 27 April 1969 and back to Weverton 1 March 1987. On 27 January 1974, the Cumberland Division East End became the Cumberland Subdivision of the Maryland Division. If this isn't confusing enough, the W&P branch was part of the East End until the 1920s when it was made part of the Baltimore Division, although separated from it by several miles. Puzzled? Just call it East End.

Studying the East End, one is reminded of that ancient joke about two retired businessmen who met on a southern beach. George said to Joe, "I had a wonderful business, but it burned down and I was too old to start over, so I just hung it up." Joe said to George, "The same with me, except a flood took out my business." After a pause, George asked Joe, "How do you start a flood?"

B&O found a way.

An Eastern Gold Rush

The East End became a conduit for massive tonnages of coal, flour, grain and manufactured goods . . . almost all originating somewhere else, usually to the west.

Yet, for the first time to any significant degree in B&O's westward quest, the East End produced on-line tonnage merely because the railroad existed. One of those sources of ladings owed its birth to the availability of cheap and fast transportation, providing an excellent example of the developmental value that the railroad brought to society.

Before the Civil War, one William S. Miller settled on a farm in what is now the Eastern Panhandle of West Virginia. After learning how to bud and graft fruit trees, he started a nursery in the area. His timing and location proved to be unfortunate . . . the whole region became a battleground and there was little call for nursery stock. So Miller planted an orchard. As most people had a few trees "out behind the barn" for personal use, there wasn't much of a market for a large quantity of fruit.

Then, in 1873, a New York fruit and produce man paid Miller $6,000 in cash for his apple crop. As with the California Gold Rush, the apple industry exploded.

To process and handle this blossoming source of edible gold, a rapidly expanding industry was born. Some examples: the C. L. Robinson Cold Storage Company in Winchester had to double its size in 1915; the American Fruit Grower/Eastern Fruit Growers facility at North Mountain had a 1,000 barrel *per day* capacity; C. H. Musselman at Inwood, National Fruit Products at Winchester and Martinsburg, Associated Orchards at various locations, the Martinsburg Fruit Exchange, the Cumberland Fruit Exchange and others.

Martinsburg in the 1920s had a total cold storage capacity for 50,000 barrels. The 1914-15 apple crop in Virginia amounted to 1,315,508 barrels of which 411,828 barrels moved on B&O lines . . . one third of the crop.

Although the 1920-22 crops were poor, 1923

EAST END

produced an excellent harvest and the Winchester cold storage plant capacities reached 450,000 barrels. As evidence of the importance of fruit growing to the regional economy, the poor crop in 1922 resulted in the need to import Washington State apples to keep the storage and processing plants in full operation.

And the Eastern Panhandle was no small source ... in 1923 the region produced an estimated one million barrels.

In that year, the Cumberland Division alone handled three thousand cars of apples, being partly broken down to the following communities: Kearneysville 400 cars, Martinsburg 300, North Mountain 800, Berkeley Springs 200, Paw Paw 250, Romney 400 and Keyser 300 cars.

It may be a bit of irony that in 1931 a record was set in apple shipments. One wonders how many went to be sold on street corners during the Depression. Much of the crop was exported to Great Britain, France, Germany and Belgium from such points as Romney, Hancock, Okonoko, Berryville, Paw Paw and North Mountain.

Fruit growing and processing remains an important part of the region's economy, but sadly not for B&O. Highway competition ultimately won all the tonnage.

On record for Berkeley County was an old Hemp Apple Tree at the home of one D. N. Kees in Jones Spring, who ate apples from the tree as a boy and remembered thinking of it as an old tree at that time. In 1923, Mr. Kees was 87 years old and he was able to document through local records that the tree was planted at least 150 years earlier. The roots of the industry ran very deep.

TOO LITTLE ATTENTION is paid by railroad historians to the importance of sturdy packaging in the movement of freight. A classic example is the old style, standard wood apple crate as shown here which was universally used by apple growers throughout the region until finally displaced by the paperboard carton. Note the clean, simple, functional lines ... bare of non-essentials.

Chapter 2

Harpers Ferry

"One of the most Stupendous Scenes in Nature"

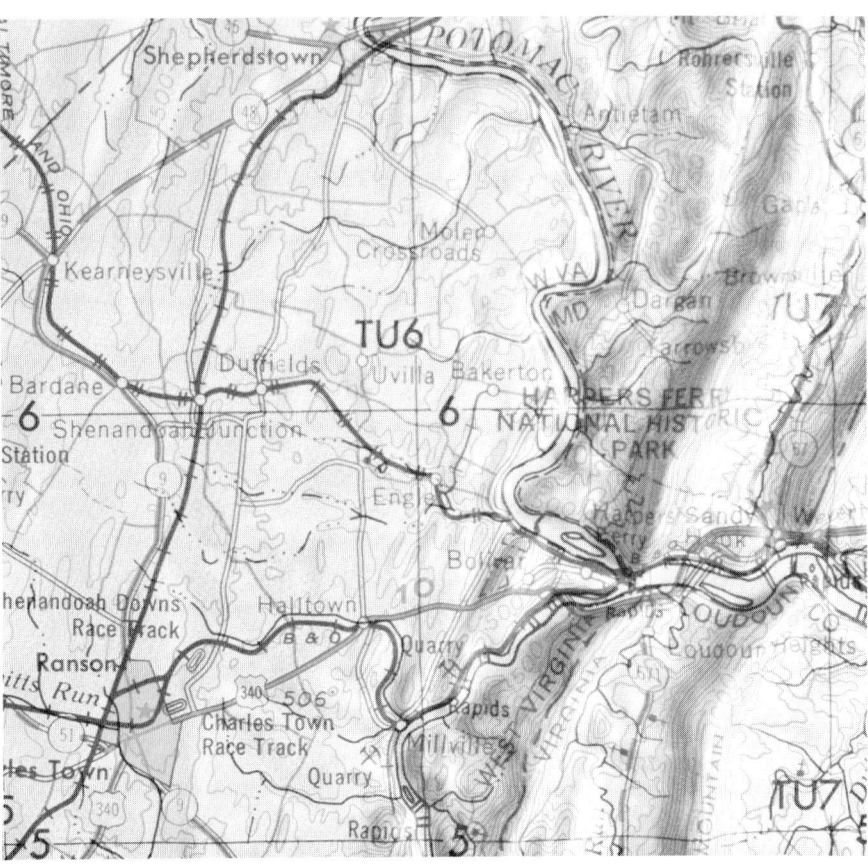

THOMAS JEFFERSON may be pardoned for his error in concluding that the mountains rose first and the rivers cut through later (actually, it was the other way around) because the visual impression of the scene clearly favors his theory. The two rivers appear to have slashed through the mountain almost as if with a swipe of a broadsword, leaving the banks steep and jagged. B&O, squeezed between the C&O Canal and the mountain side, had to wiggle around the north shore and change direction to cross to meet the Winchester and Potomac. No historian has yet divined what was in the minds of W&P management when they refused to give B&O permission to use their rails to Halltown, but the map clearly shows that this route would have been superior for all concerned. Once clear of the Potomac Valley, B&O enjoyed an easy passage west … note that hardly a wrinkle shows on the map as the Shenandoah Valley is crossed. The narrow cleavage at Harpers Ferry also produced an effect only subtly apparent on the map. When rivers flood in flatland areas, the water simply spreads out over the banks. When constricted funnel-like in a narrow passage, water rises rapidly, increases velocity, assumes the consistency of concrete and smashes through anything so unfortunate as to be in its way. B&O's bridges at Harpers Ferry were corks in the bottle and went "pop" more than once.

EAST END

There are many locations in the Western Hemisphere rich in the history and lore of man's innate urge to expand his horizons. Few can match Harpers Ferry in grandeur, glory, perversity, discord and quirks of fate.

As to grandeur, no one has been able to top Thomas Jefferson's strikingly graphic description of the locale, penned while he was standing on what became known as Jefferson Rock.

"The passage of the Potomac through the Blue Ridge is perhaps one of the most stupendous scenes in nature. You stand on a very high point of land; on your right comes up the Shenandoah (daughter of the stars), having ranged along the foot of the mountain a hundred miles to seek a vent; on your left approaches the Potomac in quest of a passage also. In the moment of their junction, they rush together against the mountain, rend it asunder, and pass it off to the sea."

"The first glance of this scene hurries our senses into realizing that the mountains were formed first; that the rivers began to flow afterwards; that in this place particularly they had been dammed up by the Blue Ridge of mountains and had formed an ocean which filled the whole valley; that continuing to rise, they had at length broken over at this spot and torn the mountain down from its summit to its base. The piles of rock on each hand, but particularly on the Shenandoah; the evident marks of their disrupture and avulsion from their beds by the most powerful agents of nature, collaborate the impression."

"You cross the Potomac above the junction, and pass along its side through the base of the mountain for three miles, its terrible precipices hanging in fragments over you . . . this scene is worth a voyage across the Atlantic, yet here as in the neighborhood of Natural Bridge, are people who have passed their lives within half a dozen miles, and have never been to survey these monuments of a war between rivers and mountains which must have shaken the earth itself to its center."

While it is easy to fault Jefferson's knowledge of geology and sentence structure, his word-picture of the scene was eloquent. And he was also prophetic with that line about the earth being shaken, although not in the sense he had in mind. The coming of the railroad, John Brown's raid and the Civil War which followed certainly shook the history of the United States like a bowl full of jelly.

It was all innocuous enough in the beginning when a trapper named Peter Stephens sold one Robert Harper the plot of ground that would become Harpers Ferry for thirteen British guineas. In 1747, Harper created a ferry system across both rivers and, of course, the place became known as Harpers Ferry.

After the Revolutionary War, the United States Government decided to manufacture its own arms rather than depend on foreign manufacturing sources. The War Department wanted to create a government facility in Springfield, Massachusetts, for good and valid reasons.

In one of the earliest examples in United States history of political interference in the awarding of lush government contracts, George Washington decided he wanted the facility in *his* district (Harpers Ferry was then part of Virginia) and since the Father of His Country had a certain amount of political clout, in 1799 construction started on the U.S. Armory and Arsenal at Harpers Ferry. Since at that time Harpers Ferry was in the middle of nowhere, a question of probity does arise. But we are writing a history of the East End, so we will pass the torch to other historians to explore this fascinating little transaction.

Certainly Harpers Ferry had water power, was central to some local forges and furnaces and timber was available to make charcoal to fuel the furnaces. But by this time in history, Robert Harper's land had passed through family hands to the Wager family who had, at the time of armory construction, a monopoly on all mercantile transactions simply because they owned the only land suitable for such activities. And the Wagers drove a hard bargain with the government, forcing the War Department to agree that all purchases for the armory be made locally. Since they owned it all, the Wagers cleaned up on the sale of food, clothing, liquor and other day-to-day needs. This neat little arrangement lasted, to one degree or another, until the Civil War. Since the cost of living was high, the War Department had to pay very high wages to the three or four hundred workers at the facility. At least in this case, soldiers could not complain that their weapons were made by the lowest bidder, and one suspects the War Department was just as happy that the Rebel army put paid to the whole thing.

The B&O arrived on the Maryland shore late in 1834, faced its first major river crossing and, for the first time, had to leave Maryland to enter a "foreign" state. The far shore was occupied by the

HARPERS FERRY

Winchester and Potomac Railroad, the Federal Arsenal and some voracious landowners. In between was the Potomac River, a riverway which delighted in alternating between savage ferocity and docile submission.

B&O's story of crossing the river (and staying across) will be told in captions to photographs. The saga of John Brown and the Civil War will be treated in a separate chapter later in the book. But one leap forward in time is appropriate now.

In 1857, William Prescott Smith (B&O officer and the railroad's first historian), described the B&O's crossing at Harpers Ferry in flowing prose:

"The beautiful and romantic Shenandoah enters the Potomac immediately below the bridge by which we crossed the latter, and their united currents rush swiftly over the broad ledges of rock stretching across the river bed. The bridge referred to is constructed somewhat in the shape of the letter Y, dividing as we approach its western end, the left hand branch connecting with the Winchester and Potomac Railroad passing up the Shenandoah and the right hand carrying the main road, by a bold curve, up the Potomac. The bridge is about nine hundred feet in length, and consists of six arches of one hundred and thirty, and one arch of seventy five feet span over the river, and an arch of one hundred feet over the canal. These arches are all of timber and iron, and covered in, except the western arch connecting with the Winchester Road, which is constructed entirely of iron, on Bollman's plan."

"It is remarkable not so much for its length as for its peculiar form, the ends being curved in opposite directions, and the structure bifureated towards the western extremity."

"The town of Harpers Ferry is built upon the narrow declivitous tongue of land lying directly in the confluence of two rivers. As the mountain steeps converge precipitously at all points about the gap, but small space is left for building with accessible convenience. The National Armories located here, and taking their manufacturing 'power' from the torrents of the Potomac, quite exhaust the level land on the Potomac River margin, so that the town is compelled to go clambering picturesquely up the hills and bluffs, whose summits are crowned with church spires and sepulchral monuments and groves."

"Jefferson's Rock, a great overhanging cliff, is in sight, balancing upon its base, and even threatening to come down upon the gorges below in a destructive avalanche. It was from this rock, that Jefferson pencilled his graphic descriptions of the scene which there bursts upon the view."

We might point out that the bridge to which Smith refers was *not* the first, nor would it be the last, structure to carry man across the Potomac. It would take almost one hundred years for B&O to finally solve the "little" problem of crossing the Potomac River.

Apply Air Brakes—Swung horizontally above the head.

Release Air Brakes—Held at arm's length above the head.

21

THE FIRST BRIDGE at Harpers Ferry was built by Lewis Wernwag in 1824-25 to replace the ferry crossing ... it is the closest structure in this scene and was known locally as Wager's Bridge. The downstream bridge was B&O's first crossing, uncovered at the time this drawing was made. Lewis Wernwag and B&O engineer Benjamin H. Latrobe collaborated on the design, which was not a happy one. Six spans of varying lengths were employed to cross the river and a seventh to cross the C&O Canal at the east end on a curve. A wood truss affair on masonry piers, the bridge was opened to traffic in January 1837 with a single railroad track and wagon roadway side by side, with the rails on the downstream side. Until the opening of the B&O bridge, freight from the W&P (which opened in March 1836) was hauled by horsepower across the Wager Bridge all the way east to Point of Rocks, primarily because of an awkward agreement with the C&O Canal. Of course, the Wager Bridge was a wooden affair and almost certainly would not have been able to carry the weight of locomotives and trains. As it turned out, neither could the B&O bridge. B&O soon discovered that the pier masonry was defective and had to be replaced, so back came the horses. The tribulations did not end there, but more of this in later captions. The Wager bridge was dismantled in 1839. B&O scored two more "firsts" at this location ... first junction with a separate railroad and probably the first freight car interchange agreement, signed in 1841.

Smithsonian Institution

ARTISTIC LICENSE is all well and good, but this chap went so far as to put the railroad on the wrong side of the bridge. Apparently done in the late 1840s, this scene shows the bridge with a tin roof installed to protect timbers from the weather. On 3 September 1837 an engine and tender collapsed a center span and the whole mess with crew dropped into the river. Miraculously, there were no serious injuries except to the reputations of Messrs. Wernwag and Latrobe as bridge builders. In the spring of 1838, down she went again with a train of "nine freight cars and eleven gondolas." This time engine *Gladiator* with tender was over a pier and did not take a swim with the train and bridge timbers. Again no serious injuries, but surely the crews were beginning to demand combat pay. "Decayed timbers" were blamed ... faulty design could not possibly have been the culprit. A long process of reinforcing the bridge began after these incidents, principally the addition of iron struts to strengthen the structure. During this era Wendel Bollman and Albert Fink were evolving their iron truss designs and in 1851 a "Bollman" truss was installed as the "Winchester Span." It was located to connect with the W&P as a left arm west of the midriver wye. While not clear in this rendering, B&O also had to skirt the Arsenal on a long trestle which appears here along the river to the right of the tall smokestack.

HARPERS FERRY

National Parks Service

THIS VIEW of the bridge must date to the late 1840s as we cannot find evidence of the "Winchester Span," although the view is obstructed. This photo was taken from the trestle work employed to skirt the Arsenal and probably fairly represents the appearance of the bridge on the eve of the Civil War. We will relate the details of the bridge's adventures during that unpleasantness in a chapter to come, but we can assure the reader that the appearance of the bridge changed drastically and frequently during that vibrant four years.

Smithsonian Institution

DURING THE CIVIL WAR, B&O struggled to replace the bridge's wooden trusses with Bollmans, a process constantly interrupted by both Rebel and Federal destructive forays. This scene, at the close of the war, shows that four of the Bollman spans built in 1862-63 had survived after a fashion, but temporary trestling was still in place at both ends.

EAST END

B&O Museum

BOLLMAN AT ITS BEST is an appropriate title for this splendid early 1870s view of the bridge at Harpers Ferry. Spiffed up and gaily painted, the bridge graces the scene. As Harwood in his epochal *Impossible Challenge* put it in his elegant prose, "This superlatively complex collection of Bollman truss spans was at least the aesthetic epitome of Victorian bridge design... with eight spans of different lengths and alignments—including the oversized birdcage-like junction span—it was the most magnificent of Bollman truss bridges and the ideal engineering companion to the ornate Victorian house architecture." This bridge also epitomizes something else and that is the crushing burdens B&O had to endure as the price of being the pioneer and victim of political ploys. On the far shore, the canal presses B&O against the wall of Maryland Heights and forces it into a hairpin turn to enter the bridge over the canal. The bridge, of course, is pointing in the wrong direction and forces another sharp curve in midstream to align itself with the Arsenal property, which in turn involves still another bridge. And the B&O had to share the bridge with a roadway, which precludes double tracking. Also, B&O was on the wrong side of the road, making the midstream junction even more of a bottleneck. Increasing train length and traffic magnified the shortcomings of this statuesque structure and by the 1890s B&O had to do something about it.

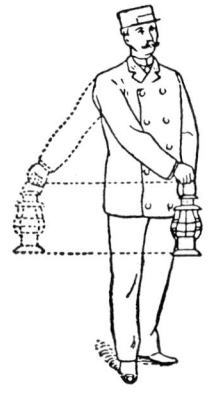

Stop—Swung across the track.

Proceed—Raised and lowered vertically.

WE CANNOT LEAVE this regal structure without offering two more views and pointing out that the various colors painted on the bridge were a form of purposeful decoration. Different colors denoted various members of the structure ... tension struts would be one color, compression members another and so on. While we have yet to find a code, apparently most early Bollman/Fink bridges were treated in this fashion. Vivat Regina, colors and all.

EAST END

B&OHS

THIS POST CIVIL WAR view shows the retaining wall and part of the trestle structure paralleling the Arsenal property . . . some of the ruins of the latter can be seen in the distance. It is possible that the building barely seen through the Bollman latticework may well be the three-story wood frame tavern which doubled as a station in this era. The duckbill passenger cars and diamond stack power certainly do not detract from this perspective.

HARPERS FERRY

B&OHS

THE CRUSH of ever increasing tonnage, number of trains and train lengths as the nineteenth century wore to a close forced B&O to focus on eliminating chokepoints. The Harpers Ferry bridge and approaches, no matter how aesthetic, were prime examples urgently requiring solution. B&O decided to tunnel Maryland Heights to clean up the eastern curves, bridge the Potomac at a more workable angle and use the Arsenal grounds to ease curvature at the western end and discard the trestle "hanging over the river." And, of course, double-track the whole area. The old arsenal grounds, now owned by a Thomas E. Savery, were purchased in 1892 and covered with a 20 foot embankment and fill. An 875 foot double track tunnel was bored through the Heights in 1893 and enlarged with masonry lining in 1895-96. The iron and steel bridge pictured was completed in 1894, lying upstream from the Bollman beauties which in turn were converted to a single lane roadway bridge. That three-story frame tavern which had doubled as a station since Civil War days was torn down and buried in the fill, although it was replaced with a gem which became famous in its own right. The newly aligned bridge was placed in service 12 April 1894 and consisted of nine spans ... three iron through-trusses (shown), five deck plate girder and one through-girder. The new bridge was nine feet higher than the Bollman classic to allow flood waters more vertical room and ease the grade. At the same time, the W&P approaches were realigned and a 67 foot bridge over Shenandoah Street in Harpers Ferry was added.

THIS VIEW of the eastern portal of the new tunnel dramatically shows the rugged nature of Maryland Heights ... so rugged, in fact, that B&O had to extend the tunnel 36 feet on each end and then backfill over the extensions to keep rockfalls off the railroad, a project completed in 1897.

EAST END

ADMITTEDLY CRUDE, this reproduction of a turn-of-the-century postcard nonetheless gives a splendid overview of Harpers Ferry and B&O's bridging history to that point in time. The bridge on the left is, of course, the Bollman complete with "Birdcage" remnants and with the railroad span in place sans rails... note that the left span points directly at the W&P. Just to the right on shore, one sees the new Shenandoah Street bridge and realignment to the W&P. Then, on the right, the 1894 bridge reaches land and curves to the right over the old Arsenal grounds on a fill. Study the retaining walls along the river and trace B&O's original route from the birdcage to land to the route west along the river. Note the new station in the Y and its companion shelter across the tracks.

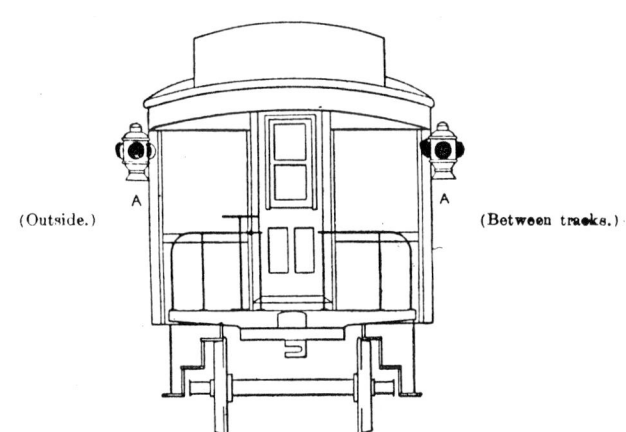

Rear of Train by Night Running Against the Current of Traffic.
Lights at **A A**, as per Rule 19.

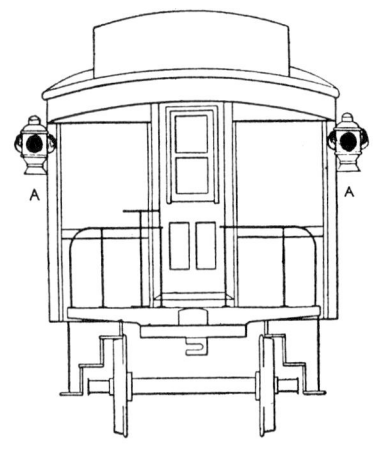

Rear of Train by Night Running With the Current of Traffic on a High Speed Track.
Lights at **A A**, as per Rule F-274.

HARPERS FERRY

ONE OF THE FRUSTRATIONS that confront historians arises when an answer to one question is found only to create still another one, and this photograph is a case in point. At lower left, at long last, the authors have found a graphic portrayal of the "hanging trestle" through the Arsenal grounds, even though obviously abandoned. The Bollman has been reduced to one span. The new station sits nice and pretty and the Shenandoah Street bridge is in view to the right. At the juncture between two Bollman spans the switchman's shanty remains, hanging out over the water (also apparent in an earlier photo in this chapter just after the Civil War). Now the reader should study the *preceding* photo and note that the "railroad" Bollman span *is still in place*, the Arsenal trestlework is gone and the station boasts a shelter across the tracks. Which one is the earlier picture? Please let us know if you figure it out. On second thought, don't. *B&OHS*

B&OHS

WE KNOW the exact date *this* photograph was taken . . . 12 November 1930. Actually, this structure was a combination station and interlocking tower . . . the connection to the old W&P (by this time B&O's Shenandoah Subdivision) peels off to the left. The B&O standard "State Line" marker appears just to the left of the station and introduces a curious point most readers might not realize. Throughout most of the world, political divisions that meet at waterways split the difference by putting the boundary down the middle of river. Not in Maryland . . . the boundaries are frequently on the far shore. Thus the entire Potomac River, for example, rests in Maryland and this marker is in precisely the right place. As to the station/tower, this will be its last season in this location . . . on 2 February 1931 it will be moved to another location. Not apparent in this photo is a subway, built in May 1913, that goes under the tracks to the waiting shed just out of sight to the right.

EAST END

B&OHS

THE 1894 BRIDGE was completed near the end of one motive power era and just before the dawn of another one. The early twentieth century would see an explosion in tonnage and a revolution in power development to handle that tonnage. Train length would increase dramatically and the 1894 bridge, perfectly adequate for train and power weight in the "middle ages" of railroading, was woefully inadequate for the "new age." So, naturally, B&O had to build still *another* goddam bridge at Harpers Ferry. In 1930-31, B&O built what they hope and fervently pray will be the *last* crossing of the Potomac at this location. This time they constructed a 1400 foot, 11 span deck plate girder bridge with 4,400,000 pounds of structural steel and 4000 cubic feet of concrete in the piers. They increased the angle of crossing so the west curve would be modest and they got a little lucky ... at least at first. Mother Nature had taken a vacation and had not left the weasel in charge of the railroad hen house. The river was so low during construction that steam shovels could work on the bed of the river and workers could cross shore-to-shore dryshod. This panoramic scene, taken in 1942, speaks for itself. Where is the Bollman bridge? More about that later. Note that the station has been moved and carefully study the consist of the train behind the S1 "Big Six" ... it is almost all tank cars. German U-Boats had virtually closed down tanker traffic off the East Coast in 1942 and the railroads saved the day by hauling vast quantities of petroleum products overland from the southwestern oilfields, still another example of the importance and versatility of railroads in wartime. Look at the extreme right where the railroad leaves the photo and you will see "Little Tunnel Cut."

HARPERS FERRY

B&OHS

AN EASTWARD VIEW of the 1931 Bridge at the height of the age of steam, with a ubiquitous Big Six rushing a Quick Dispatch train west under a delightful canopy of smoke and cinders. See how low the river. Where is the Bollman bridge? Be patient, be patient.

EAST END

TO BUILD the 1931 bridge, it was necessary to widen, or "bell out," the tunnel under Maryland Heights. During construction in 1930-31, a gauntlet track was installed to allow room for workmen to widen, reline and reface the tunnel walls... it was removed 6 April 1931 and the line went back to double track. The track in the center of the photo is the Shenandoah Sub branch which joins the mainline inside the tunnel, one of the few in-tunnel interlockers in the nation.

B&OHS

John P. Hankey

THE THOUGHT may have occurred to the reader that the Almighty has been using Harpers Ferry as a testing ground for B&O. After all, the Bible relates to the first destruction by flood in Genesis and to the second destruction by fire in the Book of Revelations. The authors concur that it couldn't be true because the Almighty only punished his children once in each case... B&O has been stung so many times it is easy to lose count. Take the 1931 bridge, for example. On 6 March 1931, before it was even open, the hummer caught fire. The cause was never finally determined even though there were workmen on the bridge with forges... it spread at such a rapid pace that it was out of control within minutes. Almost all the ties and wood parts were burned and the steel badly buckled... these two photos show how virulent the blaze. The rapid spread may have been caused by a new "Full Cell" creosote process in use at the tie plant at Green Spring since 1927, but it also could have been that the wooden parts had not been sufficiently weathered. Ballast decking was considered, but rejected as "too expensive." On April 11 1951 Extra West 7627 passed over the bridge with its ash pan door open about a half inch because of an obstruction and started another blaze. Ballast decking was again "too expensive." On 9 June 1956 a journal on a hopper of coal in Extra East D-969 burned off on the bridge (naturally), caused a derailment and set the coal on fire as well as the bridge. Enough was enough, so this time B&O installed fireproof coatings and firestops. God, why us? We've been good!

HARPERS FERRY

IN B&O's 1843 Annual Report, reference was made to "freshets of unexampled power than ever before observed" on the East End. If there were any prophets on the scene at that time, he or she would have said, "you ain't seen nothing yet." This mid-1920's performance did not take out the Bollman, but it was close. Compare the water level on the 1894 bridge with earlier low-water scenes in this chapter for a sense of just how much water the Potomac could spew forth when it was angry.
B&OHS

ON 17 MARCH 1936, the Potomac decided that it was tired of looking at the Bollman bridge and took it out. It also did a number on the rest of the East End, but that's a story yet to be told. For good measure, the Shenandoah blew away the road bridge between Harpers Ferry and the south shore. All this didn't do the town a lot of good, either. As to the Bollman, five spans virtually vanished ... only two more modern trusses on the Maryland shore and one Bollman pillar with a Toll sign survived. B&O, in consonance with its "Good Neighbor" policy, planked the 1894 bridge and shared it with motor traffic until the early 1950s when a new auto bridge replaced the blown Shenandoah bridge. This flood was so violent that it even washed away two Bollman piers ... the remaining ones can be seen in the river to this day, testimony to Mother Nature's femininity and proof of the axiom that the female is the deadlier of the species.
B&OHS

EAST END

B&OHS

AS WE HAVE mentioned, the 1894 station/tower was moved to serve the 1931 bridge and here it is seen on an unknown date. The move occurred 2 February 1931 by sliding the station along the old mainline rails as far as possible and then lifting it with cribbing to its new home. The in-tunnel interlocker was handled remotely from the tower. Space for a separate ladies waiting room in the station was converted to a heating/storage room at this time and from 1931 on the sexes mixed in one room. Whether or not this action triggered the women's lib movement is not known. Another subway was built to connect the station to the waiting shed on the other side.

B&OHS

THE STATION has shed its tower by the time of this view. On 3 February 1950, the interlocking was moved from the tower to the agent's office and the tower dismantled between August 1950 and March 1951. The cars of the work train on the right trace the route of the old mainline to the 1894 bridge, which was left in place as an emergency detour for many years ... in fact, they were used as such during the various firestorms previously reported. In the fall of 1958, the line was reduced to a 19 car siding which tends to date this view in that era. The station is extant, we are happy to say.

THIS ILLUSTRATION of the first tunnel on the East End was taken from an 1850's rendering and is the only representation we have found of Potomac Tunnel, a ninety foot bore "through a mass of dark blue limestone." The tunnel was daylighted in March 1902 and is known today as Little Tunnel Cut.

Warren Somerville

Winchester and Potomac

The Winchester and Potomac (or Potowmak as originally spelled) was chartered 8 April 1831 and began operations 14 March 1836. We have already related the contretemps between the W&P and B&O at Harpers Ferry and the reader may have come away with the impression that the management of the W&P was not too swift. That thought has certainly occurred to the authors, particularly when it appears that they picked the losing side in the Civil War.

Whatever the validity of this reasoning, the W&P was devastated during the war and B&O ended up taking over the railroad 1 July 1867. The 32 mile line runs southwest from Harpers Ferry through Charlestown to Winchester and is still being operated as a branch by CSX in 1992.

The Winchester and Strasburg Railroad was chartered in 1867, building a 19 mile line southwest from Winchester to Strasburg. This road was a creature of the B&O and operations were taken over by it 28 July 1870. At Strasburg Junction, connection was made with the Orange, Alexandria and Manassas Railroad, extending B&O's reach 51 miles farther south to Harrisonburg. This line ultimately became part of the Southern Railway and was used but not owned by B&O.

The Valley Railroad was chartered in 1866 to build a 61 mile line from Harrisonburg to Lexington and it was built as far as Staunton by 1869. Robert E. Lee of Civil War fame, now retired from the vocation of destroying railroads, was president of this line.

The Valley Railroad was built with B&O backing from the beginning and was leased by B&O 1 September 1873. It wasn't until 1883, however, that the line was completed between Staunton and Lexington.

All this is rather far afield from the East End, but it is interesting because there is ample evidence that Garrett had dreams of creating a major extension all the way south to Tennessee, the so-called "deep south route" which would have reached, through connections, to New Orleans.

In any event, during this era the Shenandoah Valley Railroad was completing its parallel line from Hagerstown to Roanoke and a connection with the Norfolk and Western at the latter point, putting paid to still another Garrett scheme.

The W&P crossed the SV at grade at Charlestown and B&O met SV on the East End at Shenandoah Junction, creating a minor interchange point at the former and a major one at the latter ... about all B&O would get out of this grand plan other than local traffic off the W&P.

B&O began dropping leases over time, sold the lines south of Harrisonburg to the Chesapeake Western in 1943 and abandoned the line from Staunton to Lexington between 1941 and 1946.

In 1992, B&O retains only the line from Harpers Ferry to Strasburg Junction, not all that far from where it started.

EAST END

B&OHS

BEGINNING at the beginning of the W&P, in this 1920s era photo we see a motor car with trailer on the branch meeting an eastbound passenger train at Harpers Ferry. Train service to the Shenandoah Valley varied over the years, of course, and as one would expect was more frequent in the early years. For example, the December 1884 employee timetable called for four daily westbound freights and two passenger trains with an equal number eastbound. However, there was only one Harpers Ferry to Lexington run each way ... a hint that the "deep south route" would have to find a lot of traffic from somewhere other than on-line. This train, incidentally, left Lexington at 7:35 a.m. as No. 231 and arrived at Harpers Ferry at 3:02 p.m. Westbound as No. 210, it left the Ferry at 12:05 p.m. and arrived at Lexington at 7:30 p.m. The alert reader will note that the train numbers are askew ... the even number is running west and the odd number east. That's the way the B&O did it in the 1880s, adding to their precious reputation for eccentricity.

HARPERS FERRY

Jeff Madden

MILLVILLE is the first place of importance west of Harpers Ferry on the W&P. Quarrying of limestone was big in the early years and remains so to this day. Name trains such as the Millville Digger and the Rock Runner took their titles from this little hamlet and its quarries. Located on the Shenandoah River, fishermen flock to this area because of a Potomac Edison dam nearby. B&O once hauled coal into a power facility here, adding some welcome loads in returning cars.

Jeff Madden

IN THIS WORKADAY scene, the Millville Digger is going about its routine switching chores by the station. Both this and the preceding photo were taken in the summer of 1972 ... by this time, an agent was there only for the preparation of bills from the quarry and the odd order or two.

THIS POSTCARD view of the B&O station at Charlestown was taken pre-1917 ... the depot was built in 1880. The town is famous for its race tracks and their promise of easy wealth "if." Special trains were known to have plied W&P rails to this spot, delivering passengers into the rubbing hands of touts in a sort of track-to-track transaction. Since B&O always took a paternal interest in their passengers, ticket agents no doubt urged travelers to buy round trip tickets in advance so they could at least get home if things did not go well.

37

EAST END

THE FIRST large town west of Harpers Ferry, and the last on the W&P, is Winchester. Rail facilities here included this 1893 era stone station which survives in 1992 under the threat of abandonment by CSX. Other Winchester facilities include a 2100 foot connection with the Cumberland Valley Railroad built in 1914 to upgrade the 1888 interchange installed when the CV was opened. CV was absorbed by PRR and, of course, is now part of Conrail. References to an 1881 ice house, a temporary depot in 1875, a brick freight station in 1876 and a two story dwelling for the road supervisor as well as an original wooden turntable replaced by one of iron can be found in B&O Annual Reports, indicating that Winchester was a lively location in its day. A coaling station and water penstocks also graced Winchester, but they were removed at the end of the steam era on 15 October 1953.

ON AN AUGUST DAY in 1946, B18d 2028 pauses at Winchester to load milk and express at the completion of which she will dash to Harpers Ferry with aplomb. Built by Rhode Island in October 1901, the 2028 will last until 1953 and expire at the ripe old age of fifty-two.

HARPERS FERRY

B&O Museum

WE WOULD not want the reader to think the valley lines were bereft of stately structures, so we offer this c. 1920 valuation shot of the downtown B&O depot at Stephens City just south of Winchester. The significance of the period after "City" on the station sign mystifies us ... perhaps this is another B&O "first."

STRASBURG JUNCTION is the present day end-of-the-line for B&O's Shenandoah Subdivision, but it was a way point for many years. One of the structures serving this community was this apparent combination station/office built in 1915. There was also an engine house at the junction, built in 1874. On 20 August 1949, Train Valley 55 made its last passenger run from Harpers Ferry to here, ending 114 years of passenger service in the valley.

B&O Museum

ONE CAN BE SURE that the W&P had many "shovel job" steam locomotives, but at Strasburg Junction the poor fireman had to shovel to get coal into the tender as well as the firebox. And we guess someone had to shovel the coal to get it into the bin.

B&O Museum

39

EAST END

SURELY tongue was in cheek when Harrisonburg's depot was labeled "Union Station," but one must admit there were a surprising number of passengers in this pre-1922 postcard view. The message on the card is from a father to his daughter, saying "you should see the valley and the mountain scenery ... it is surely beautiful." In the mid years of this century, B&O used Brill motor car 6001 and trailer 6101 in regional service between Harrisonburg and Lexington, making two roundtrips daily. The automobiles in this scene presage the decline in branch line passenger service.

PERHAPS this classic structure at Staunton, designed by E. Francis Baldwin in 1883, was built when the dreams of deep south sugarplums were dancing in Garrett's head. Actually, the deep south route did have some strategic potential as witnessed by the success of rival N&W/CV (PRR) lines. At least one noted historian feels that B&O's failure to realize the dream was as much a product of bumbling on Garrett's part as it was a lack of traffic potential.

Chapter 3

Into the Valley

Harpers Ferry to Martinsburg

"A short distance west of Harpers Ferry, the road leaves the Potomac, and passes up the ravine of Elk Branch, which presents itself at this point in a favorable direction. This ravine, at first narrow and serpentine, becomes wider and more direct until it almost loses itself in the rolling table land which characterizes the Valley of Virginia. The head of Elk Branch is reached in about nine miles, and thence the line descends gradually over an undulating champaigne country to the crossing of Opequa (sic) Creek, which it passes by a stone and timber viaduct of one hundred and fifty feet span and forty feet above the water surface. Beyond the crossing the road enters the open valley of Tuscarora Creek which it crosses twice and pursues to the town of Martinsburg, eighteen miles from Harpers Ferry."

So begins William P. Smith's description of the B&O line of road west of Potomac Tunnel in the early 1850s. His use of the word "champaigne" is interesting ... a modern dictionary defines the word (without an e) as (1) level, open country; plain (2) a battlefield. Within a few years, B&O would learn that the latter definition was as apt as the first.

At the entry point to Elk Branch, the railroad passes a spot known as Peachers Mill. Today there is a signal at this location and crews call the signal by that name. Since the 1856 B&O Annual Report mentions a Peachers stone bridge of eighteen feet in length, it is reasonable to accept local lore that a John Peacher lived near and kept a mill at this place.

Now legend takes over. There were reports that his property was frequented by gypsy caravans, witches, warlocks and the like. And Peacher was said to have had an enchanted wheel which he could employ to evoke a spell upon those who had stolen from him and his friends and cause the miscreants to return such items forthwith.

During the Civil War, as we shall see, the Rebel forces stole B&O engines, cars and rails with abandon ... after the end of the war, B&O managed to get at least some of the stolen goods returned. We have no evidence that B&O used or even knew of Peacher's wheel, but one should not argue with success. There are, however, considerable grounds for believing B&O attributed magical qualities to one Thomas "Stonewall" Jackson.

Crossing the lush Shenandoah Valley to just east of Martinsburg, B&O found itself in limestone territory with the result that at least five separate quarrying operations added to B&O traffic.

Another more grim and unusual recipient of rail traffic was the Newton D. Baker Hospital/Veterans Administration Center, which had a siding to receive hospital trains with World War II wounded. Built beginning in 1941 with a siding to aid with deliveries of construction materials, the hospital opened in 1944 with over seven miles of rails. It was named for Newton D. Baker of Mar-

EAST END

tinsburg, Secretary of War 1916 to 1921 and B&O Director from 1923 until his death in 1937. Curiously, Baker's father had served B&O as a company surgeon. Thus the East End heard the cries of the wounded for a second time in history.

Farther west, the flagstop of Shoop (locally known as Blairton) served a large quarry with a branchline and inevitable side tracks.

After passing Opequon Water Station and Flaggs Crossing, B&O's Kelly Island Branch departed south from the mainline at Rattling Bridge for three miles to the Kelly Island-National Limestone Works which began operations in 1910. The quarries on this branch are no longer active, but in 1992 the branch still serves several active customers.

Approaching Martinsburg, B&O passes the site of Meads/Bulleye Bridge and reaches the Martinsburg Yard Limit sign. Now let us return to the beginning of this stretch of railroad and explore the line in detail in captions to photographs, a pattern which will continue throughout the book.

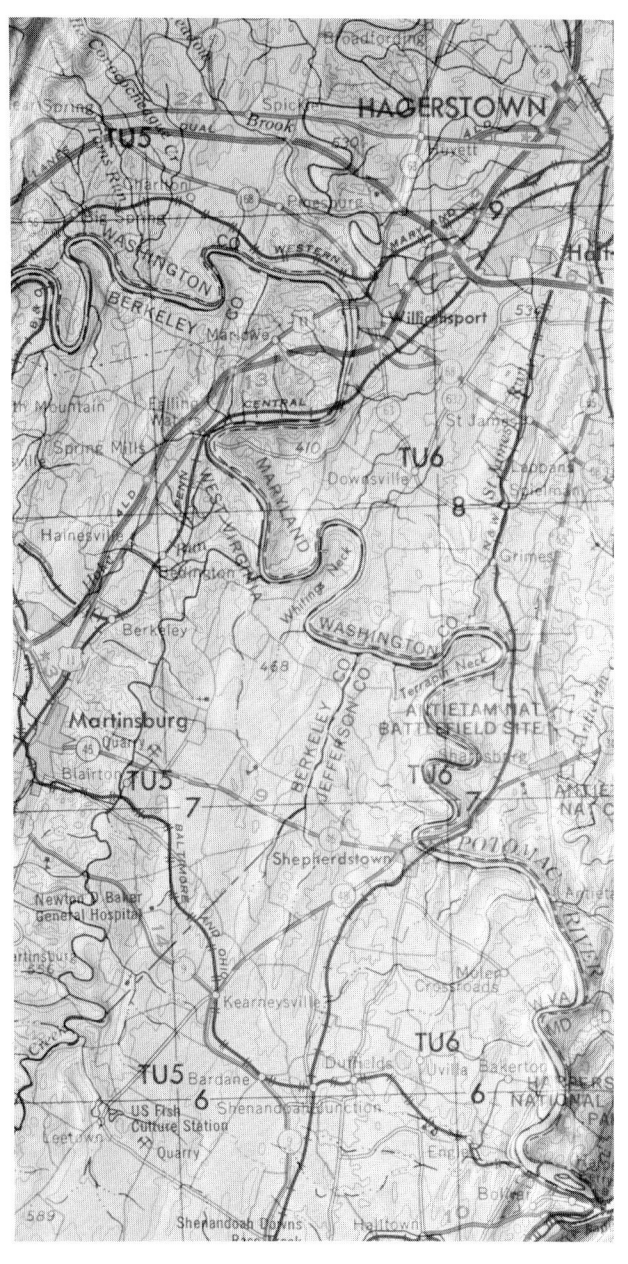

WEST OF THE FERRY at last, B&O literally dashed across the easy country to Martinsburg. Starting at lower right on this map at Harpers Ferry, the line paralleled the Potomac for a short distance and then took off cross-country to Engles, Duffields, what would become Shenandoah Junction, Hobbs (Bardane on the map), Kearneysville, Blairton and the outskirts of Martinsburg. Aside from the pleasures of passing through delightful and relatively flat country, B&O was well away from the Potomac River and nemesis C&O Canal. Here we find the well known, mirror image Nine Mile Grade, beginning westwardly about a mile west of the Ferry bridges and topping nine miles farther along at Hobbs, about a mile west of Bardane. This part of the grade ranges from .57 to .75 percent, nickel and dime when one considers that it has always faced mostly empty traffic. The grade facing eastward traffic (and moving from west to east) begins about a mile west of Blairton at Opequon and, of course, tops at Hobbs. Actually, this grade is only about seven miles long and boasts grades ranging from a slight .35 to a maximum of .75 percent. That it would become, and remain, a helper grade was a product of simple arithmetic... it is cheaper to maintain long train length with helpers than to break up trains to avoid helpers. Please note the N&W line running from mid-bottom north through Shenandoah Junction to Hagerstown. To the south, this line runs to Roanoke... but more about this later.

INTO THE VALLEY

A LARGE ISLAND squats in the middle of the Potomac River just west of the Ferry and it became B&O's first stop in its westward trek. In this early twentieth century postcard view, that island appears in the upper right. Named Byrnes Island, B&O bought it in 1878 and built an amusement park which opened the following year with a 1200 square foot dance pavilion twelve feet high and attached music stand. This mini day resort, renamed Island Park, was connected with the "mainland" by a long footbridge which crossed the river and Arsenal Millrace as seen in the center of this scene. The park must have been popular because B&O expanded it in 1890 with a larger pavilion, new bandstand seats, a 1696 square foot dining room and a new waiting shed. Note the skewed Bollman truss bridge just below the footbridge... this structure got B&O off "Arsenal" Island, across the millrace and back on the south shore of the Potomac. The C&O Canal can barely be seen on the far, or north, shore. Poor B&O had to cross still another waterway to get out of the Ferry.

THIS EASTWARD, or downstream, view of the Island Park area from a turn-of-century postcard presents your authors with a problem. The B&O mainline hugs the south shore to the right of the Arsenal Millrace and was built in conjunction with the 1894 realignment at the Ferry. The skewed Bollman, which was built as a double track structure in 1866 to replace an earlier wooden bridge, is in this view used as a siding to serve industrial customers on the Arsenal peninsula... it was removed in 1933. There is no doubt that the Bollman siding follows the trace of the original B&O mainline out of the Ferry which, the reader will recall, was on the river side of the Arsenal area. The millrace was built long before the railroad as a power source for the Arsenal, which was defunct by the end of the Civil War. The problem is Potomac Tunnel or Little Tunnel Cut. B&O Tunnel Records show the tunnel just a half mile west of the Ferry, which would place it around to the right out of sight in this view but within sight of Maryland Heights as we reported in an earlier caption. But the "shore" mainline was not built until 1894. And a 1981 operating sketch shows Little Tunnel Cut almost two miles west of the Ferry station, which places it near Peachers Mill. Perhaps the enchanted wheel can answer all.

EAST END

Smithsonian Institution

HAVING FINALLY gotten out of the Ferry for three plus miles, we arrive at Engle (call letter N). This c. 1900 view portrays a neighborly little depot where locals could come and set awhile, but there's no bench. Further, there is precious little ballast and no tie plates. That B&O is now deep into limestone country explains the existence of Engle, for it is from here that the Bakerton Branch left the mainline to go 4.1 miles northwest to a huge quarry opened in 1895. By 1916 this quarry was the largest lime burning operation in West Virginia and an interesting variety of sidings and yard tracks dominated N for many years. In 1933 the location was reduced to part-time because of the Great Depression and on 1 October 1936 Engle was operated remotely from the Ferry. The switch leading to the branch was pulled 15 January 1958 and Engle was no more.

TRAIN NO. 9, Engine 5085 and nine cars, shows no sign of stopping at Engle on 24 June 1945. The track diverging to the left is the Bakerton Branch.

*B&OHS/
E. L. Thompson Collection*

INTO THE VALLEY

ANOTHER NEIGHBORLY STATION was Duffields (DU), about three and a half miles west of Engle and with a bench for the comfort of those wishing to discuss philosophy. Built in 1884, the structure shown replaced a stone station which was in turn converted to a private residence. One Alfred Duffield was B&O's first agent at this location, hence the name. In the early years there was a stone water tower next to the original depot and during the Civil War a blockhouse was built nearby to guard the tank. In July 1856, a second track was started from here west to Martinsburg and a third track was being added between here and Kearneysville in 1873. Ultimately three tracks were completed all the way west from Engle to Martinsburg. About midway between Engle and Duffields, Reedson was to be found with a depot and it is important to note that this facility received an indoor water closet in 1886. The line of road from Engle to Duffields follows Elk Run, which it crosses twelve times en route.

REARVIEW SHOTS of rural depots are not frequently seen, so we thought that it would be appropriate to show the backside of Duffields for the benefit of those who care.

B&O Museum

EAST END

Margaret Moreland Collection

SHENANDOAH JUNCTION (SV), about a mile west of Duffields, did not exist as such until 1880 and was then created as a mere junction with the Shenandoah Valley Railroad, a role which it plays to this day. This poor photograph looks eastward with B&O/N&W nee SV connection rails curving to the right and the B&O station appearing in the distance on the right. Yet this location epitomizes the result of a struggle between titans in the last century ... John W. Garrett of the B&O, Thomas A. Scott of the PRR and Frederick Kimball of the SV. Garrett and Scott tangled early in the Civil War, which will be related in a later chapter, and after the war ended they clashed again with rival plans to create a "deep south route" ala Garrett and a Great Valley Line ala Scott. Garrett's plans were centered on the W&P, Valley Railroad et al and Scott's vision focused on the Cumberland Valley Railroad, under PRR control as early as 1859, the East Tennessee, Virginia and Georgia and the SVRR. A postwar financial panic in 1873 clouded the waters, almost crushed Scott and rearranged the playing board. CVRR managed to get from Hagerstown to Martinsburg by 1873, but was stalled at that point until 1889 when it managed to limp into Winchester. The SVRR passed to the control of Philadelphia investment firm E. W. Clark & Company in the late 1870s and, under the leadership of young and vigorous Kimball, the road was completed from Hagerstown to Waynesboro through Shenandoah Junction and Winchester by 1881. The Clark/Kimball group controlled and reorganized an earlier road into the Norfolk and Western in 1881 and connection between the SVRR and N&W was made in 1883. Kimball won, Garrett lost and PRR recouped by gaining control of N&W in 1901 at a time when it also controlled B&O. To form Penn Central, the PRR gave up control of N&W and the latter went on to merge with Southern to form Norfolk Southern. So, for over a hundred years, B&O has had to watch all that tonnage pass overhead at Shenandoah Junction rather than over the Ferry bridges. Curiously, the traffic potential dream after the Civil War was cotton from New Orleans to northeastern mills. In the end, it turned out to be Pocahontas coal to northeastern furnaces.

B&OHS

A POSTCARD view of Shenandoah Junction circa turn-of-century looking westward ... the depot is almost completely hidden by the building closest to the boxcar. The N&W connection can be seen curving off to the left of the car.

Alice Leavell

THE CHARMING B&O station at Shenandoah Junction from the rear c. 1920 ... the B&O mainline crosses in front of the depot, going off to the left toward Cumberland. The photographer was standing on the B&O/N&W connecting tracks.

INTO THE VALLEY

JUST WEST of the depot area on a cold winter day in 1972, we see a southbound N&W freight passing over the B&O main. The Junction is an excellent location for the railroad student as traffic on the N&W (now NS) has materially increased in recent years. NS uses this line to reach its Conrail connection at Hagerstown and it is a major north-south route which avoids use of Amtrak's Northeast Corridor.

Jeff Madden

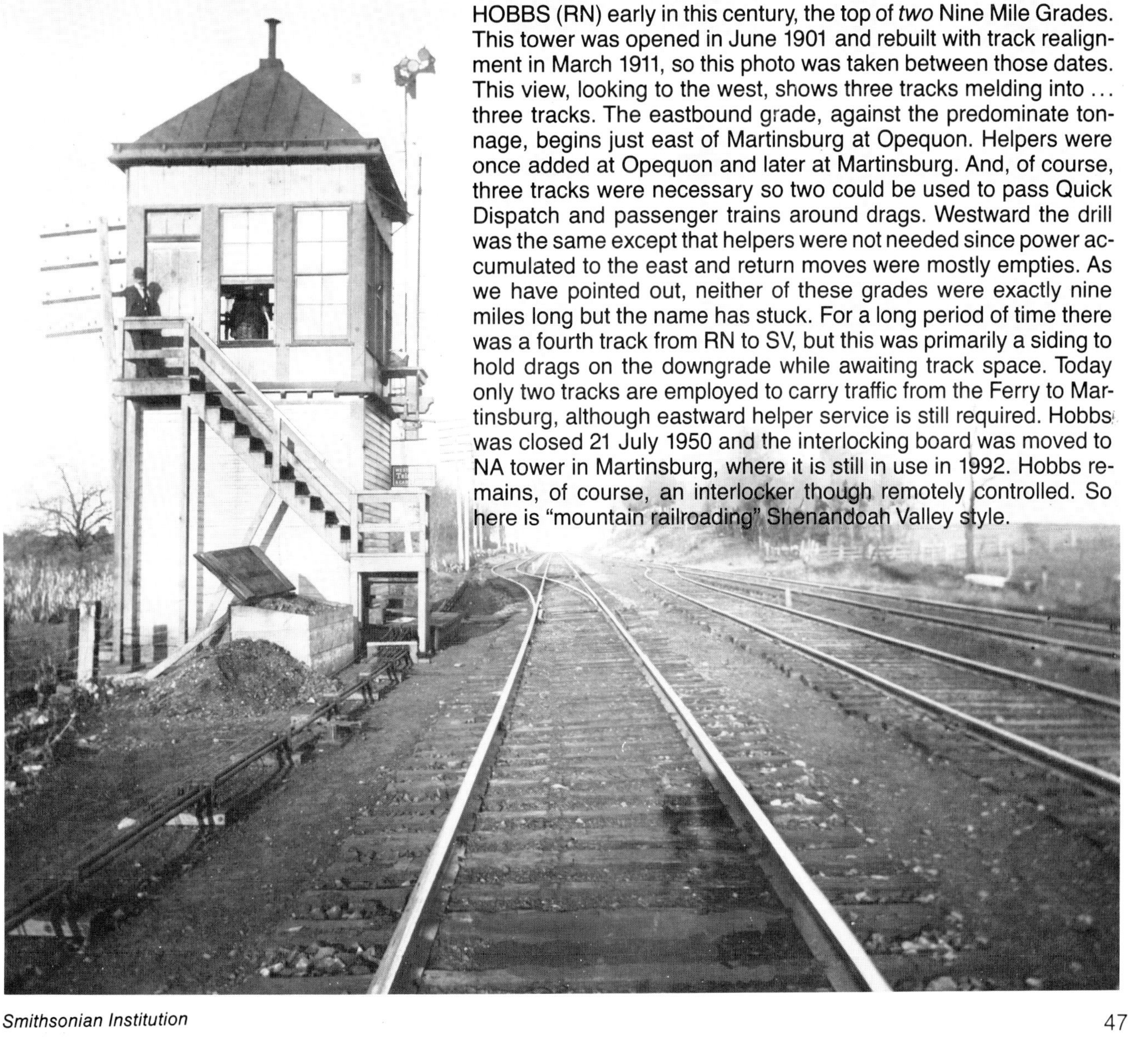

HOBBS (RN) early in this century, the top of *two* Nine Mile Grades. This tower was opened in June 1901 and rebuilt with track realignment in March 1911, so this photo was taken between those dates. This view, looking to the west, shows three tracks melding into ... three tracks. The eastbound grade, against the predominate tonnage, begins just east of Martinsburg at Opequon. Helpers were once added at Opequon and later at Martinsburg. And, of course, three tracks were necessary so two could be used to pass Quick Dispatch and passenger trains around drags. Westward the drill was the same except that helpers were not needed since power accumulated to the east and return moves were mostly empties. As we have pointed out, neither of these grades were exactly nine miles long but the name has stuck. For a long period of time there was a fourth track from RN to SV, but this was primarily a siding to hold drags on the downgrade while awaiting track space. Today only two tracks are employed to carry traffic from the Ferry to Martinsburg, although eastward helper service is still required. Hobbs was closed 21 July 1950 and the interlocking board was moved to NA tower in Martinsburg, where it is still in use in 1992. Hobbs remains, of course, an interlocker though remotely controlled. So here is "mountain railroading", Shenandoah Valley style.

Smithsonian Institution

EAST END

B&OHS

ABOUT TWO MILES west of Hobbs is Kearneysville, a small but ancient valley town and point on the B&O. Beauty is in the eye of the beholder, certainly, but the rough appearance of the Kearneysville Station does not inspire the authors. The spire on the left end of the roof and the pointed window in the eave on the right seem to be apologies for the lack of any other fancy trappings. This c. 1920 valuation photo does imply, with justice, that Kearneysville was the source of some business for B&O. Just east of this point, sidings ran to the Standard Limestone Company which, among other things, supplied concrete for three of the Magnolia Cutoff tunnels. And there was a "peach" siding nearby, as well as a public apple shed built by B&O in 1927, all of which reminds us that apples were not the only tasty morsels to grow in the Valley.

B&O Museum

THIS FREIGHT STATION and cattle chute at Kearneysville add to the impression that the town was a bustling one and that the whole Valley region boasted some fine grazing land.

INTO THE VALLEY

AN EASTBOUND QD train with a ubiquitous Big Six on the point hammers past the spur to the Newton D. Baker Veterans Hospital in the middle of Nine Mile Grade in the 1940s. This spur was removed, but another was later added from very nearly the same point to serve the Arcata Graphics plant and it is still active in 1992.

VANCLEVESVILLE, about one third of the way up Nine Mile Grade's western slope, has witnessed countless trains over 150 years of history and we would venture to say that photographer Fred Schlicting was the only one in town eager to pay any attention to just another eastbound drag on this dreary day c. 1950. The plume from EM1 7604 is awesome and proves she is at full strain ... the ground shakes as the cab goes by ... Martinsburg helper Bix Six 6136 thunders by and passes into the distance. Just another drag, just another shove, picking them up and putting them down. But what a sight and what a sound!

EAST END

50

INTO THE VALLEY

EAST END

B&O Museum

OPEQUON (QN) marked the bottom of the west slope of Nine Mile Grade. This early twentieth century view looks eastward from Flaggs Crossing . . . the second building from the right is Flaggs Mill, served by a boxcar, and the tower can be seen behind the four drop-semaphores. Although there was a telegraph station and water tank here dating from the very early years, the interlocker was not built until 1906. Precisely at noon on 7 June 1916, the QN interlocker was disconnected and automatic signals activated from Hobbs to Martinsburg. The track on the right was used as a helper pocket and today is a storage track. Beyond the tower to the east, the Eastern Sewer Pipe and Brick Company built a plant on both sides of the railroad circa 1927.

B&O Museum

FLAGGS CROSSING rated a watchman complete with shanty early in this century and apparently he came to work on horseback. Close examination of the photo reveals that the gentleman has a wooden pegleg, perhaps explaining the consideration he has shown the horse by covering it with a blanket on this winter day.

INTO THE VALLEY

B&O PRIDED itself on its "Good Neighbor" policy, but was not above making exceptions and this bridge is an example. Officially Meads Bridge, and nicknamed "Bulleye" Bridge, it carried the main road from Martinsburg to Shepherdstown over B&O rails from the time of the building of the railroad until 1939. The original bridge was rebuilt in 1856, 1872, and 1876 ... the one pictured is probably a later incarnation. Incidentally, the name "Bulleye" evolved from the practice of railroad detectives, or "bulls," using the bridge as a spot to watch for hobos attempting to board slow moving or stopped eastbound trains which were in the process of acquiring helpers at Martinsburg. By 1939, the city of Martinsburg and B&O were deep in discord over who was going to make "badly needed repairs" to the structure. Tired of the city's complaints and determined not to put another penny into the bridge, B&O resorted to tactics taught it by Stonewall Jackson some years earlier. In the dark of night, B&O sent a crane and gondola to the site and demolished the bridge. The next morning a local farmer wound his way to the spot and, lo, no bridge! And B&O never did replace it ... the City Fathers had to reroute traffic to another road. The location was just east of Martinsburg's Graveyard Curve. Perhaps the remnants are buried there, presumably without a headstone.

Chapter 4

Martinsburg

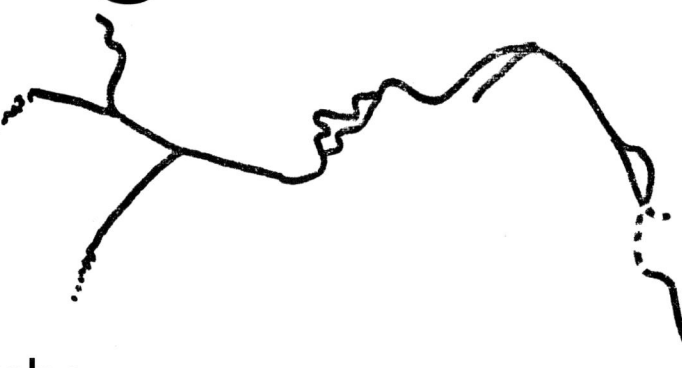

Martinsburg to Cumbo

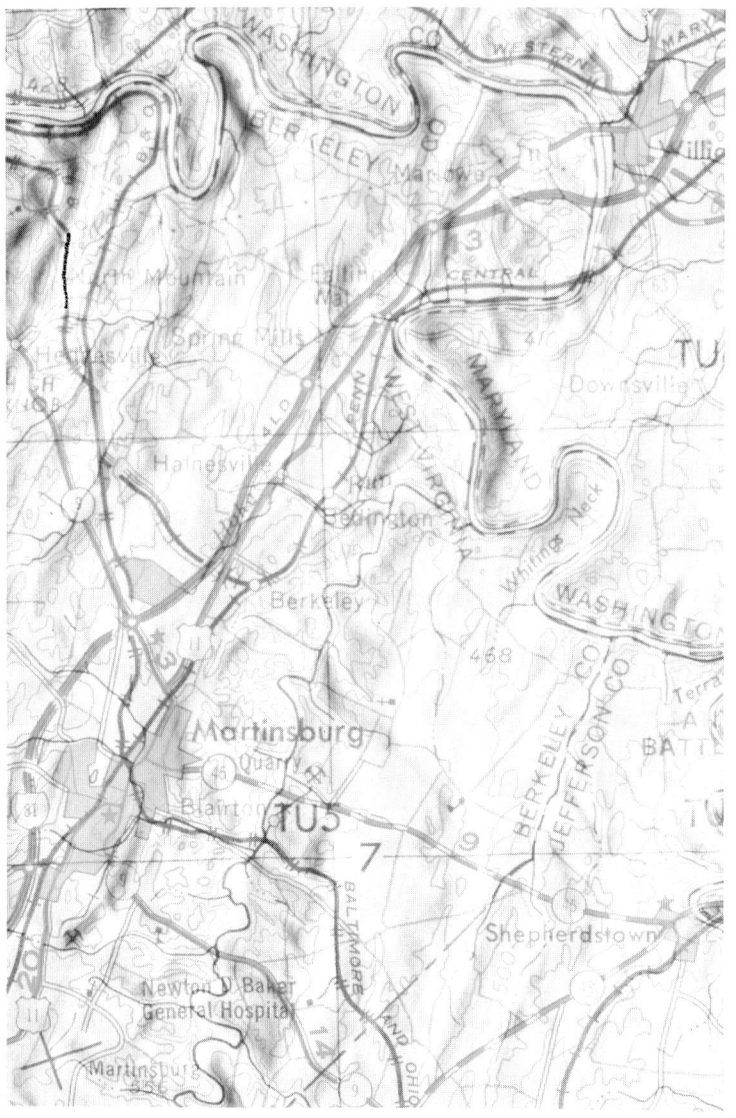

THE EAST END mainline, now traveling in a northerly direction, enters the town of Martinsburg at lower left, meets and crosses the Cumberland Valley Railroad (Penn Central on this map) just north of town, moves to a meeting with present-day Interstate 81, State Route 9 and Warm Spring at the small circle, continues northerly to an upside-down Y track complex known on the railroad as Cumbo just below the title "Hedgesville" on this map and then continues on two routes around and through North Mountain to the Potomac River. Note the single track line running southeasterly from Cumbo to Berkeley where it meets the "Penn Central" line. As shall be discussed later, this route was part of the Cherry Run and Potomac Valley Railroad lowgrade freight line (a B&O subsidiary) which was originally surveyed and planned to run from Cumbo through Shepherdstown all the way to Harpers Ferry. This chapter will present East End rails from Martinsburg to Cumbo ... the next chapter will detail the railroad west (or north) of Cumbo.

The B&O is a storied railroad and its line of road is studded with place names that loom large in the history of the United States and the Industrial Revolution. Martinsburg, a grist mill Valley town dating from the eighteenth century, ranks high on the list of prominent locales along this venerable railroad and has produced more than its share of B&O's famous "firsts." As we shall see, just north of town history produced an incident that all concerned fervently hope will be a B&O "last."

Martinsburg was a focal point for Civil War drama and a violent strike. As significant as these events would prove to be, the establishment of the town as B&O's first division point played an even greater role in the history of all railroads. Milepost 100 resides in Martinsburg, marking a crew change point. From that almost accidental act of selection evolved the principle of the "one hundred mile" working day, a labor/management bone of contention that haunts railroads to this day and gives rival truckers belly laughs as they rush their loads to destination without regard to artificial boundaries.

Of course, William Prescott Smith toured the line of road in 1853 and 1857 . . . here, with some mild editing and condensation of both accounts, we see Martinsburg as he saw it.

"At Martinsburg, the Tuscarora is again bridged twice, the crossing east of the town being made upon a viaduct of ten spans of forty four feet each, of timber and iron, supported by two abutments and eighteen stone columns in the Doric style, and which have a very agreeable effect."

"The Company has erected here large engine houses and workshops, and has made it one of their principal stations for the shelter and repair of their machinery, a measure that has greatly promoted the prosperity of the town, which like many of the old Virginia villages had previously been in a stagnant state for an almost immemorial period. Martinsburg is also the dividing station between the first and second working divisions of the road, one hundred miles from Baltimore."

Implicit in this statement is another B&O "first," probably the creation of the nation's first "railroad town."

Smith passed off the next eight miles west from Martinsburg as having "nothing striking in the scenery" until North Mountain comes into view. The authors disagree . . . the route from Martinsburg to Cumbo is rolling farm and orchard land with multicolored limestone outcrops highlighting many pastoral scenes that are a pleasure to behold.

The stretch of railroad between Martinsburg and Cumbo was built with strong Irish and German backs. The Pillar/Colonade Bridge to which Smith referred was apparently built by a Major Eads and supervised by a German named Rotterdam with German labor . . . the road west by a contractor named William O'Neal with Irish labor.

We will follow the usual pattern of providing detailed history in captions to photographs and drawings along the line of road, but wish at this point to direct the reader's attention to the small circle at Warm Spring on the preceding map. On 9 March 1949 this remote way station bore witness to the Last Great Train Robbery in U.S. history.

According to various newspaper and police accounts, the prestigious westbound Ambassador No. 19 with 147 passengers and crew had just passed the Warm Spring crossing when the train went into emergency and came to a stop at approximately 7:40 p.m.

It seems that two zoot-suited men from Ohio (Luman C. Ramsdell, 23, and George L. Ashton, 21) had been tossing down a few in the club car when they were refused further service because the train was then in West Virginia, "dry" with respect to liquor by the drink at that time.

These two stalwarts expressed their displeasure with this decision by pulling the plug on the train and their pistols from their pockets and proceeding to rob fellow passengers, in the process shooting a car steward in the leg who was trying to keep the men from entering his car. Somehow they got the train backed to the crossing, where they departed only to enter the Clover Rail Club Tavern at the crossing and commenced robbing the patrons to the tune of about $1500.

According to State Police Sergeant Emmett Roush, in charge of the subsequent investigation, the Clover Rail was the roughest of sixty-three taverns in the county at that time. The locals got religion in a hurry and it is said that so many were trying to squeeze under a backroom bed that it arose from the floor, the opposite of the procedure most nights.

In the meantime, B&O diesel maintainer Robert Mort made his escape from the train, hitched a ride with a motorist whose auto had been stopped by the train at the crossing, dashed into Martinsburg and reported the incident to disbe-

EAST END

lieving police. Finally convinced, the police rushed to the town's only police cruiser and roared into the sunset, only to run out of gas just after passing under the Queen Street tunnel.

Back at the scene of the crime, the two robbers tired of Clover Rail hospitality and commandeered the new 1949 Buick of one F. A. Townsend (also stopped at the crossing) after beating him.

They drove to a deadend road by the tracks, hiked to Kearneysville and boarded a bus for Washington. The driver, Mr. Bill Lopp, was suspicious and finally managed to inform a sheriff in Leesburg enroute to Washington. The sheriff phoned ahead and Washington police were waiting at the bus terminal. The pair, however, had spotted a pawn shop about two blocks from the terminal and had alighted to cash in some of their loot. The DC police moved quickly to the shop, a gun fight erupted, Ramsdell was wounded, the duo surrendered, confessed and were whisked away to Federal prison. They were paroled in 1956 and in 1960 they lodged suit for $50 million against B&O, claiming that the railroad had served drinks to "minors" and thus was clearly to blame for causing them to run amuck!

We are confident that the reader will join with us in hoping that the judge did not die laughing.

Berkeley County Historical Society

LOOKING EASTBOUND from the west side of the Pillar/Colonade Bridge, we see a magnificent structure of unusual and perhaps unique design in a pre-1861 view ... in fact, the only photograph taken of the bridge and known to the authors. Probably built in the 1840-41 era, the bridge was only twenty years old when it was wasted by Stonewall Jackson in 1861. The bridge crossed Tuscarora Creek and was a timber and iron affair with 44 foot spans supported by 18 stone columns and apparently was double tracked. Undoubtedly the bridge would have perished in later years as heavier equipment made it inadequate, so perhaps a quick death was the more merciful one.

ALTHOUGH THIS RENDERING of the Pillar Bridge is somewhat inaccurate, it is probably the best illustration to match Ele Bowen's 1854 quote in *Rambles in the Path of the Steam Horse*, "the bridge presents a fine architectural appearance which is heightened by the mill, the willow trees and numerous other things thereunto belonging and appertaining." This view, which was taken from Bowen's work, is from the east side of the bridge looking west with Martinsburg seen beyond the structure. The grist mill of one Adam Stephens can be seen behind the bridge on the left ... the train, of course, is westbound.

Warren Somerville

MARTINSBURG

THIS POSTCARD scene almost certainly was taken from a photograph shortly after Jackson destroyed the bridge. The view looks easterly with the Stephens mill in sight and two tracks sagging over the eastern abutment. The puzzling aspect is the lateral distance between the pillars ... one would expect to find a third row of pillars supporting the center of the bridge. Whatever the design of the superstructure, it must have been satisfactory as we have found no reports of trouble.

THE FOUNDER of Martinsburg was Adam Stephen, who counted among his accomplishments this grist mill to which we have already referred. The town was apparently founded c. 1772. After Jackson put paid to the Pillar Bridge, B&O replaced it with temporary trestlework which lasted until 1872 when B&O filled in around it and constructed the substantial stone retaining walls (seen here in the background) to contain the fill. It was not a small project ... 9,749 cubic yards of masonry and 16,589 cubic yards of fill were involved, in addition to 31,000 cubic yards of earth removed from the site. The result was a structure even Jackson's ghost could not blow away. This photo is post-1876 because in that year B&O added the handrails shown. The mill building itself is interesting and it should be noted that the Frog Hollow Branch would soon run in front of it.

EAST END

Warren Somerville

AGAIN we can thank Ele Bowen and his 1854 work for this illustration, which has been adapted from an etching in his book. This view looks westward and on the extreme left we see the edge of a building and a shadow which probably represents the original depot destroyed by Jackson in 1861. The platform structure just beyond appears to be an early coaling structure, with a water jug across the tracks. The large structure on the left is the hotel which became the B&O station after the 1861 destruction. Bowen reports that coal train lengths were shortened at Martinsburg, preparatory to climbing Nine Mile Grade, which implies that helpers were not used at that time.

THREE-POSITION SIGNALS.

Indication—Proceed at slow speed prepared to stop.
Name—Slow-speed-signal.

B&OHS

ATOP THE REPLACEMENT for the Pillar Bridge (now inelegantly named Bridge 49½) on 6 April 1937, the viewer is looking northward (westbound) into B&O's Martinsburg complex. The first structure in sight on the left is the Martinsburg Fruit Exchange, behind which can be seen two cars sitting on the "pay car track" next to a branch to Frog Hollow. Beyond the fruit exchange, and almost out of sight, is the "new" station and NA Tower. On the right, first we see the "East" Roundhouse built in 1872 and then the domed-top "West" Roundhouse built in 1866. Between the two roundhouses can be seen the roof of the Machine Shop Building and beyond the West Roundhouse another major shop building topped with a curious tower. Incidentally, Bridge 49½ was built to four track width in 1872 and could more properly be called a viaduct as two 13′6″ brick and stone arches pierce the walls.

MARTINSBURG

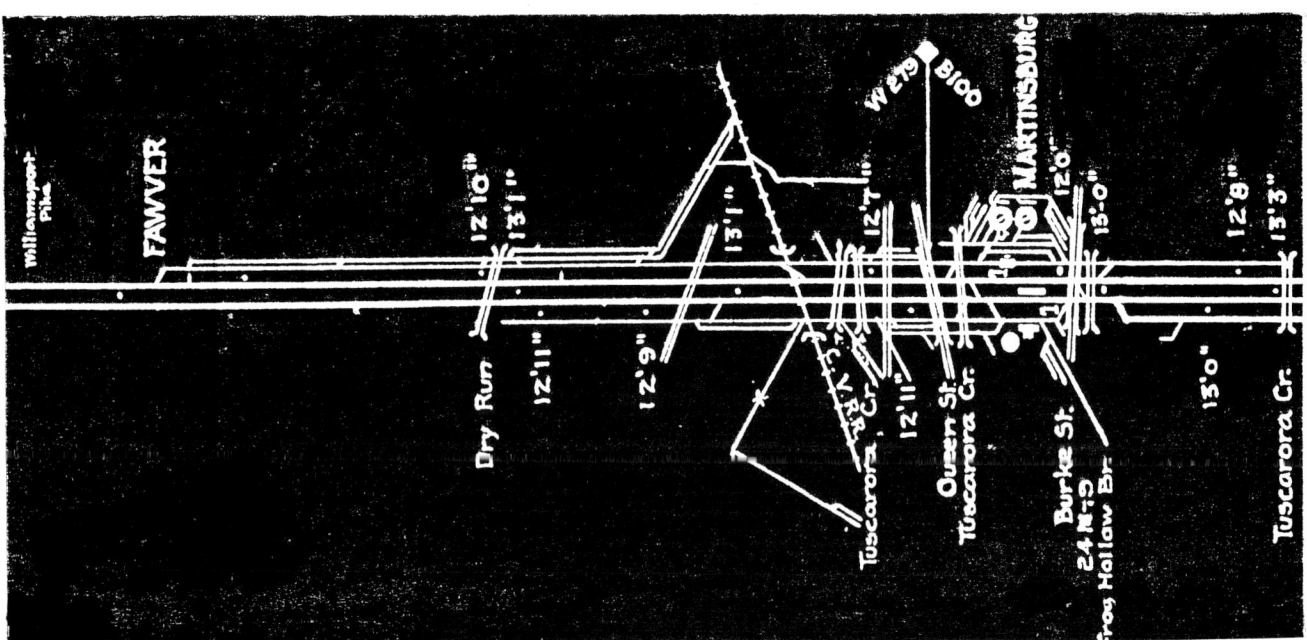

THIS C. 1930 track chart of the Martinsburg/Fawver area presents an excellent straight-line overview of the three-mile long complex. Going from right to left, note Burke Street, the Frog Hollow branch leaving from the station area, the shops across the tracks, Queen Street, Milepost B100, the Cumberland Valley Railroad overpass with connecting tracks from Fawver and, of course, Fawver itself, Much of the following story will relate to these places along the railroad.

THE FROG HOLLOW Branch leaves the B&O main just east of the "new" depot and runs southeasterly for several miles to tap traffic from limestone kilns and a large quarry. Built in the late 1880s, the branch has followed quarry expansion to the southeast to the extent that today it is over two and a half miles long, complete with a loop at the end. This photo shows the line under construction in the last century and is amusing because the railroad is removing only a small amount of picket fence to minimize interference with local residents. Today, when an interstate highway is built, the bulldozers plow away everything in sight. This branch also has a siding near the mainline called the "pay car track," so named in ancient times when railroad employees were paid in cash from a traveling bank on wheels. The name has stuck and is used to this day, proving that railroaders are very reluctant to change traditional nomenclature.

EAST END

THE CREW of the "Frog Hollow Jet" poses at a road crossing on the branch of the same name in 1910 in front of husky 0-8-0 1092, a slide valve job that looks quite capable of lugging tonnage. One assumes that a fringe benefit of service on the branch was the ability to spot the pay car as soon as it arrived.

B&O's ORIGINAL Martinsburg station was east of this location and, of course, was destroyed by Stonewall Jackson in 1861. The structure seen here was built in 1849 as a hotel by a man named Kroeson and went by various names, including Kroeson's, Depot House, National Hotel and Berkeley Hotel. B&O leased part of the building as a depot in 1861 and purchased the whole property in 1866. This c. 1870 photo shows the main building apparently as originally constructed and sporting the name Berkeley Hotel . . . rail historians, of course, are delighted to see fine examples of short wheelbase pot hoppers and a two-digit Camel. The two additions to the right probably were added shortly after B&O purchased the property . . . as we shall see, the main building was expanded up and back at a later date. Hotel operations continued until at least 1925, although it is possible that it may have primarily served as a crew base.

Smithsonian Institution

MARTINSBURG

THIS PRE-1900 photo, when compared to the previous view, clearly shows that the Berkeley Hotel had a top floor added and a large wing built on the rear. Note the switch stand by the stone wall ... this marks the beginning of the Frog Hollow Branch.

B&OHS

LOCATION is supposed to be everything in real estate, but surely one would not put a hotel in the middle of a busy railroad mainline and shop area in the steam era if any other rational choice was available. This c. 1916 valuation photo of the Martinsburg Station/Hotel clearly shows the effects of being sited in a constant cloud of cinders, smoke, unburned carbon and general grime.

EAST END

THIS POSTCARD scene of the station area dates to the early years in this century to judge by the locomotive pilot, early auto and horsedrawn wagon.

SOMETHING NEW has been added to the station area in this postcard scene with message dated 1911 and, of course, it is NA Interlocker hard by the stone wall and Frog Hollow switch. NA as an interlocker was opened in February of 1900, but obviously not in this location ... some evidence suggests that it was originally a half mile or so to the west. As reported, the interlocking board from Hobbs was moved to NA in 1950 and a back room was added to this structure to accommodate it ... the "tower" is active in 1992. Sadly, the station building is not ... it was condemned in 1992 for broken windows which led to pigeons which led to excrement which led to health hazards which led to a death sentence for the House That Kroeson Built. Happily, the station was recently purchased by a local historic property developer along with the shops across the tracks. No firm plans have been announced, but at least the buildings have been stabilized to prevent further damage.

MARTINSBURG

Theodore Hare Collection
THE FIRST TRAIN arrived in Martinsburg on 21 May 1842 and the last true B&O passenger train on 1 May 1971, ending a 129 year tradition. Here we see the eastbound Capitol Limited making a farewell station stop at 8:15 a.m. Of course, Amtrak and commuter trains continue to stop at Martinsburg ... indeed, Amtrak's new Capitol Limited pauses here. But there is no station ... passengers board from the platform and buy tickets on the train.

Jeff Madden
STONEWALL JACKSON was not the last apparition to visit the East End. Here, in March of 1972, we see the westbound Potomac Turbo entering Martinsburg. This product of wizard aircraft engineers, touted as capable of 170 mph speeds, had difficulty running at all. Begun as a six month experiment, this notable trainset only lasted about three months and lived up to its reputation by breaking down and missing its last scheduled run 13 May 1972. It was a great passenger draw, of course ... its 144 seats usually had 12-15 passengers. A senior B&O operating executive described the train as having "floating problems," eg, sometimes it would refuse to back and other times refuse to go forward. When standard power had to be added to bail it out (which was frequent), a portable coupler had to be installed to match pulling faces and even this device had a tendency to drop out, derailing the train on at least one occasion. Well, at least it was good for laughs.

EAST END

THIS EARLY B&O design water tank was located just northwest of the station in what is now a parking lot and almost certainly built in the last century ... it was replaced by a more modern jug closer to the Queen Street underpass. The East End was frequently plagued by too much water and, on other occasions, by not enough. For example, a 1934 drought forced B&O to lay a 1400 foot pipeline to nearby West Quarry to draw water to trackside ... so urgent was the need that the project was completed in a day or so, including running an electric line to run the pumps pulling water from the quarry hole.

JUST WEST of the station is Queen Street which we see here around the turn of the century after crossing gates were installed in 1891. The stone warehouse on the right was built by the Kroeson family and in 1866 was supplied with telegraph facilities and an agent. The building on the left housed a tavern which had a somewhat bloodthirsty reputation in its day and apparently was an early manifestation of the Clover Rail bistro alluded to in this chapter.

MARTINSBURG

THE QUEEN STREET crossing became, it is easy to see, a bottleneck and this underpass (or "subway" to the locals) was completed in 1924. By that time the problem must have been serious with traffic backing up for miles. B&O and the city reached an agreement in 1917, but it took seven years to complete ... surely some sort of record for dawdling. Being only two lanes wide, it is still a bottleneck in 1992. This photo was taken in the early 1950s ... note the diesels swinging by.

IF THE READER will refer back to the Martinsburg track chart in this chapter, he will see a location called Dry Run about a mile west of the Cumberland Valley Railroad overhead bridge. Here was still another East End limestone quarry. The substantial limekilns pictured here are mute evidence of what was once a thriving industry ... the nine ovens in this structure were fed by railcars on tracks running on top. Lime was dumped in and coked off at the bottom. The branch was opened in the 1880s, but by 1929 the quarry was full of water which was flowing in too rapidly to pump out.

BEFORE the West Quarry Branch lies the B&O freight house in Martinsburg, built in 1881 and shown here in 1978. The handsome structure is extant in 1992, although derelict and frequented by the local "homeless." Tastes vary and beauty as always is in the eye of the beholder, but to us this is one of the most graceful structures we have ever seen. John Garrett's reign may be criticized for many things, fairly or not, but surely all would agree that comeliness in structure design was one of his lasting visual contributions to the B&O.

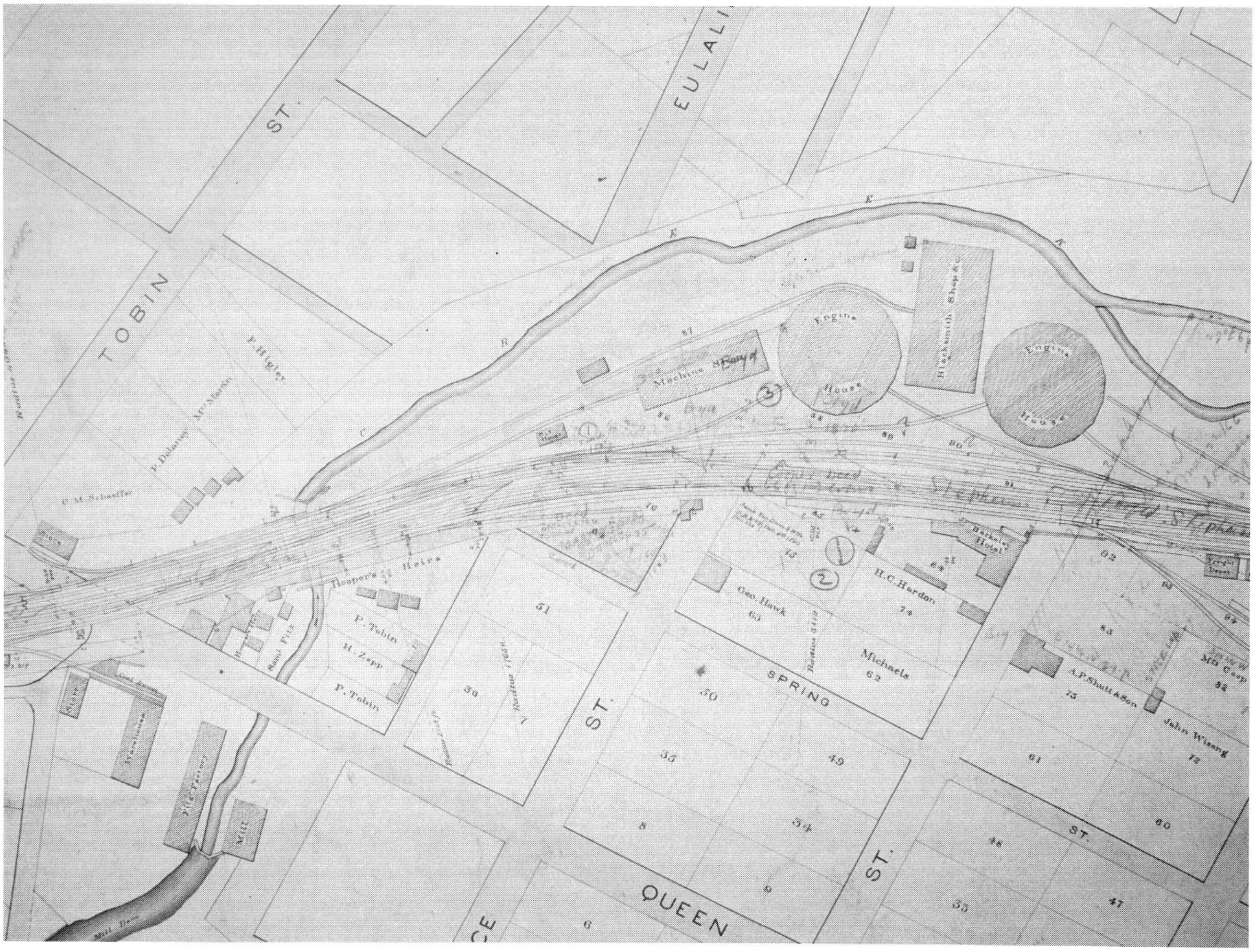

EAST END

B&O Museum

DATING TO THE EARLY 1870s and taken from a company map, this interesting overview of the Martinsburg complex shows, south of the mainline, an agent's office, early freight depot, the budding Frog Hollow Branch, Berkeley Hotel, water jug, mill with dam and, diagonally across the lower left, Queen Street. North of the tracks, from right to left, appears the East Roundhouse (1872), Blacksmith Shop, West Roundhouse (1866) and Machine Shop with oil house, all interlaced with tracks and turnouts. The penciled notations refer to updates and changes.

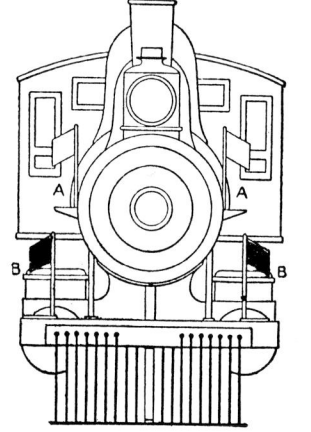

Engine Running Backward by Day as an Extra Train, Without Cars or at the Rear of a Train Pushing Cars.
White flags at A A. See Rule 21.
Green flags at B B, as markers.

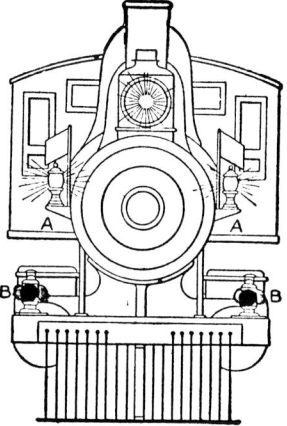

Engine Running Backward by Night as an Extra Train, Without Cars or at the Rear of a Train Pushing Cars.
White lights and white flags at A A. See Rule 21.
Lights at B B, as markers, showing green at side and in direction engine is moving and red in opposite direction. See

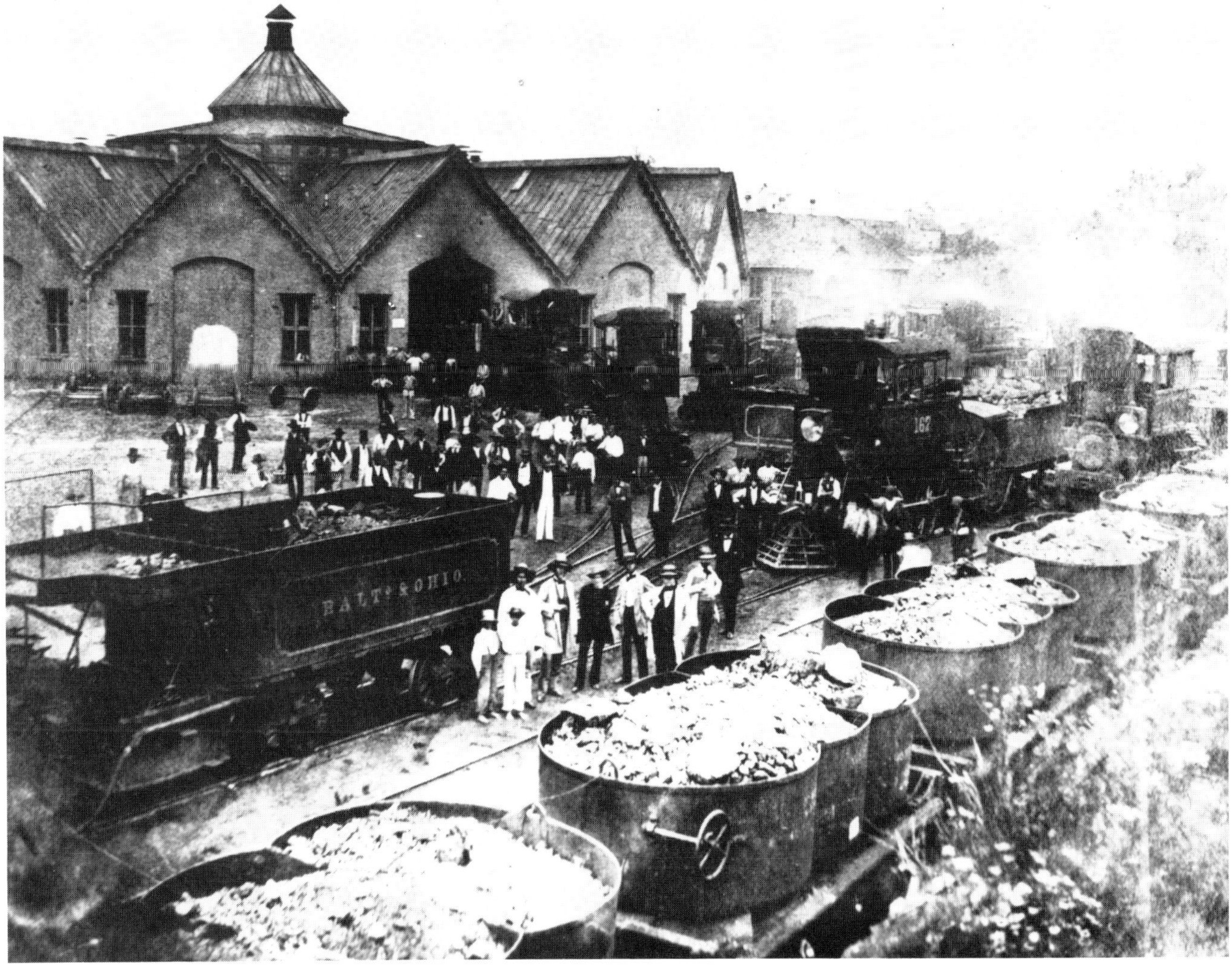

MARTINSBURG

B&OHS

MARTINSBURG had been a railroad center for fifteen years when this photograph of the original engine house was taken in 1857 and the spectre of a Civil War was only a vague vision. Winans Camel locomotives and pot hoppers fill a scene framed by a very attractive as well as utilitarian structure which is flanked on the right by a barely seen machine shop. The only engine number visible, at middle right, is that of the 167 which was built by Denmead in September 1853 ... she was dropped from the roster in 1880 and did not make the long trek to Dixie in 1861 after Stonewall Jackson laid waste to just about everything in sight. It is quite possible, of course, that some of the other engines seen here did take a four year holiday in the Sunny South. Those pot hoppers introduce another bit of B&O lore. In the mid 1920s, B&O official Revell Brown found two of them, along with an iron boxcar, lost in the weeds on the Bakerton Branch near Engle and had them removed ... they ended up in B&O's Fair of the Iron Horse in 1927 and are in the B&O Museum to this day. Mr. Brown went on to become president of the Reading Railroad, no doubt in reward for this sterling historical service.

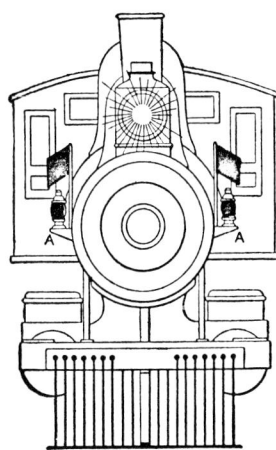

Engine Running Forward at Night Displaying Signals for a Following Section.
Green lights and green flags at A A.

67

EAST END

B&O Museum

TAKEN IN 1871 or mid 1872, this eastward view of the complex shows, from left to right, the oil house, Machine Shop, 1866 West Roundhouse, Blacksmith Shop and, faintly seen behind the A frames on the extreme right, the walls of the new 1872 Roundhouse standing about three feet high and under construction. The derrick cranes are in use building a stone retaining wall which stands to this day. The Blacksmith Shop bears metal trimwork marked "B&O RR 1866."

THE EAST ROUNDHOUSE, probably in the second decade of this century, is a bit grimy but at least is in the use for which it was intended. This house had sixteen engine pits and was in active use by the railroad until 1985 when it was closed... the West Roundhouse was used until 14 March 1988. In the later years, the buildings were used in reclamation work. The jobs were moved to Barboursville, West Virginia, with the last nineteen men transferred or laid off. On 14 May 1990, juveniles set fire to wooden pallets in this building and it was gutted with only the brick shell remaining.

B&OHS

MARTINSBURG

THESE INTERIOR views of the Martinsburg roundhouses were taken early in this century. A 1970 Historic American Engineering Study states that the roofs of these structures were originally of cast iron and allowed maximum center floor area free of obstructions. The clerestory domes apparently employed two concentric circles of cast iron to support the roof, later changed to wood trusses.

THIS STUNNING photograph, c. 1950, was taken by B&O Conductor Melvin Hollar who, together with four of his children (two sets of twins), was a member of the West Virginia Civil Air Patrol. The odd patterns on the roofs of the roundhouses were actually aeronautical symbols identifying Martinsburg. By the time of this photo, the complex was devoted to reclamation and bridge work. Note that the wing to the right of the station has been replaced by a one-story structure.

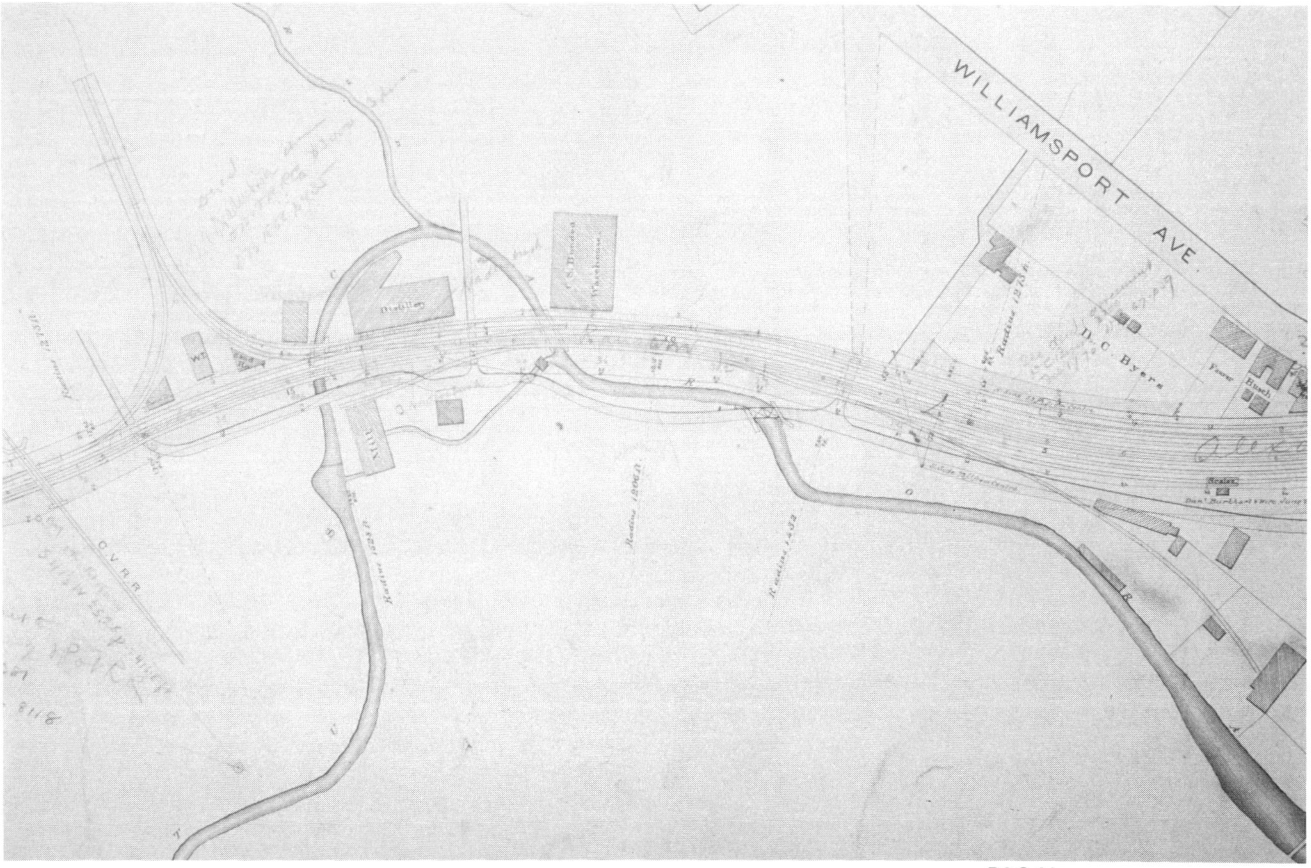

EAST END

B&O Museum

THIS COMPANY MAP of the terrain west of the Martinsburg shop complex records the scene in the early 1870s . . . note, at lower left, the CVRR bridge over B&O. Moving from right to left, note the warehouse, distillery and gaggle of buildings in the triangle of the wye as well as the mill across the tracks . . . they will be seen shortly.

THIS PRE-CIVIL WAR photo shows a Camel working west past the warehouse on the right and approaching the Hannisville Distillery. The distillery was closed, of course, during prohibition and National Fruit Products Company used the buildings into the 1980s. The road bridge reached a mill as shown on the preceding map, later served by a B&O siding. The leftmost track in the scene was a siding leading to a team track known locally as the Maple Avenue siding, which lasted until the late 1980s. One thinks of Martinsburg as being a small town, yet the size of that warehouse indicates that it was a major commercial center. And the distillery establishes that Martinsburg was fully civilized a century and a half ago.

70

MARTINSBURG

B&OHS

PROBABLY A VALUATION shot taken in the second decade of this century, this view shows the east leg of the CV connection track wending off to the right past a corner of the distillery. Please notice the B&O boxcar just appearing to the right of the center pump house building... it is sitting on the west leg of the wye, which as we shall show was a very busy piece of track in the early 1900s.

THE WYE TRIANGLE did not want for buildings... this valuation shot c. 1916 shows an eclectic mixture of structures supporting a water station, including an early B&O penstock. Water for this facility came from nearby Tuscarora Creek which must not have been of the highest quality because a water treatment plant was installed here as early as 1858. We assume that the distillery used water from the same creek untreated, which gives the reader an insight into the potency of the local whiskey. These buildings probably date from the late 1860s... water quality must not have improved because B&O built a new treatment plant here in 1928. The track serving this facility was not removed until 15 June 1958, although the structures were probably gone a few years prior to that date.

B&OHS

EAST END

B&OHS

THE PANIC of 1873 resulted in an ever deepening depression during the 1870s and railroads, including B&O, reacted with pay reductions for employees. For the second time in less than a year, John Garrett ordered another 10% pay cut to be effective 16 July 1877 while maintaining a high dividend rate and waxing eloquent about B&O's financial condition and prospects. He soon learned workers could also read and a bloody strike began in Baltimore, spreading quickly to Martinsburg and, indeed, throughout the country as other railroads joined him in slashing wages. In Martinsburg, the railroad was blockaded by workers and a pattern of troop call-ups and violence ensued. Actually, the strike at Martinsburg was rather mild compared to other points around the nation ... PRR's Pittsburgh facilities became a war zone and ten thousand troops were required to put down the "insurrection." This photograph shows power accumulation at Martinsburg during the strike, which petered out by early August. Some good came out of this unpleasantness ... Garrett made some concessions to workers and created the B&O Employees Relief Association in 1880, which provided some health care and retirement provisions for workers. Earlier in this chapter we have referred to the "100 mile" working day as being a burden for railroads in modern times ... it was not, however, unreasonable in the last century. With train speeds of ten or so miles per hour and inevitable delays, one hundred miles made for a very long day for operating employees, and constant layovers waiting for a returning train added to the burden. While the strikers lost the battle of 1877, in the end they won and proved the wisdom of the adage that "any company with a union probably deserves it."

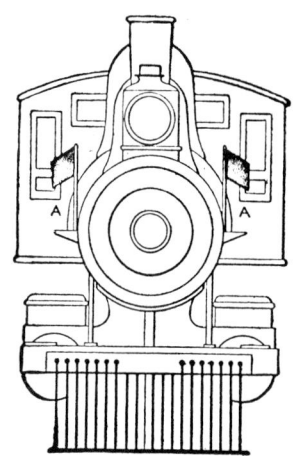

Engine Running Forward by Day Displaying Signals for a Following Section.
Green flags at **A A.**

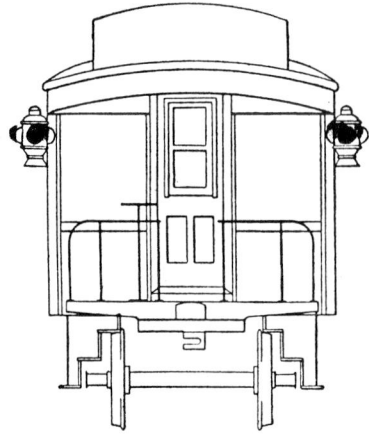

Rear of Train by Night Running on Any Track Against the Current of Traffic.

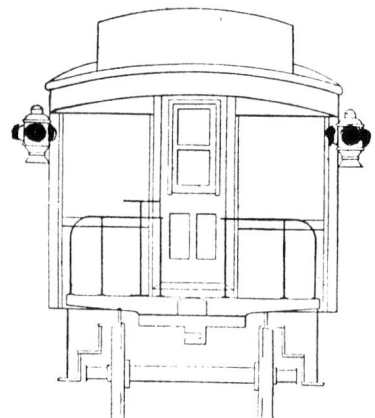

Rear of Train by Night Running With the Current of Traffic on a Slow Speed Track.

MARTINSBURG

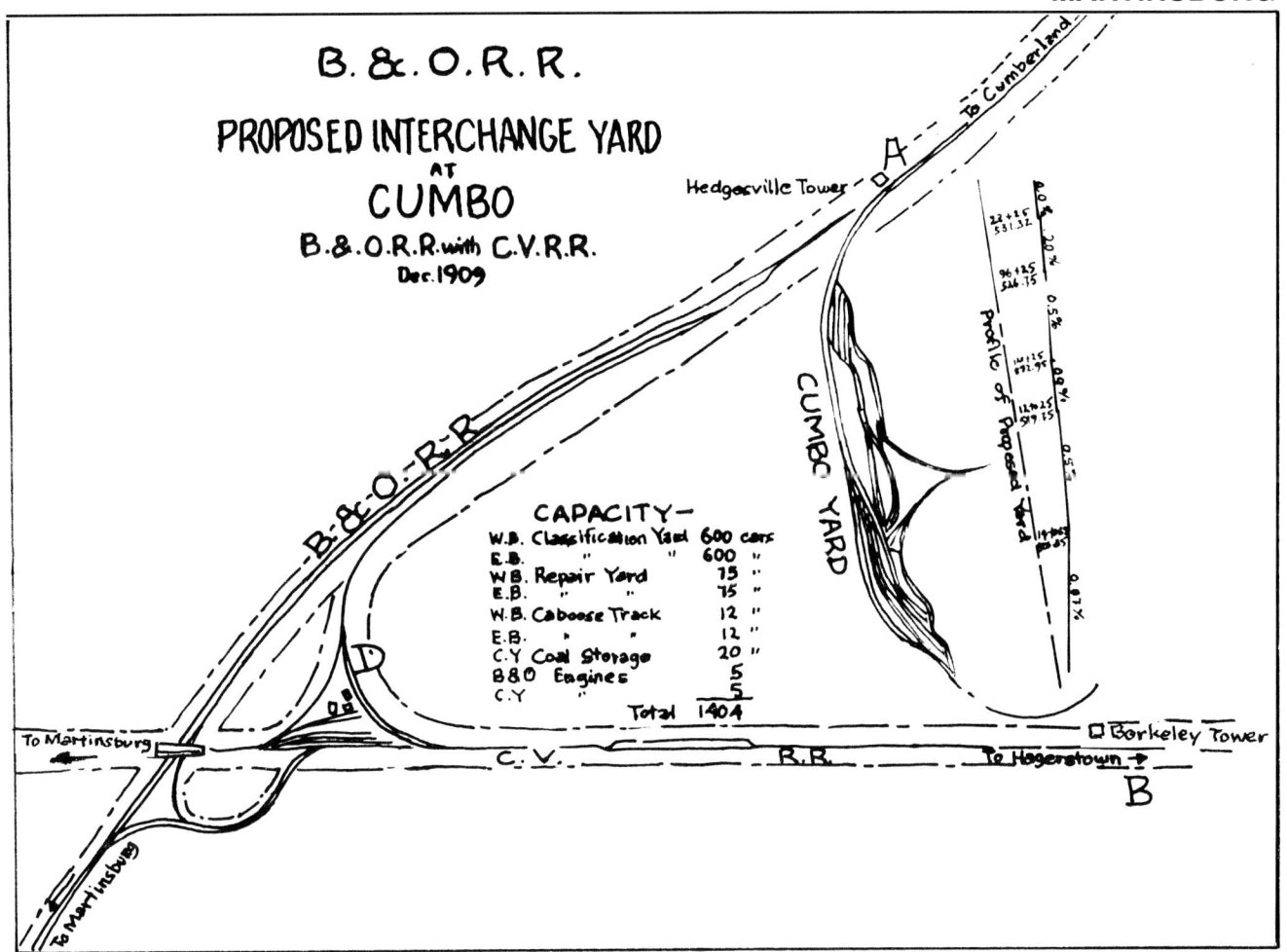

THE EAST END has never wanted for drama throughout its history and the line of road just west of Martinsburg did not prove to be an exception. The lower left area of this sketch shows the original CVRR connection and wye as well as the CV bridge crossing B&O rails to downtown Martinsburg and beyond to Winchester. B&O rails continue to Hedgesville Tower. In and of itself, this stretch of railroad is merely a tiny part of the East End of little significance. In 1964 Interstate 81 swept across B&O, taking with it the Clover Rail Club Tavern, and in the mid-1960s General Motors built a parts plant just west of that highway ... B&O reached that facility with Pearson siding and yard. By the turn of the century, Hedgesville was just a little town along the railroad ... the tower there was not built until 1904. Yet this sketch for a proposed interchange yard dated December 1909 implies that something happened in the first decade of this century that affected this sleepy piece of railroad. Something did, in spades, and it was called the Great Coal Push. First, some background. The Western Maryland had completed a line from Hagerstown to Cherry Run on the B&O (about nine miles west of Hedgesville) in 1892. Heavy traffic, primarily coal, flooded west from Cumberland to Cherry Run, thence to the WM and from there through Hagerstown to the Reading and northeastern markets ... it was called the Central States Dispatch route. By 1902, PRR controlled B&O and, through B&O, the Reading. In that era, George Gould was busily building a huge transcontinental railroad empire and, toward that end, acquired WM as well as the West Virginia Central and Pittsburg, a coal line that reached from Cumberland deep into West Virginia coal and timber lands. PRR felt threatened by the Gould aspirations and when they felt threatened, they had a tendency to take action that shook the earth. In the fall of 1902, they issued orders that henceforth all eastward tonnage would bypass Cherry Run, go to Martinsburg, transfer to CVRR (controlled by them for years) and then go to Hagerstown and market. Since WM did not at that time have a line from the Cherry Run area to Cumberland, this action put Gould in a bit of a bind ... in fact, so much so that this development played a major role in collapsing the Gould enterprise in 1908. When one annoyed the Penn in those days, one took his private parts in his hands ... they cut to kill. As far as B&O and CV were concerned, this action dumped vast tonnages of traffic on parts of their railroads where they were ill equipped to receive it and that, in turn, triggered a vast expansion of yard facilities as shown in this sketch. We believe the area "D" at lower left represents the initial reaction of B&O and CV to handle this flow ... Cumbo Yard itself was not entirely completed until February of 1915 in response to an ever increasing wave of traffic that crested between 1907 and 1914. By 1927, B&O (and Reading) were long free of PRR domination and WM was under B&O control, so much of volume was shifted back to Cherry Run. But it was all something to behold for a number of years.

EAST END

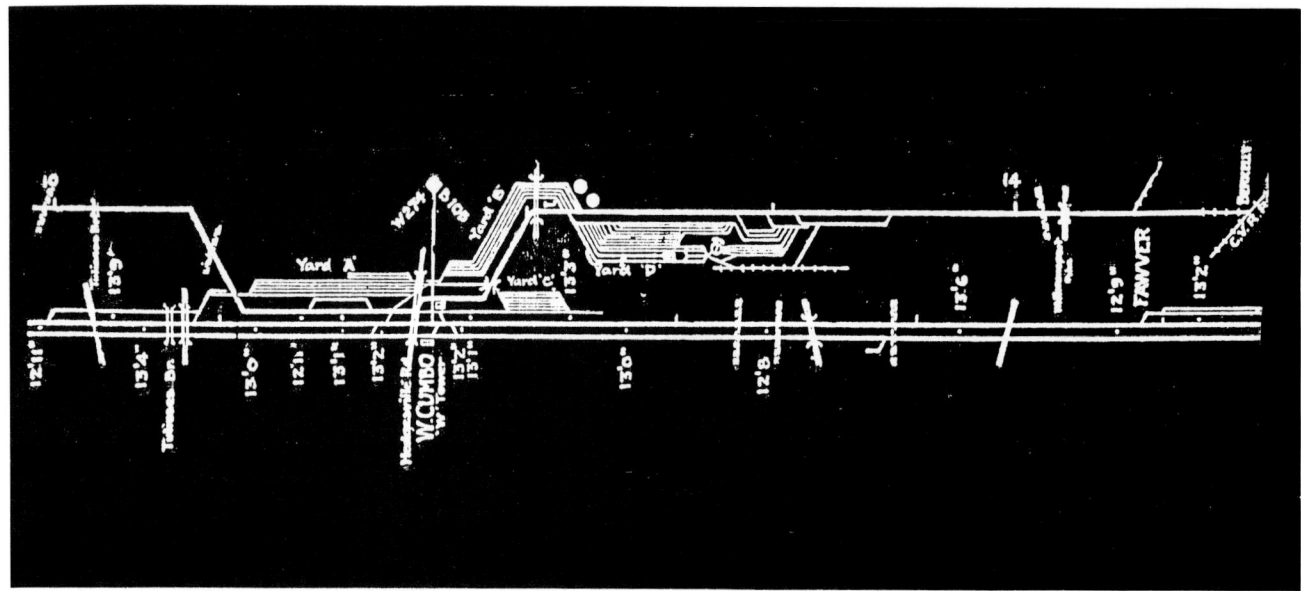

THIS 1930s TRACK CHART probably represents the Cumbo complex at its height. As far as the B&O was concerned, Hedgesville became West Cumbo ... East Cumbo was generally associated with the CVRR which actually owned some trackage and engine servicing facilities as can be seen by slashed lines just to the right of Yard D and farther to the right as their lines were approached at Berkeley. By the "D" in "Yard D," please note the symbol indicating a coaling trestle ... more of this later. As previously mentioned, the line eastward from Yard D was part of the CR&PV low grade line that did not get farther east than Berkeley. On the upper left, the reader should note the single track line leaving the Yard A area and leading westward ... this is the low-grade CR&PV line to Cherry Run. As will be shown, this line has always been primarily an eastbound track and carries the number four even though it lies to the east of the mainline. This complex handled a lot of cars ... in 1929, 30,000 interchange cars per month flowed through it in both directions. While B&O shifted much CSD traffic back to WM at Cherry Run in 1927, Cumbo was a major facility with much trackage as late as 1981. Today, in 1992, it is all weeds and memories.

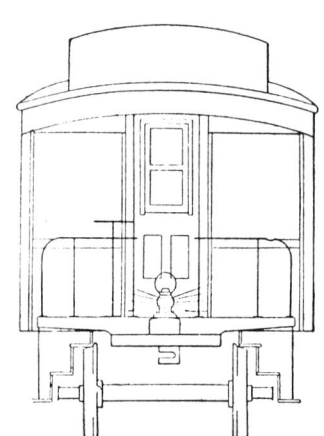

Passenger Cars Being Pushed by an Engine by Night.

White light on front of leading car.

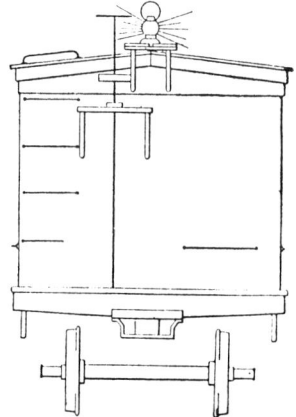

Freight Cars being Pushed by an Engine by Night.

White light on front of leading car.

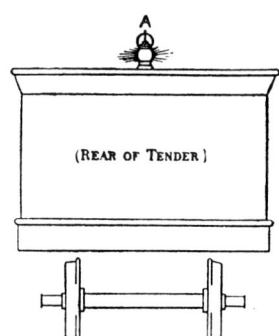

Engine Running Backward by Night, Without Cars or at the Front of a Train Pulling Cars.

White light at A.

MARTINSBURG

ON THE PREVIOUS track chart we have drawn the reader's attention to the location of the Cumbo coaling trestle . . . here it is in all its glory on 6 September 1916. The following three photographs were taken from atop this utilitarian structure.

B&OHS

THIS WESTWARD view from the coaling trestle in 1917, for all its graininess, at least gives the correct impression that Cumbo was a yard in the middle of nowhere.

EAST END

STILL ATOP the coaling trestle but with the camera sighted a bit more to the left, this c. 1920 view brings the c. 1911 YMCA building at Cumbo into the photograph. The foundation of this building was used as late as 1985 to temper switch frogs.

THIS EASTWARD view from the coaling trestle at Cumbo reminds us that the steam era, with all its charms, was also the age of cinders, smoke, coal gas and grime. Through the smoke, one can make out the engine servicing facilities and attendant structures.

Back—Swung vertically in a circle at half arm's length across the track.

MARTINSBURG

Berkeley County Historical Society

PEOPLE are also part of the picture ... here, in the East Cumbo yard area, we see a number of men leaving their mark for posterity along with the 1230. The structure at extreme left appears to be the body of an early caboose and, just to the left of the engine and in the distance, there appears to be a tank car body mounted for water use.

Jeff Madden

WEST CUMBO, Hedgesville and Wilsons have all been used to identify this location at the western edge of the yard complex. The first tower (W) was on the south side of the tracks somewhat west of this spot, but that tower burned down 17 February 1912 and was replaced by this structure ... there were many misadventures on that day, incidentally, which we will treat in a later chapter. This August 1979 scene shows the Chessie Steam Special westbound with ex-Reading 2101 on the point and a curious crewman watching from the platform of the caboose on the far left.

77

Chapter 5

Back to the Potomac

Cumbo to Cherry Run

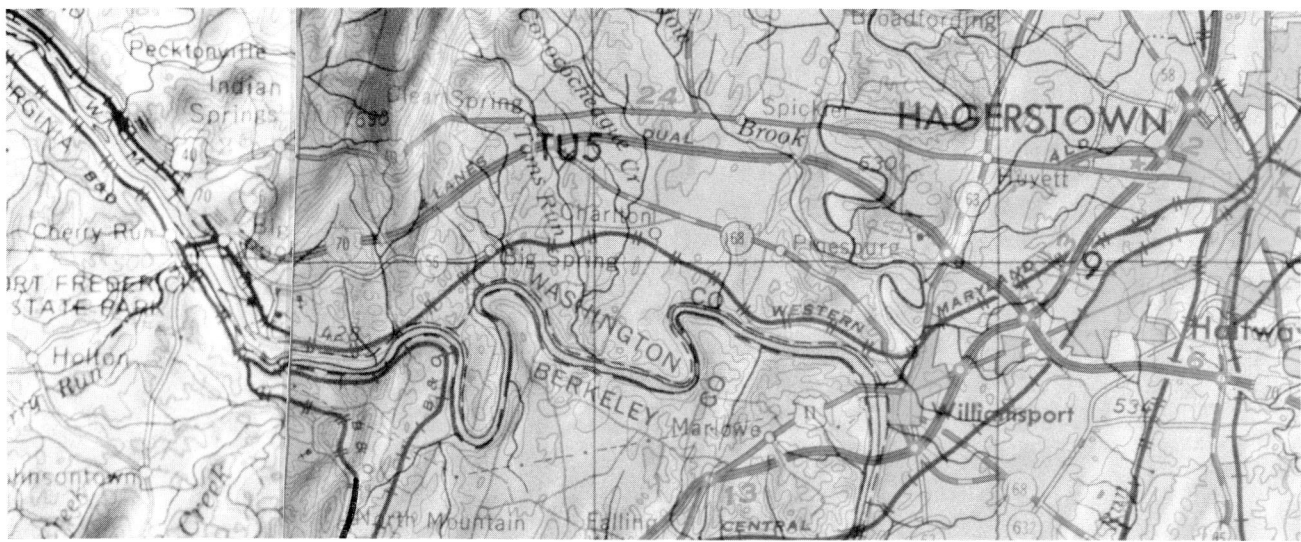

A BATTLE has been defined as an unpleasantness that occurs at a junction between two maps and your authors had to face the same problem when depicting the mainline from West Cumbo to Cherry Run. Left of center at the bottom one finds North Mountain, which is only a mile or so west of West Cumbo and at the top of a short, mild .58% grade westbound which slices through a cut in the mountain ... this line was double-tracked early in history and remains so to this day. The low-grade, single track cutoff line appears slightly to the right of the mainline and meanders northward to the Potomac and then westward along the Potomac River to rejoin in parallel the double-track main ... all three tracks then proceed northwestwardly to Cherry Run just past Fort Frederick. The cutoff is really an eastbound track and was built for that purpose ... the steepest grade facing eastbound tonnage is only .28% whereas the "old" main has some stretches of .76 and .78 percent grades. To the casual reader, the difference in the gradients may not seem like much but when a railroad must ram heavy tonnage through a stretch of line the gain is significant even though the lowgrade route is longer. The reader should also trace the Western Maryland line from the crossing of the river at Cherry Run to Hagerstown ... this piece of railroad, while less important today, has played quite a role in eastern railroad history.

After passing Hedgesville/Cumbo, the builders of the Baltimore and Ohio left the arcadian Great Valley and saw mountains looming in the distance, pierced by one of the most majestic rivers in the world, the mighty Potomac.

Of course, the railroad would have been impossible to build without the existence of the Potomac and, as it turned out, would be almost impossible to operate because of it. The crossing at the Ferry, as fraught with troubles as it was, would prove to be a mild annoyance compared to what lay ahead.

As always, William Prescott Smith's 1850's descriptions were adroit:

> "Westward from Martinsburg the route for eight miles continues its course over the open country until it strikes the foot of the North Mountain and crosses it by a long excavation, sixty-three feet deep, in slate rock, through a depression therein, and passes out of the Valley. On leaving these rich and well tilled lands we enter a poor and thinly settled district, covered chiefly with a forest in which stunted pine prevails."

> "The route encounters heavy excavation and embankment for four or five miles from the North Mountain, and crosses Back Creek upon a stone viaduct of a single arch of eighty feet span and fifty-four feet above the stream. The view across and up the Potomac Valley is magnificent as you approach this bridge and extends as far as the distant mountain range of Sideling Hill twenty-five miles to the west . . . the river is reached at a point opposite Fort Frederick . . . an ancient stronghold, erected a hundred years ago and still in pretty good preservation."

> "How suggestive of our country's gigantic strides is the fact that this frontier outpost (erected in 1755) is passed as now almost at the beginning of a continuous railroad stretching a thousand miles west of these ruined relics of our fathers!"

Just west of that Back Creek bridge was a rise that would become known as Block House Hill during the Civil War, refuting Mr. Smith's inference that wars in this area were a thing of the past.

The reader is aware that the history of the East End, for almost three quarters of a century, was one of struggle to accommodate ever increasing waves of eastbound traffic. By the early 1890s, almost all of this traffic flowed from Cumberland all the way to Baltimore with no diversions of any significance. Up until that time North Mountain and Cherry Run were merely points along the way with telegraph offices, turnouts and water stations existing to control and smooth train movement. To be sure, some traffic was deflected to the CV at Martinsburg, but that was an enemy railroad controlled by PRR.

Curiously, as early as 1836 in an era when B&O's route west from the Ferry had yet to be decided and ten years before PRR was born, the State of Pennsylvania embarked on a very ambitious railroad project to connect Columbia PA (then the terminal of the state-owned Philadelphia and Columbia Railroad) with the B&O somewhere west of Hagerstown, which as a practical matter meant somewhere on the way to Cherry Run.

Pennsylvania's request for a Maryland charter put B&O in a bit of an awkward position. The reader will recall that B&O wished to reach the Ohio River via Pittsburg and at that time had a charter from Pennsylvania to do so. It would not be diplomatic nor wise to irritate the Keystone State by refusing permission, so B&O waffled by saying "yes" while asking for authority to set minimum rates on all traffic diverted to Philadelphia.

Much to B&O's chagrin, this new railroad began to fly . . . the line was to run from Columbia to Hanover, Gettysburg, Blue Ridge Summit, possibly Waynesboro and ultimately to connect with B&O. A lot of heavy construction work was done between Gettysburg and Highfield . . . the project, promoted by the famous Thaddeus Stevens, soaked up almost a million dollars of state funds before it sank into the pits of controversy and acquired the derisive name "The Tapeworm." The route was finally abandoned late in the 1830s, to B&O's relief, and much of the right-of-way was later sold to a predecessor of the Western Maryland to become, in part, Western Maryland's line between Gettysburg and Highfield.

Then, in 1892, the Western Maryland reached the B&O at Cherry Run and the pattern of eastward traffic flow began to change. The Central States Dispatch route (CSD) began to take shape and at least some of the volume began to leave B&O rails short of Martinsburg. A tower was installed at Cherry Run in 1893 and another at North Mountain. There is some evidence that helper service was employed by this time and these new interlockers were probably needed to speed traffic over the North Mountain "bump."

We have already related the Great Coal Push

EAST END

war that erupted in 1902 and removed traffic from the Cherry Run interchange to Cumbo and the CV ... the low grade cutoff was completed c. 1903.

However, all traffic did not flow to the CV ... in 1905 the courts insisted that West Virginia Central and Pittsburg traffic be given to parent WM at Cherry Run. But then WM completed its own "Cumberland Extension" in 1906 and hauled its own tonnage.

All of these developments did not save Gould, but it did result in a lot of confusing traffic flows on the East End. In the end, of course, PRR lost control of B&O and Reading, WM control passed to B&O, and Cherry Run again became a major interchange point. The Cherry Run yard was constantly expanded westward until it reached Miller where an interlocking tower was installed in 1900 and improved in 1910-11.

West of Cherry Run, little changed ... waves of traffic continued to inundate B&O lines. Much of it, however, debouched at Cherry Run and Cumbo ... by c. 1918 about 43% of all B&O eastbound tonnage left its rails at these two points and, among other things, made unnecessary any extension of the CR&PV to Harpers Ferry.

Today, almost no traffic leaves B&O at these interchanges ... the more the world changes, the more it stays the same.

Back to the early 1840s, B&O again became a riverline railroad at Cherry Run, subject to floods of water as well as traffic. The way west was wet.

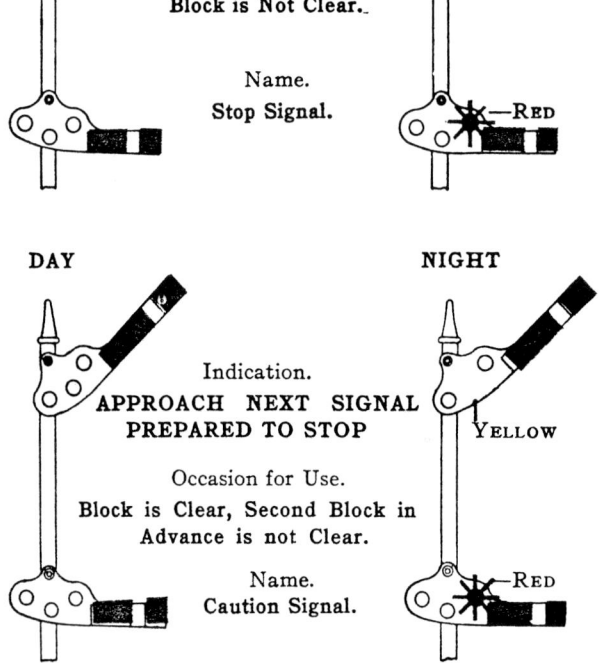

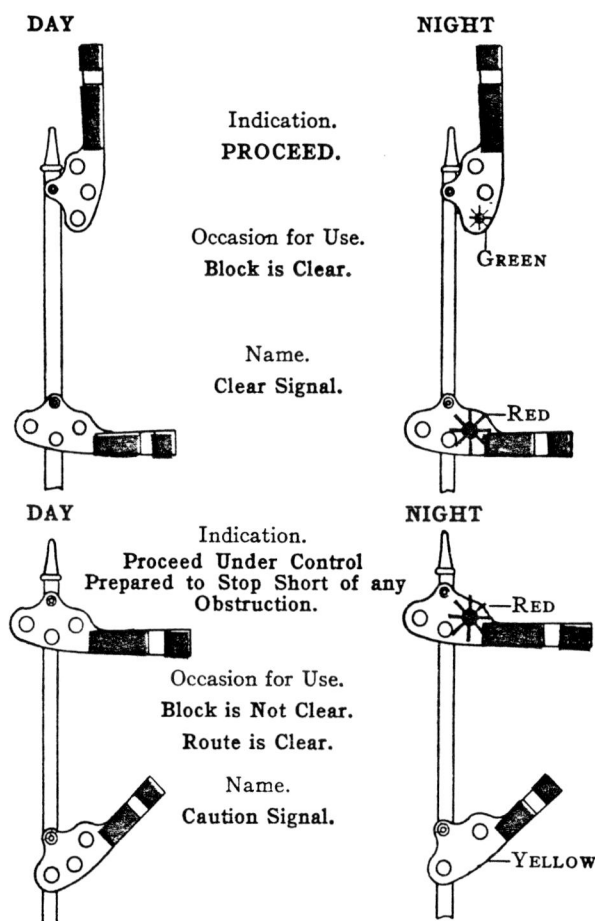

BACK TO THE POTOMAC

B&OHS

WHILE NORTH MOUNTAIN was never a thriving metropolis, this diminutive waiting shed understates by inference the size of the town ... at one time, brick and tile manufacturing facilities, a large roller mill and a host of apple packing agencies were located here. This shed was on the corner of the road crossing, serving the westbound track, and was across from more elaborate depot facilities in a general store. This photo was taken c. 1916 ... note that it appears some headend parcels, as well as two passengers, await the next train.

A WESTBOUNDER roars across the North Mountain road crossing in June of 1976, ignoring the white building on the right which once housed the main depot in the town. Sidings in North Mountain were removed c. 1938 and today the locale is merely a name along a two-track mainline.

ALMOST CERTAINLY, this tower at North Mountain (MN) was the initial one erected in 1893 ... it was located just west of the road crossing. MN burned 4 January 1910, was replaced with a temporary block signal 11 February 1910 and some records suggest that a new replacement tower was built shortly thereafter. The train order signal at MN was placed out of service 5 March 1914, but the tower was still active by October of that year. By 1 February 1916, however, the call letters were no longer in use ... it is possible that the interlocker was operated remotely from Cumbo. The locomotives in this scene are obviously helpers ... apparently helpers were used on this grade well into this century even after the low grade line was in service.

EAST END

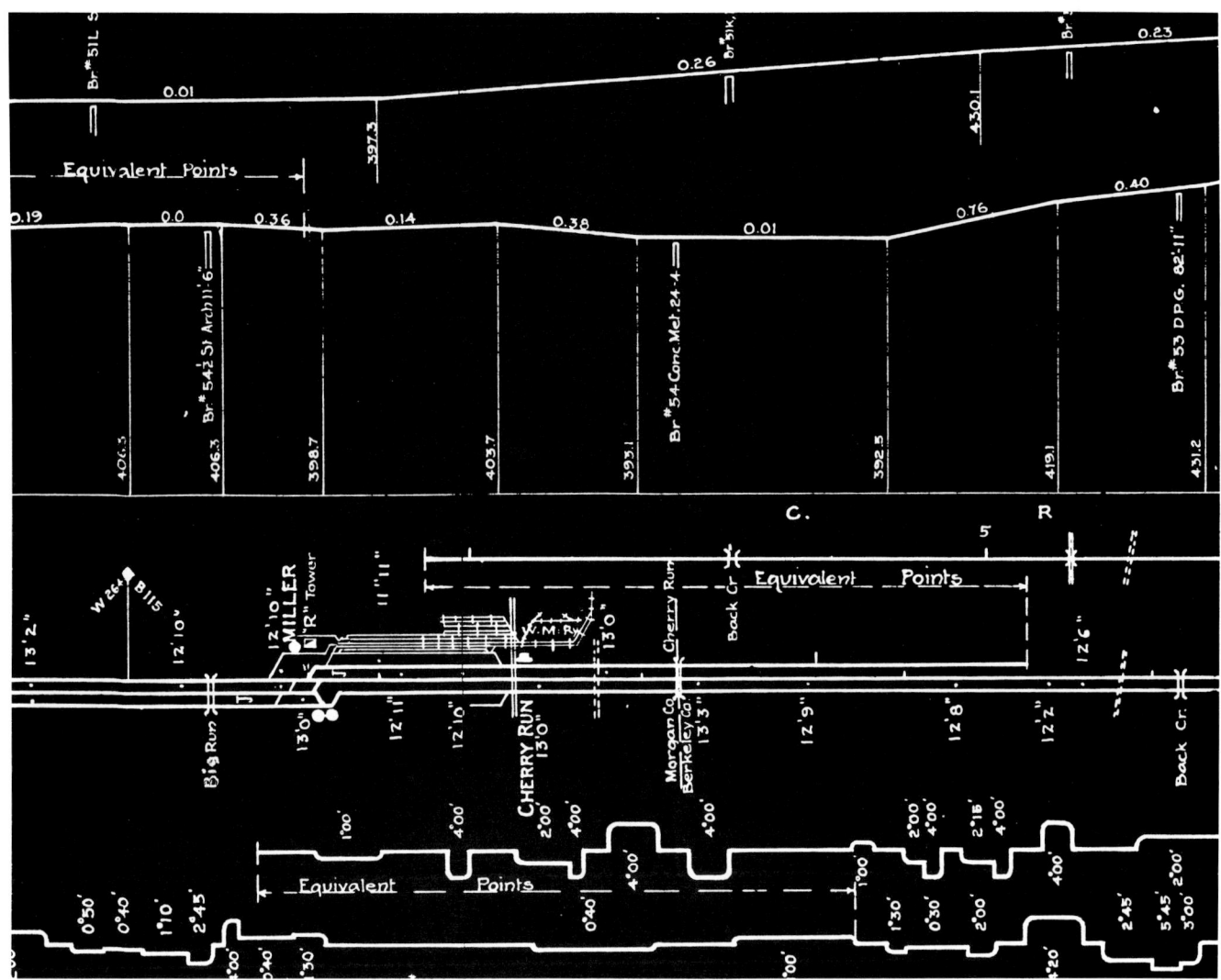

THIS C. 1930 track chart shows the Cherry Run area probably at its peak. The grade profile at the top is the low grade cutoff ... the one below it the old mainline. Note the sag in the latter ... this is known as the Cherry Run dip. Also note the Cherry Run stream just east of the town, which divides two counties. Farther east of this point was the Cherry Run (CR) interlocking tower erected in 1905 and just south of the tracks was Coal Pen Hill, location of a coaling trestle as we shall see.

Western Maryland trackage is apparent ... the line running "north" is the WM main which crosses the Potomac and runs to Hagerstown. At the west end of the yard, Miller (R) tower is located ... opened in August 1900. In between, in the town of Cherry Run, is the depot, for years identified as the "yard" call letters CX. The whole complex was busy, low and subject to floods of water as well as traffic.

BACK TO THE POTOMAC

COAL PEN HILL was aptly named, for it boasted this large coaling trestle (or "chute," as B&O called it) just south of the original mainline. We do not know when it was built, but since repairs were reported in 1897 it can be assumed that it was constructed at least as early as 1892 when WM reached Cherry Run. In 1905 interlocker CR was opened by the trestle, but those call letters were used earlier than that date. We guess that this "chute" was primarily used to coal helpers, as the tower was closed 23 August 1911 and we have found no further reference to either after 1913. All this probably coincides with the creation of a major coal and water facility at Sir Johns Run, about fifteen miles west of here. There is also some evidence that helpers were no longer used from Cherry Run to North Mountain after this era.

THIS TRANQUIL SCENE at Cherry Run belies the reality of activity that marked this important interchange ... the photographer managed to get a shot without a single human being in sight. The three tracks are B&O, with the closest to the station being the low grade cutoff. From left to right, one sees the freight station, grade crossing, passenger station and office building ... WM trackage is on the far side of the buildings. The two railroads definitely used the station and office buildings jointly and possibly the freight station. We believe most of these buildings date from 1893 ... we know call letters CX were used as early as 1904 and in all following years until the late 1930s, although curiously not in 1913 and 1914.

EAST END

B&O Museum

THIS EASTWARD VIEW c. 1917 shows a westbounder on the middle, or No. 1 track, approaching CX as kids dance around to annoy the photographer. The left track is the low grade cutoff line. In the distance on the right of the tracks can be seen a water jug which serviced penstocks in the station area ... this facility was definitely gone by 1930 when water service was provided west of here at Miller.

BLAND BUT UTILITARIAN, the joint B&O/WM office building at Cherry Run in this valuation shot is sooty, to say the least. With rail lines at both the front and back doors, office workers had a dangerous time of it just getting to and from work. In the background, we see a WM water jug on the left and a WM locomotive with train passing to the right on Western Maryland rails.

B&OHS

BACK TO THE POTOMAC

AS THE VIEWER looks westbound from the Cherry Run road crossing in this c. 1917 valuation photo, he sees the caboose of a westbounder disappearing in the distance and a rather forlorn freight station on the right. At least the yard in the center distance shows some signs of life.

B&OHS

A WESTERN MARYLAND drag, with H5 Consolidation 509 on the point and a mid-train helper only four cars back, is about to leave Cherry Run in this c. 1920 photo. The joint B&O/WM station is on the left and the WM yard tracks in the distance on the right ... just behind the photographer was a WM turntable, active for many years until replaced by a wye. At this time, WM approached the Potomac crossing on a trestle and the power spacing on this train is probably related to weight restrictions on that structure.

B&OHS

EAST END

THIS IS WM's Cherry Run turntable and roundhouse, in a state of disrepair and soon to disappear. Western Maryland rails left Cherry Run, climbed a trestle to reach their Potomac River bridge and then descended on a similar trestle on the other side of the river. In the early 1920s, the trestles were filled in and trackage in the Cherry Run yard realigned for better curvature, all of which caused the demolition of the freight station, depot, office building and this roundhouse and turntable. A caboose was set off as a ticket office and waiting shed and a spring-switch wye installed for turning power. Today it is still possible to walk the trace of the wye and kick up a few rotted crossties.

THIS EARLY 1920s view of the Western Maryland trestle approaching the Potomac crossing near Big Pool on the Maryland shore, as poor as it is, hints at the construction method used to convert the trestle to a fill . . . just bury the trestle. The crane is sitting on a siding and the jerry-built structure in the foreground is a servicing facility for the crane. *Raymond Litten Collection*

BACK TO THE POTOMAC

B&OHS

ODD AS IT MAY SEEM, the floods of water that have plagued East End operations for a century and a half are almost impossible to document graphically. Everyone is running for high ground while they are going on and taking photos or dashing off sketches is not a high priority for anyone with any sense. When the waters recede, all attention is devoted to repairs and photographers get in the way. The net result is that there are very few photos of floods and most of those merely note the damage done. This scene of the west approach embankment to the WM bridge at Cherry Run after the March 1936 flood is a good example ... all the new fill material merely hints at the savagery with which the Potomac assaulted this impediment to its dash to tidewater. Only in the upper right corner can one see the remnants of a structure that certainly did not begin its trip toward the ocean in that location. Would the old trestle have fared any better? That question is moot, but co-author Roberts has personally experienced the 1972 Agnes flood in the Patapsco Valley near Baltimore, the Cheat River flood on the West End at Rowlesburg in 1985 and has been on the water when a giant wave looms up ... he can assure all that no photo could possibly be made nor prose written that would adequately describe the awe and terror that grips a puny human being when faced with Mother Nature unleashed.

BLOCK SIGNAL RULES.

THREE-POSITION BLOCK SIGNALS.

501. The following signals will appear where conditions require their use:

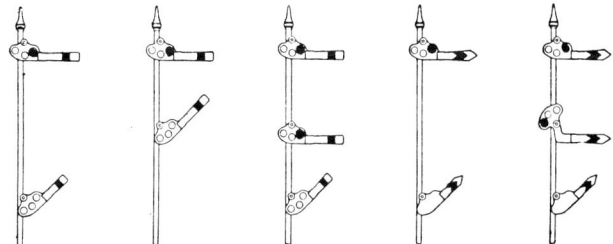

Indication—Proceed at slow speed prepared to stop short of train or obstruction.
Name—Permissive-signal.

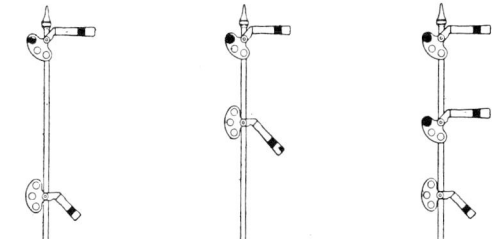

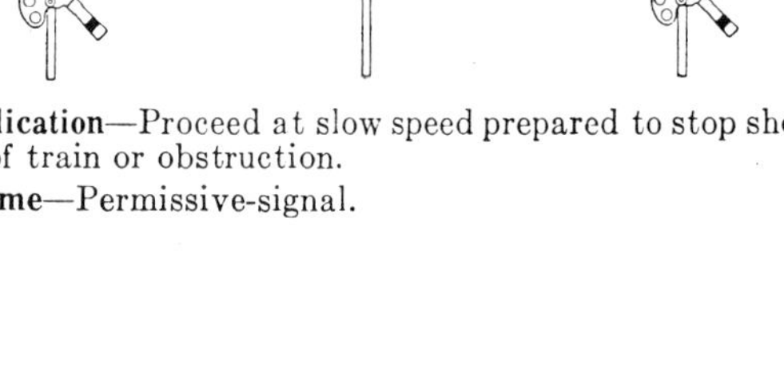

Indication—Proceed at slow speed prepared to stop short of train or obstruction.
Name—Permissive-signal.

EAST END

B&O Museum

WE HAVE YET to see a valuation photograph that could be described as anything better than poor, but without them we would have almost no visual record of most of the structures along any railroad's line of road. Here we see Miller (R) interlocker at the west end of the Cherry Run yard with attendant water treatment plant and pump house c. 1917. The tower was opened in August 1900, improved in 1910 and 1911 and then was closed between 1911 and late 1915 when it was reopened for a brief period with the call letter M. By early 1917, it was back to R and has remained open to this day. The closure in the teens is puzzling, particularly since CX at Cherry Run was also out of service in 1913 and 1914 as we have reported. As to the pump house, we know such a facility was located at Miller as early as 1872 and that a new treatment plant was installed in 1928. The facility shown was obviously coal-fired ... electric motors were ultimately installed and coal/ash tracks removed. Water was pumped to two large concrete water tanks across the tracks ... they show on the track chart earlier in this chapter and the skeletons remain today. The feed pipe from the river to the house remains as well as the foundation and rubble of the house itself.

THE MARCH 1936 flood, as this photo of Miller tower attests, produced rather high water levels ... the white marking "H.W." stands for "high water" and that spot is over fourteen feet above the top of the rail. This means that the entire Cherry Run yard complex was under water almost as far east as Back Creek, including some portions of the low grade line. Water depth probably averaged about ten feet. West of Miller was no picnic, either. And the poor operator was faced with a decision rather early on. Do I get out now while the getting is good or stick to my duty? If he stuck to his duty, he must have had second thoughts when the water got to his feet. Will the tower stand fast or will I have a cruise downstream? This time, of course, the love boat did not leave harbor, but as we shall see it wasn't always that way.

B&OHS

BACK TO THE POTOMAC

B&OHS/E. L. Thompson Collection

CSD 94 ENGINE 6185 with 71 cars pounds through Cherry Run on 27 October 1946 on WM rails, thrilling a number of photographers en route. The scene on the left, of course, is barren with only the three B&O tracks marking what was once an active junction with a medley of buildings. Behind this train and out of sight on the right is an ancient B&O baggage car used, in 1992, as a tool house with no tracks nearby. This photo confirms a practice of long standing ... B&O trains running through to Hagerstown on the Western Maryland.

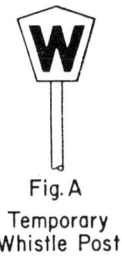

Fig. A
Temporary
Whistle Post

Fig. B
Permanent
Whistle Post

EAST END

B&O EXTRA EAST 6203 with 102 cars on 27 October 1946 approaches Big Pool Junction on the Western Maryland, noting the WM's "Cumberland Extension" rails barely seen on the right. This photo introduces a subject that may confuse students of the East End and, indeed, has puzzled more than one author. Why did B&O allow *any* traffic to be diverted from its rails at Cherry Run or West Cumbo? And why were two such diversion points allowed to exist so close to one another? The answer to part of that question is obvious ... traffic destined for nearby points such as Hagerstown, Harrisburg and so on would naturally be turned over to WM or PRR. But why drags as in this photo or CSD manifest trains as in the preceding shot? As to drags, a large portion of the coal hauled by B&O in the steam era was destined for use by other railroads in the northeast as fuel ... some estimates ranged as high as fifty percent. Naturally, these railroads wanted their coal delivered to their nearest junction, resisting attempts by B&O to move the tonnage to Baltimore and then north via rather circuitous routes. As to manifest freight, the reason was more subtle but nonetheless real. Most eastern terminals were "closed" ... that is to say, railroads in given terminal areas would not switch and deliver cars to industries served by their rails if they did not get a piece of the line haul. In Philadelphia, for example, PRR and Reading controlled almost all the sidings and flatly refused to take cars from B&O at Philadelphia for delivery on their lines. PRR wanted the cars given to them at West Cumbo and Reading wanted to receive the cars at Shippensburg near Harrisburg, using the WM merely as a bridge connection. There wasn't a lot B&O could do about it ... even though B&O controlled Reading, as late as the 1960s the two roads were wrangling on this subject and B&O, wanting to handle cars via Baltimore to Philadelphia, had to agree to pay Reading for the earnings they would have received had the cars been turned over to them at Shippensburg. Traffic flows and conditions evolve, of course, but the reader may rest assured that such bargaining is going on at this very moment. While we cannot be sure, the odd closings of Miller and Cherry Run in 1913 and 1914 may well be related to such internecine warfare.

B&OHS/E. L. Thompson Collection

BACK TO THE POTOMAC

OVER A SPAN of one hundred and fifty years, the number of accidents on the East End which caused blood to flow must be almost without number. In this book, we will report only two of the tragedies. This, the first one, occurred at 2:15 a.m. on New Year's Day in 1957 on the low grade line between Cumbo and Cherry Run ... it was caused by operator error. The low grade line, the reader will recall, was primarily an eastbound railroad bearing track number four and signaled only in that direction. Frequently, however, westbound moves were made under train orders. On New Year's Eve, a westbound train of empties hauled by GP9s was to use the low grade line from Cumbo to Cherry Run and train orders to that effect were issued. The train, however, experienced difficulties in getting out of Cumbo and was delayed for some hours. An operator shift change took place and something fell between the cracks, because an eastbounder hauled by F units was released out of Cherry Run. The error was realized early on and an attempt to stop the eastbound failed by only a few seconds. Everyone except the crews of the two trains knew a calamity was inevitable. Desperate attempts to stop the trains were made, including phone calls to B&O employees and residents along the line of road. All failed and those in command ordered ambulances to rush to the scene where it was anticipated that the trains would meet some five minutes before the wreck actually occurred. The collision was devastating. The three crewman in the eastbound lead F unit, naturally being cab forward, were killed instantly. The crewmen in the GP9 were riding cab to the rear, but a total of five crewmen were injured, some severely. These two photos give mute testimony to the force of the collision ... one shows the lead GP9 on top of the mess and the other after it was removed. We have referred to floods of traffic and water on the East End ... there were also floods of tears.

Roy E. Stoner Collection

W. E. Rodgers Collection

Fig. A
Temporary speed restriction shall be covered by Train Order or General Order and designated by portable sign Fig. A placed at the point of restriction.

Fig. B
Permanent speed restriction shall be carried in Special Instructions and designated by triangular sign Fig. B placed at the point of restriction.

Chapter 6

The Funnel

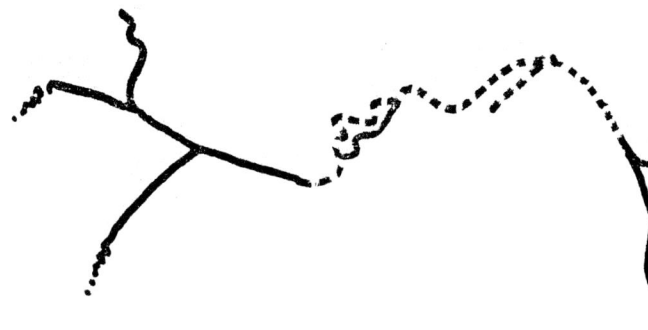

Cherry Run to Okonoko

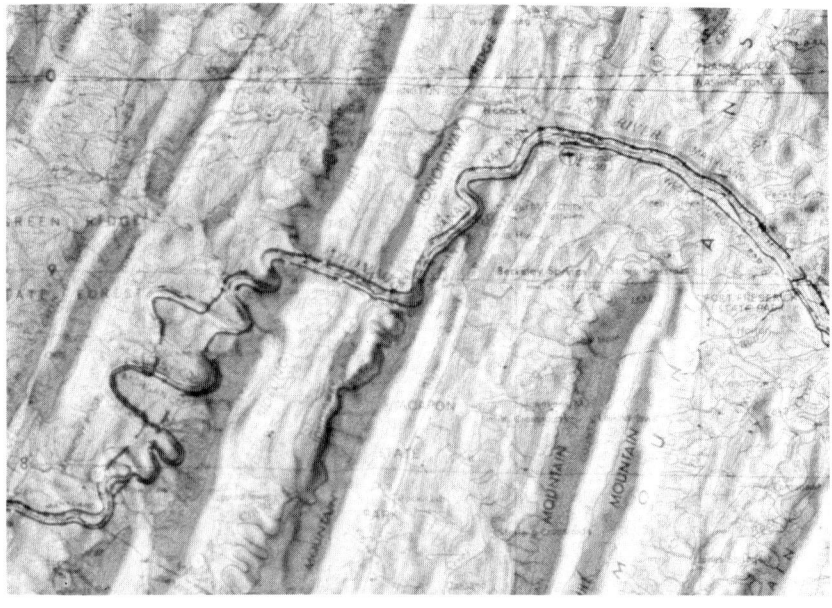

LEAVING CHERRY RUN near Fort Frederick on the extreme right center, B&Os westward lunge to Cumberland along the south bank of the Potomac boasted an easy bottomland passage until well west of Hancock. (The single/slashed line on the north bank is Western Maryland's single-track Cumberland Extension line, which plays no part in our story.) Even the line from Hancock to Orleans Road, while pressed against hillside terrain in places, was expandable and comfortable. The decision to tunnel Doe Gully (shown here as an open cut) was obviously a sound one. From Doe Gully west, however, the original line of road was crushed against steep mountainsides as it followed a serpentine river route to Paw Paw. The trace of the impressive Magnolia Cutoff shows here as a straight route through four tunnels from just west of Paw Paw to Orleans Road. Hansrote, a tiny locale that does not even show on this map, was located just east of Magnolia and can be found on the rear endpaper map of this book... this inconsequential spot turned out to be a strategic bottleneck on the East End until the opening of the Cutoff as we shall see. The Cutoff rejoined the original line just west of Paw Paw at a point on the railroad known as Okonoko at the extreme left bottom corner. A short tunnel on the original line just east of Paw Paw (not shown on this map) bypassed another large loop in the Potomac. For almost three quarters of a century, the original railroad from Orleans Road to Paw Paw was the main artery and constricted throat of the entire B&O system. The original line in this area and, indeed, the entire Western Maryland line have long since been out of service... only the Cutoff remains.

THE FUNNEL

The railroad east from Cherry Run to Harpers Ferry, for all its charms and interesting history, merely presented B&O with minor frustrations when compared to the line of road *west* from Cherry Run to Cumberland.

And, of that tormented stretch of railroad, the line from Cherry Run to Okonoko just west of Paw Paw was the worst of all. Squeezed between the tortuous Potomac River and rugged semi-mountainous terrain, this part of the East End had to accommodate enormous traffic tonnage without diversion, relief or excuse and do it in the face of interruptions from floods, war and the inevitable frictions that result from forcing large numbers of trains through what can only be described as a funnel.

The funnel analogy is a good one ... the reader should test it by pouring water into a funnel. He will discover that once the funnel reaches its capacity, the water will back up and swearing at it will not change a thing. One must enlarge the funnel or drown in the overflow.

Of course, this part of the East End was a riverline railroad and the predominant eastbound tonnage was "going with the flow" ... that is, moving downhill. Unfortunately, it wasn't quite that simple.

Between Orleans Road and Paw Paw, at a tiny place called Hansrote, the route east was *uphill*. As grades go, it was a mere anthill only two and a half miles long and with a slight rise of only .8%. The informed rail historian will react with incredulity when we state that this diminutive pimple proved to be a funnel within a funnel. Well, it was and it drove B&O crazy for years.

And then there were tunnels within the funnels, innocuously named Doe Gully and Paw Paw. When the railroad was first built, constructing these two tunnels made a lot of sense. A cursory glance at the map at the beginning of this chapter will show the famous "Loops of the Potomac" between Orleans Road and Paw Paw ... these tunnels bypassed two of the bulges. As an interesting sidenote, the C&O Canal tunneled a loop on the other side of the river near Paw Paw, the boring of which badly delayed completion of the canal to Cumberland.

Faced with the gargantuan increases in eastbound traffic and consequent increases in westbound empty movements as well as revenue hauls, B&O could only cope with the inundation by doing three things ... increasing train length, adding tracks and speeding movement with modern signaling, state of the art interlocking plants, swift communication and dispatching skill. B&O did all these things with vigor and imagination, but each time they came close to coping with the flow the traffic would increase again and again.

Adding to the problem was passenger traffic. B&O dominated this business from Baltimore and Washington to St. Louis and Chicago which meant that the East End was also cursed with being a chokepoint in this regard.

The line was originally built with single track and ample passing sidings. Even before B&O reached Wheeling, a program of double tracking was started from Piedmont east ... completed in segments, this addition was under strain by the late 1800s. In 1901 a third main track was completed from Cherry Run to Sir Johns Run. A fourth track from Hancock to Round Top was opened in August 1912 and continued to Sir Johns Run by September 1914.

A third track from Sir Johns Run to Orleans Road was finished in July 1911, thus giving the stretch of railroad from Cherry Run to that point three basic mainline tracks with the middle track signaled for movement in both directions. A major locomotive servicing facility was opened at Sir Johns Run in November 1911.

From Orleans Road to Okonoko (Little Cacapon), however, sixteen miles of double track remained burdened with two tunnels and that minor little blackhead at Hansrote. The Paw Paw tunnel was daylighted by September 1904, but to do the same at Doe Gully would involve removing a mountain (which, in the event, was exactly what had to be done). And it was one thing to add tracks on alluvial banks along the river ... quite another to slash into the sides of steep mountainsides to do the same in the "Loops" terrain.

And now to the blemish at Hansrote. The tactic of increasing train length and weight, no matter how sound, made this location a helper grade and the most B&O could jam into the cliffside was a short piece of third track. So, within an already constricted two-track funnel, B&O had to deal with helpers. Stop, wait for helper to return on the westbound track, couple up, wait for track space, watch the trains pile up one behind the other, finally get out on the main. Merely by example, it is recorded that at a certain time on the day of 5

EAST END

September 1914 there were five slow freights and a manifest train waiting for helpers or track space at Hansrote.

The solution to the Okonoko-Orleans Road problem was the Magnolia Cutoff, a subject which we will explore in the next chapter . . . here we are presenting the history of the original line. After the Cutoff was finished, at a meeting of B&O officials at Deer Park, President Daniel Willard sympathized with his operating people by describing the problem on this part of the East End as trying to put "a quart into a pint bottle." Mr. Willard's allusion was all too felicitous.

For a gentler time, let us revisit the East End from Cherry Run to Okonoko through the eyes of William Prescott Smith in 1853 and 1857:

"From Fort Frederick, the route follows the Virginia shore of the river upon bottom lands to Hancock. The only considerable stream is Sleepy Creek, which is passed by a viaduct of two spans of one hundred and ten feet each. Hancock is in Maryland, and although a town of no great size or importance, makes some show when seen across the river from the station at the mouth of Warm Spring Run."

"The route from Hancock to Cumberland pursues the margin of the Potomac River, with four exceptions. The first occurs at Doe Gully, eighteen miles above Hancock, where by a tunnel of 1200 feet in length a bend of the river is cut off, and a distance of nearly four miles saved. The second is at the Paw Paw Ridge, where a distance of nearly two miles is saved by a tunnel of 250 feet in length. The third and fourth are within six miles of Cumberland, where two bends are cut across . . ."

"In advancing westward from Hancock the line passes along the western base of Warm Spring Ridge, approaching within a couple of miles of the Berkeley Springs, which are at the eastern foot of that ridge. It then sweeps around the termination of the Cacapon Mountain, opposite the remarkable and insulated [sic] eminence called the 'Round Top.' Thence the road proceeds to the crossing of the Great Cacapon River, nine and a half miles above Hancock, which is crossed by a bridge about 300 feet in length . . . soon after, it enters the gap of Sideling Hill, that famous bugbear of the traveller which on the National Turnpike opposes such a formidable barrier to his journey, but which here is unnoticed except in the fine profile which it exhibits on each side of the river, as it declines rapidly to water level."

"The next point of interest reached is the Tunnel at Doe Gully. The approaches to this formidable work are very imposing, as for several miles above and below the tunnel they cause the road to occupy a high level on the slopes of the river hills, and thus afford an extensive view of the grand mountain scenery. The tunnel is . . . through a compact slate rock, which is arched with brick to preserve it from future disintegration by atmospheric action. The fronts or facades of the arch are of a fine white sandstone, procured from the summit of the neighboring mountain. The width is 21 feet, and the height 20½, affording room for two tracks. *The height of the hill above the roof of the tunnel is 116 feet.* The excavation and embankments adjacent are very heavy . . ."

"Above this point the line pursues the very sinuous part of the river lying between Sideling Hill on the east and Town Hill on the west. The curves are not however abrupt, but form fine sweeping circuits, passing sometimes along beautiful alluvial bottoms and again at the foot of precipitous cliffs."

"The Paw Paw Ridge Tunnel is next reached, thirty miles from Hancock . . . this tunnel is through a soft slate rock and is curved with a radius of 750 feet. It is of the same sectional dimensions with the Doe Gully Tunnel . . . arched with brick and fronted with white sandstone. Thence the route reaches Little Cacapon Creek . . . at the mouth of this stream are fine flats and a beautiful view of the mountains to the eastward."

Even by the 1850s, B&O was learning how those "alluvial bottoms" and "fine flats" were formed. They came from silt deposits from flood waters. And the more man cultivated fields and cut over forests in the Potomac watershed, the more the runoff increased and the more ferocious the floods became.

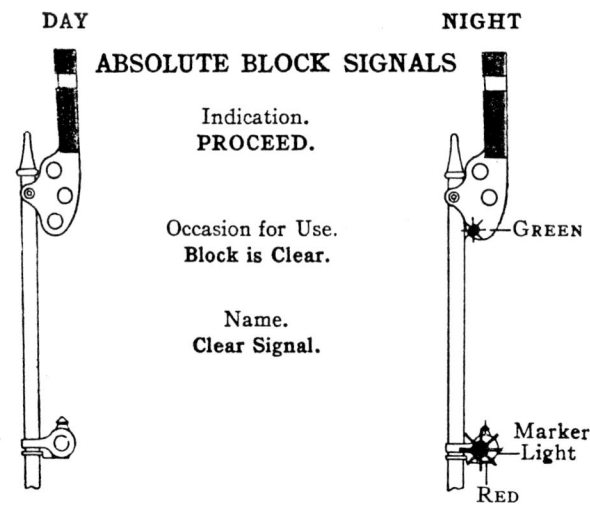

THE FUNNEL

THE TOWER at Sleepy Creek (SC) was located just four miles west of Cherry Run on the south side of the tracks ... this view looks east. This tower was opened in September 1901, improved in 1907 and rebuilt in 1911 ... since the second story extension is known to have been added in 1911, this photo was taken after that date. SC was taken out of service in 1930 and retired or torn down in 1934. A bit of lore is associated with SC during World War I ... tower operator John Rockwell, it is said, tired of his duties one day and simply locked the tower and left to join the Army. The resultant interruption of train movements did not endear Rockwell to B&O ... one wonders if the Army had similar problems with him.

B&O Museum

SLEEPY CREEK looking west from the westbound home signal bridge sometime after 1911 ... we have found references to an 1893 tower about a mile east of this point on the other side of the tracks and it is known that a telegraph station was located in this area well before the Civil War. Obvious from this photo is that SC is located on a flood plain and we can assure the reader that the entire scene has been under water many, many times. A geologic oddity exists farther up Sleepy Creek ... semi-anthracite coal deposits that once bore the name Meadow Branch coalfields. Noted before the coming of the railroad and mentioned by William Prescott Smith, these deposits spawned the Berkeley Coal Mining and Railroad Company as well as plans for a canal by one James Rumsey who operated a grist mill here. Neither the railroad nor the canal was ever built ... the seams were too fragmented to exploit regardless of the conveyance chosen. Yet coal was worked locally well into the 1940s.

EAST END

B&OHS

THIS EASTWARD view of the Sleepy Creek depot and freight station was taken to record repairs after the flood of 29-31 March 1924 ... the high water line on the boxcar is about one third of the way to the roof. Note that all the trackage in sight had to be reballasted. The crest of this particular flood was reached at 3:30 p.m. 30 March at the tower and the operator was marooned by water three feet deep stretching for three miles over the tracks, although not right at the tower itself. The problem began on the West End at Altamont where it had snowed for eight days to a depth of three feet ... this was followed by a temperature rise to 64 degrees on 29 March and fourteen hours of warm rain. Cumberland Division damages alone totaled $154,500 without regard to lost revenues.

HANCOCK is now and has always been in Maryland on the other side of the Potomac, but that little accident of geography has never stopped B&O from calling this location by that name even though locals call it Brossius Station. This interesting structure was built in 1876 and was moved easterly in 1911 after this photo was taken, probably to make room for additional yard tracks serving the Berkeley Springs Branch which joins B&O here. The train board is leaning rather casually against the telegraphers extension which might indicate that the move is imminent, but other reports suggest that even the station clock was not removed and simply went along for the ride.

B&OHS

THE FUNNEL

B&O Museum

SECURE in its new resting place by the time of this valuation photo in the mid-teens of this century, the Hancock Station does not seem to have suffered from the uprooting. The highway bridge to the town has not been so lucky ... in a 1936 flood most of it was washed away, introducing the question of just who was isolated from what ... the town or the station.

B&O Museum

LOOKING EAST from an early road crossing (long since replaced by an overhead bridge), we can vaguely see the Hancock complex including HO Tower ... surely a perfect subject for a model railroader in that gauge. The tower was opened in November 1901 and modernized in 1912 ... it is extant in 1992. This mid-teens valuation photo also vaguely shows a water jug which is near the junction of the branch line going to Berkeley Springs to the right.

B&OHS
E. L. Thompson Collection

TRAIN 21 Engine 5066 with six cars paints the Hancock area with condensate on 16 March 1947. HO can barely be seen on the right and the covered hopper just above the exhaust hints at the traffic B&O receives at Hancock. The flood plain is painfully apparent.

EAST END

B&OHS/E. L. Thompson Collection

HANCOCK probably proved to be Ten Wheeler 2014s last stop before Valhalla. Seen here on 16 March 1947 being serviced for branch line work to Berkeley Springs, the 2014 was out of service by 1 January 1948 and scrapped in March of 1948. She had a long and interesting history ... built as B18 by Rhode Island in August 1901 in a two-cylinder compound configuration, she was converted early in this century when compounding was found to be nothing more than an interesting theory and is seen here as B18d replete with superheater, piston valves and Baker valve gear.

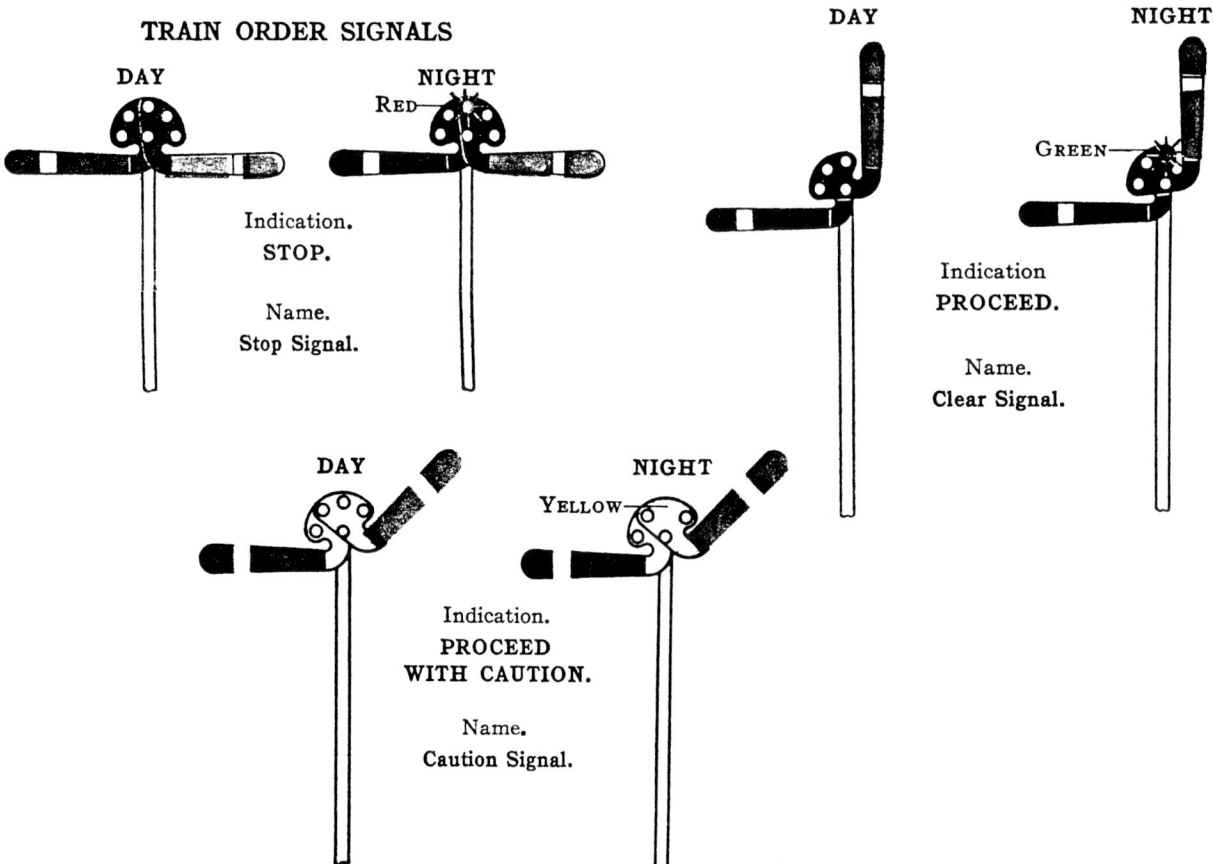

THE FUNNEL

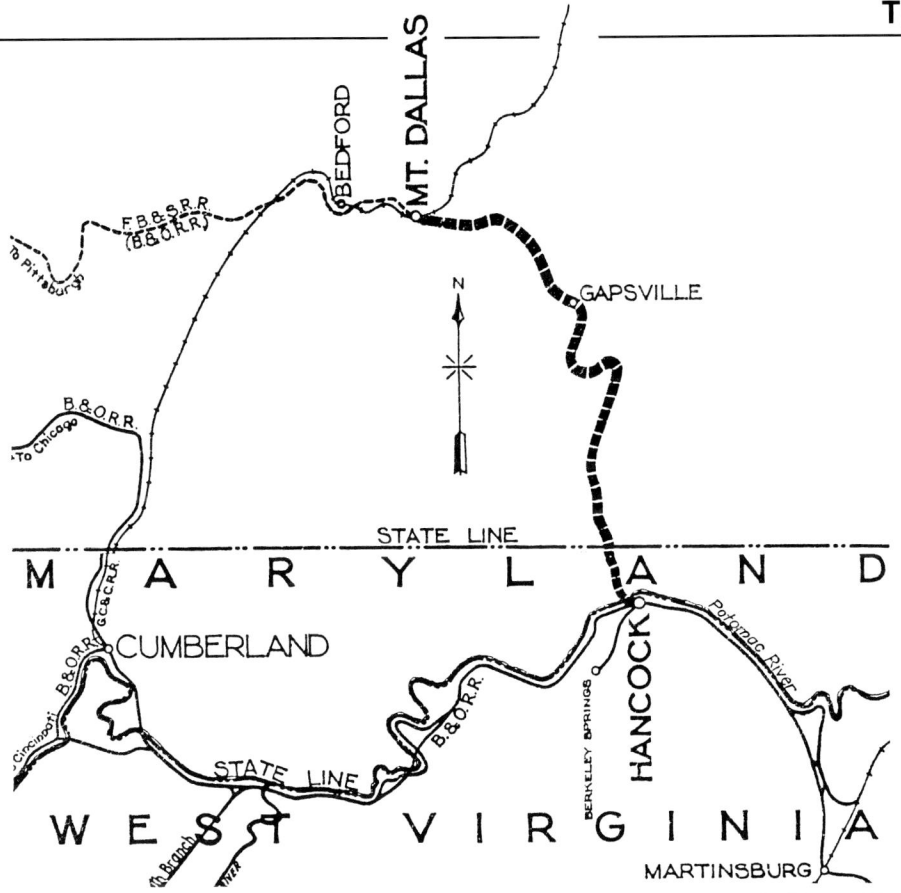

PHILOSOPHICALLY as well as historically, B&O was a railroad of dreamers imbued with the axiom that one should always aim at the stars, never at the sand. Early in this century, the sleepy town of Hancock was to be a junction point for a B&O dream that never quite came to pass. Very early in trunkline railroad history, surveyors noted that a line of road from Harrisburg to Pittsburg via Chambersburg would be superior to the more northerly path chosen by the Pennsylvania Railroad in terms of grades and distance. Such a railroad, by the name of the South Pennsylvania, was created by Pittsburg industrialists in league with the New York Central to punish PRR and construction was started in 1883. Many tunnels were partially completed, along with a lot of roadbed grading and bridge pier construction, when in 1885 a deal was cut between NYC and PRR, guided by the fine Italian hand of the House of Morgan. The industrialists were shafted and construction stopped. Early in this century, B&O picked up pieces of this partially completed railroad at a foreclosure sale for the princely sum of $37,500 as part of a grand scheme to build a super double track railroad from Port Perry (Bessemer), about five miles south of Pittsburgh (as it was then being spelled), over the South Penn line of road to Mt. Dallas and from there south to Hancock. Young Francis L. Stuart, then a lowly B&O assistant engineer, submitted a breathtaking plan to this end in 1902 and predicted that B&O would be in a position to "dictate rates and share of business" with completion of this railroad. Stuart proselyted his plan with vigorous prose, listing advantages such as the lowest crossing of the mountains of any eastern trunkline, the wealth of untapped coal traffic that would fall into B&O hands and the relief it would give to B&O congestion west of Hancock. Apparently B&O lawyers had too little to do in this time frame, because railroads were chartered right and left ... the Potomac and Allegheny Railroad in 1902 was the one shown on this map running from Hancock to Mt. Dallas. Others, by various names at different times in the first decade of this century, were planned to run as far west as Wheeling and east to Harrisburg. As to the stretch between Hancock and Port Perry, Stuart estimated the cost of the mainline, branches, yards and shops at a mere $21,438,262.50. One assumes the fifty cents was for a cigar for Mr. Stuart at the victory celebration ... the amount on the other side of the decimal point must have caused his superiors to wonder about his sanity. He did continue a career with B&O and even had the honor of seeing his name on one of four tunnels on the Magnolia Cutoff, which was built about thirteen years later for about six million dollars. Daniel Willard, on 1 July 1910, asked for a report and was told "it seems difficult to see any justification for the construction of a trunkline which is practically out of date in the grade scheme and also when it fails to serve so many of the interests that a new line demands." Another review in 1912 was equally scathing. The road was built, however, but as a highway ... in the late 1930s the State of Pennsylvania used most of the old South Penn as an integral part of the nation's first true superturnpike and Interstate 70 was constructed from Hancock roughly along the path of the unbuilt Potomac and Allegheny Railroad. As for B&O, the arrow aimed at the stars literally ended up in sand south of Hancock at Berkeley Springs as we shall see.

EAST END

Warren Somerville

JUST A FEW MILES south of Hancock, on Warm Spring Run, lies the town of Berkeley Springs, probably the oldest resort in the nation. This sketch, taken from Bowen's work, presents the scene c. 1853 ... he described the waters as "light, sparkling, tasteless" and always at 74 degrees. Indians were known to have frequented the springs before Europeans took over ... George Washington visited them 18 March 1747 as a surveyor and ended up owning several houses. Whatever the "remedial qualities" of the waters, many notables summered here including Charles Carroll of Carrollton of Revolution and B&O fame. Known first as Warm Springs, then Bath and finally Berkeley Springs, an 1844 fire and the birth of rival resorts elsewhere slowly eroded patronage ... a 600 guest capacity was sufficient by the time of rebuilding completed in 1848. B&O was not in a hurry to build a line here and was happy to let patrons alight at Sir Johns Run to travel the rest of the way in carriages. Finally, with a tannery threatening to leave town to seek a railhead, the county contributed $30,000 to B&O for a branch and the Berkeley Springs and Potomac Railroad was born. The line opened in November 1888 and the first train was led by Camel 128. The 6.1 mile long line had to cross Warm Spring Run fifteen times to get to the town, but the discovery of a very high quality of glass sand nearby made it all worthwhile and B&O bought out the county's share in 1915. At one time half a dozen sand mines operated along the line ... today all operations are under U.S. Silica.

THIS IMPRESSIVE little station at Berkeley Springs, complete with tile roof, was built by B&O in 1915 ... note the jitneys waiting for passengers from the steam powered train arriving. In 1922 B&O also turned to gasoline power for the branch, purchasing all-steel Gas Motor Car 6000 with 23-foot long trailer 6100 for service here. With room for 56 passengers with baggage, this little 65 hp four-cylinder contraption provided three trips each way daily from Hancock ... by 1933, there were none, but happily the station survives.

Virginia Walker Collection

THE FUNNEL

B&O Museum

SLIGHTLY WEST of Hancock near Grasshopper Hollow we see the Roundtop Cement plant which straddled the mainline. This photograph was taken in the early 1870s ... some of the ruins are still visible.

THIS VIEW greets the eye from the summit of Roundtop Mountain just west of Hancock, or so the title to this postcard proclaims ... we suspect that Roundtop is the mountain on the right and this photo was taken from Tonoloway Mountain on the north side of the river. Either way, the four-track B&O main dominates the scene on the right and the C&O Canal and Western Maryland on the left in this easterly panorama. The name Tonoloway evolved from the Tonoloway Confederacy of the Algonquin Indians who controlled this region in Colonial Days and, almost inevitably, a "Lovers Leap" is nearby. Young frontiersman Palston Vera saved beautiful Indian maiden "Sunny Eye" from drowning and a passionate love affair resulted. Naturally, her papa didn't like the idea and he gathered some warriors to chase the couple to (where else) Lovers Leap, from which arm-in-arm they leapt to their deaths and no doubt raised a happy family in the next world. At least B&O rails had not yet reached here in that era, so no traffic interruptions resulted.

EAST END

SIR JOHNS RUN (CK), about five miles west of Hancock, has played a role in history quite aside from its part in the drama of the East End. Named for Captain Sir John Sinclair, quartermaster to Braddock's ill-fated army, the location was a supply point for that expedition. And, in 1784, a very early steamboat designed and built by James Rumsey was demonstrated here in the presence of George Washington, who was very impressed. Fifty feet long and drawing steam from a tub boiler, the craft pulled water from the river and impelled it out the stern ... this jet exhaust pushed the boat upwards of 40 mph. Mr. Rumsey also had plans for a steamboat which deployed long poles against the river bottom, a design which thankfully did not reach the prototype stage. Nonetheless, Rumsey's skill in boiler design earned him a gold medal from Congress, presented to a son after his death in Great Britain where he was raising money and is said to have expired from the shock of actually getting some. As for B&O, this point was a telegraph station in the early days ... the interlocking tower seen on the right just beyond the frame building was installed in 1902 and improved in 1911. This scene dates from World War I era c. 1917 ... note the waiting shed on the left.

THIS INTERESTING structure graced the scene at Sir Johns Run from c. 1866 to early in this century ... this photo was taken c. 1900. It was located on the site of the waiting shed in the preceding view ... note the overhanging telegrapher's office and the freight station just beyond. If this building seems somewhat grand, it should be remembered that Sir Johns Run was the depot for Berkeley Springs until a direct line was built from Hancock in 1888.

THE FUNNEL

B&OHS

AS FAR AS B&O was concerned, Sir Johns Run became a strategic point on the East End when the decision was made to locate a major coaling and water facility just east of the village about midway between Cumberland and the Ferry. Here, in 1924, we see the complex looking easterly with a westbound train approaching on the left. Opened for service in November 1911, the centerpiece of the facility was this reinforced concrete 600 ton giant built by Roberts and Schaeffer Company ... it straddled the two middle tracks, but was capable of servicing four tracks. A double-track ashpit was placed under the two middle tracks about 600 feet east of the coaling station to permit fire cleaning. Note the two white marks above the tracks on the foundation of the coal bin ... they mark high water during the 1924 flood. Also note the water jug on the right ... built in 1913, this was one of the first water tanks constructed of reinforced concrete in railroad history. This tank was fed with water from a dam/reservoir in Sir Johns Run which flowed by gravity through a 10 inch cast iron pipe for some 7,000 feet ... a pump in the basement of the tank could also draw water from the Potomac River if necessary.

THIS WESTWARD view of the coaling dock at Sir Johns Run c. 1916 hints at its size when compared to the men on the extreme left. The complex remained in service until the end of steam ... it was definitely active in 1954 and gone by 1964. Supplying coal and water was an expensive proposition for all railroads eliminated by dieselization ... less remarked is the fact that this stop, among many others, was no longer necessary.

B&OHS

EAST END

THE READER is aware that there was still another flood on 17 March 1936 . . . it also came to the attention of CK. This tangle of levers and pipes were all that was left of the tower. The whole area was covered with four to seven feet of dirt and debris. B&O, in financial trouble in 1936-37, gave up on Sir Johns Run, "retired" the tower which no longer existed and resignaled the tracks from Orleans Road to Hancock to allow for one way traffic only with crossovers at CK operated by hand. World War II volume, however, pressed B&O to reconsider and on 29 February 1944 an interlocker remotely controlled from Hancock went into service with restoration of multi-directional signaling. A study before and after this modernization showed that an average of fourteen minutes per train was saved along this route. Even this new interlocker did not last long, however . . . by 1964 it was all gone and Sir Johns Run went back to being just another name along the railroad.

B&OHS

ABOUT FIVE MILES west of Sir Johns Run at Great Cacapon was interlocker GC, built c. 1903, improved in 1907 and 1911 and permanently out of service in 1934 . . . we have found no photo of this tower. Another six miles, however, brought B&O rails to Orleans Road (AD), shown here in 1966. AD, opened in 1906 and improved in 1911, went from obscure to prominent to obscure in its life cycle. Orleans Road turned out to be the eastern junction of the Magnolia Cutoff where the new High Line and old, original Low Line met and was a busy place for half a century . . . closure of the Low Line in the middle of this century returned AD to being just another tower along the line of road.

Duane Carrell/courtesy Brian Paulus

THE FUNNEL

ON 12 FEBRUARY 1827, B&O forefathers first met to plan the enterprise that would become the nation's first true railroad ... one hundred and fifty three years later to the day, Barbara Jean Hopkins became the first woman engineer to be killed in the service of the company at Orleans Road on 12 February 1980 at 5:55 a.m. Hopkins, a qualified engineer riding on a westbound trailer train as fireman, had taken the throttle some miles east of Orleans Road. The dispatching move was a good one ... her westbound train to take eastbound main track 2 to Orleans Road, hold to allow an eastbound Amtrak train to pass on track 1 and then cross over. An eastbound train on track 2 was also to hold at Orleans Road ... it did not do so and the collision shown occurred. All signals were functioning properly. This book is dedicated to her memory.

James F. Eells III

JUST TWO MILES west of Orleans Road was Doe Gully Tunnel ... this 1880s depiction is looking easterly at a westbound train which has just exited Murray's Cut just west of the portal. The C&O Canal can be clearly seen on the left and, of course, the Potomac River in the middle. That minor little "Hansrote" grade to which we have referred ended at a spot near the end of the train in this view near the Cut, not a good place for helper cutoff. As will be shown in the next chapter, the building of the Magnolia Cutoff deroofed Doe Gully Tunnel, although the location of the High Line required the boring of new Randolph Tunnel to pierce the ridge apparent just above the locomotive in this scene. The line of road appears to be comfortably above the river, but that is an illusion. Flood waters would aim directly at the embankment where the train is located and regularly tear a new one for B&O.

SWITCH INDICATORS

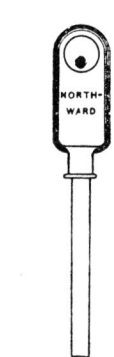

Block is Not Clear.

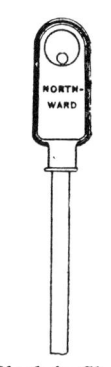

Block is Clear.

EAST END

HANSROTE TOWER (HX), installed c. 1906, surely became known to B&O operating officials as Heartburn Tower before completion of the Magnolia Cutoff. A relative of fireman John W. Rockwell, second from the left in this scene, confirms that this photo was taken shortly after the tower opened. Until the early years of this century, B&O probably adjusted to this grade by limiting train length so no helper service would be needed, but huge increases in traffic forced B&O to increase tonnage per train and helper service would prove to be the lesser of two evils ... a slight dip west of here probably provided some eastbound momentum prior to 1906. When the cutoff opened, Hansrote Tower disappeared from history although, curiously, B&O built a single track connecting line from here westward to the High Line for emergency purposes.

MAGNOLIA'S place in railroad history would have little to do with its pristine location on the south bank of the Potomac River, but rather because this tiny town lent its name to the famed Magnolia Cutoff ... a giant bridge would cross this scene from right to left and put the town literally in the shade. The tower (WO) seen in the middle of this photo was built in 1906 ... just to the left of the tower appears some evidence of an unplanned unpleasantness. From the very early days, Magnolia was known as No. 12 Water Station and indeed supplied water until 1928 ... the tower supposedly went west in 1914 as we shall see. Since the track on the left is probably a holding track installed in 1906 to Hansrote, the date of this photo is probably within a few years of that date.

THE FUNNEL

Smithsonian Institution

FOR ALL THE CHARM of its name and its attractive 1882 Baldwin station, seen here c. 1900, Paw Paw is merely another little town along the original line of road to Cumberland. For the curious, let us point out that a paw paw is a banana-like fruit that grows in damp areas in eastern and southern states. Certainly B&O received considerable fruit traffic from this pleasant town, but there is no record of any paw paw shipments. The Magnolia Cutoff passed south of town and in recent years the area near this station has been served by a siding ... the station is extant. Paw Paw's place in history was guaranteed in 1948 when B&O purchased eight new lightweight S2 14-4 Pullman cars and named the first one Paw Paw (7010) ... there was even a christening ceremony in the town, complete with the presence of B&O President Roy White and sparkling bottles of West Virginia apple cider. Another East End point was also honored ... Cacapon (7015), although no distinction was made between Big and Little.

PERHAPS THE READER feels the authors have employed hyperbole in describing floods on the East End ... this photo of Paw Paw in 1936 surely will put such thoughts to rest. The Paw Paw station is just off the lower left edge of this photo and the water reached almost to the roof. Both High Line and Low Line traces can be seen. Former Paw Paw mayor and resident Eldridge Kerns was a B&O operator and worked towers at Okonoko, Orleans Road, Hancock, Miller and Patterson Creek ... to reach the latter he would drive to Spring Gap in Maryland and row a boat across the river to the tower, displaying determination we all would like to see in modern politicians. We would not criticize him if he did not make it to work on this particular day.

B&OHS

EAST END

B&OHS

OKONOKO (NO), four and a half miles west of Paw Paw and one and a half miles west of Little Cacapon, became the western junction of the Magnolia Cutoff where it met the original Low Line. This tower, it seems, was originally located at Magnolia ... it was cut apart, moved by flatcar and reassembled here. There was a telegraph office here in the very early days and a tower was constructed in 1893 and improved in 1903, although all were probably closer to Little Cacapon ... the one pictured went in service at noon 9 July 1914. NO received a rebuilt interlocker from a tower in Ohio in August 1945, but did not get color position signals until 1957. The tower was closed 24 March 1958 and interlocking handled remotely from Patterson Creek's FN Tower. In the late 1800s, the Green Ridge Railroad of Maryland operated trains from Maryland timberlands, owned by the Merten family and others of Cumberland, to the river at Darkey's Landing in Maryland and floated logs on the river and canal. The river was soon bridged and connection made with B&O. At one point in 1893, two passenger trains left Okonoko daily for Town Creek in Maryland and connected with B&O trains. By 1918, the timber was gone, Merten bankrupt and the GRRR a fading memory.

Chapter 7

The Magnolia Cutoff

Orleans Road to Okonoko

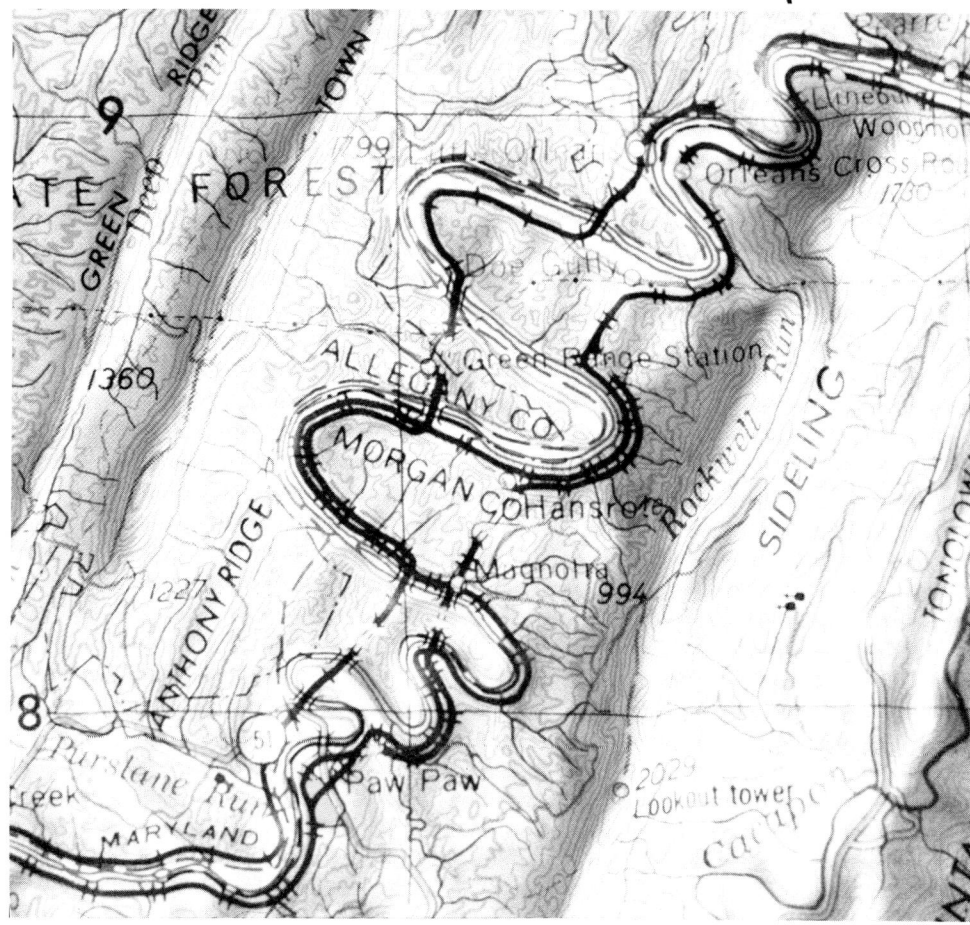

SIMPLY BECAUSE THE serious problem on the East End was eastbound traffic, we have chosen to describe this map in that direction starting at lower left. The reader should ignore the single/slashed line that darts back and forth across the Potomac ... that is the Western Maryland's Cumberland Extension. The original, or "Low" line, followed the river all the way to Doe Gully except for a short "loop cutoff" tunnel just east of Paw Paw ... after tunneling Doe Gully, the old line continues to Orleans Road and east. The Magnolia Cutoff "High Line" begins west of Paw Paw and starts a mild but steady eastward climb ... Paw Paw is bypassed by a deep cut and short Carothers Tunnel. The High Line then parallels the Low Line but at a much higher elevation where one will find famous "Concrete Wall," crosses the Potomac and the Low Line, plunges into Graham Tunnel, crosses over the Low Line again at Magnolia, runs through Stuart Tunnel to exit near Hansrote, again parallels the Low Line at a higher level, punches through Randolph Tunnel by the word "Range" on the map, meets the Low Line at grade in Doe Gully (the tunnel was daylighted) and all four tracks run together to Orleans Road over a large fill and Rockwell Run. The Magnolia Cutoff had two main purposes ... first, of course, to add trackage but also (and of equal importance) to ease the grade facing eastbound tonnage over a long distance to eliminate the need for helpers. Even this mild grade was compensated, i.e., slightly steepened on tangent (straight) track and slightly eased on curvature. While they were at it, B&O also lowered the line of road through Doe Gully and thus reduced the Hansrote Grade from .8% to .48%.

EAST END

Thomas Jefferson passionately described the gorge at Harpers Ferry as "stupendous" and stood in awe at the works of God.

Seventy-seven years after its opening, the authors have meticulously studied the Magnolia Cutoff and marvel at this grand achievement by the works of man.

Tourists pour into Harpers Ferry to admire the scene. The Magnolia Cutoff is hidden in the wilds of the Potomac River, visited only by train crews, MOW people and the odd rail historian. And yet this isolation is probably its greatest tribute . . . the planning and execution of this monumental project was so well done and the problem so completely solved that today it is hard to grasp that a problem ever existed.

We have amply described the problem between Orleans Road and Okonoko . . . perhaps the best summary would be that the original line was a tunnel within a funnel within a funnel. For twenty years B&O struggled with this riddle and applied patchwork solutions . . . candidly, in this era B&O was in the throes of receivership, control by PRR, vast increases in tonnage and the legacy of earlier managements, many of whose policies turned out to be unwise.

By early in this century, B&O was a wreck in terms of equipment, line of road, finances and service to its patrons. Even Vaudeville comedians drew belly laughs with B&O jokes.

As had happened so many times in its history, B&O managed to find a new saviour . . . in this case, Daniel Willard as president. He took office in 1910 and managed to find over $100 million to finance desperately needed improvements. About half of this money was to be expended on the line of road and terminals, the balance for equipment. Everywhere Willard looked he saw alligators and the biggest of all was perched on the East End. Congestion here was choking the entire system. He took immediate steps.

First, he issued instructions that "B&O" would no longer be used anywhere . . . *all* references would be "Baltimore and Ohio." That change cut down on some of the parody. And he stuck to it . . . it wasn't until late in his reign that he reluctantly allowed "B&O" to be used again.

Second, he looked at the East End and groaned. Tonnage was soaring (it would go up 26% by 1913) and *no* line of road improvement could be completed in time to help with the immediate problem. He instantly ordered a fleet of Mikado locomotives to improve hauling capacity over Consolidations by 26.2% and dispatched teams of officers to customer sidings, instructing them to force car loading to capacity . . . the average increase per car came to 13.4%. He also forced tight supervision and inspection to minimize break-in-twos, along with crash improvements in signaling and dispatching communications.

And, most important of all, he demanded that his civil engineers eschew their wet dream schemes for new low-grade passages of the Allegheny barrier and concentrate on solving real problems with available means. At the top of the list was the "Neck of the Bottle" on the East End.

One has to be fair . . . once Willard got their attention, his team of civil engineers came up with a brilliant and affordable plan to solve the problem once and for all. The project was okayed on 13 March 1913 for an estimated $6 million with the cognomen "Magnolia Cutoff" and the first eastbound train made passage on 5 December 1914 . . . the High Line was completely opened for service by January 1915. And it came in under budget for $5,467,950 in spite of serious, unanticipated problems with geology. In these days when huge cost overruns are endemic, this is probably the most amazing development of all. And Mother Nature didn't help . . . there were serious floods in the Spring of 1913 and the following winter was very severe.

The Magnolia Cutoff was not a minor engineering achievement. The High Line involved the boring of *four* double-track tunnels, the removal of a mountain at Doe Gully, two *major* bridge crossings of the Potomac at great height, a huge fill at Rockwell Run which included heavy hillside cutting, gigantic Concrete Wall built *after* slicing deep into an almost sheer mountainside, a very deep cut near Paw Paw and a River Wall between Paw Paw and Okonoko to gain room for two more tracks.

And all this construction was done *without any significant interruption to operations on the Low Line, where traffic was soaring.* Large portions of the Cutoff were built *alongside* the Low Line, in many places separated by only a few feet.

We have had a little fun with Francis L. Stuart and his colleagues earlier in this work, but we must point out that he was the Chief Engineer on

THE MAGNOLIA CUTOFF

this amazing project. There are four tunnels on the Cutoff, by name Randolph, Stuart, Graham and Carothers ... all named for B&O chief engineers. The Magnolia Cutoff has to be Mr. Stuart's finest feat and we sincerely believe that he is one of the major heroes in B&O's long and glorious history. We recommend that the B&O Historical Society appropriately acknowledge his role in the transportation saga.

When completed, the Cutoff was praised throughout the world. Not only was it "the largest single piece of work ever undertaken by this Company," the Cutoff was also called the most significant railroad improvement project ever constructed and this in an era when Americans beamed with pride upon completion of the "impossible" Panama Canal.

The Magnolia Cutoff also turned out to be the last major physical improvement on the railroad. Simply put, eighty-eight years after its birth, the B&O was finally completed and fully ready for whatever the future might bring.

The High Line was built to relieve congestion and operating savings were originally estimated to be only about $17,000 a month ... within a few months the actual savings amounted to $25,000 a month, so the project even became self-financing.

On time and under budget. The Neck of the Bottle was smashed open.

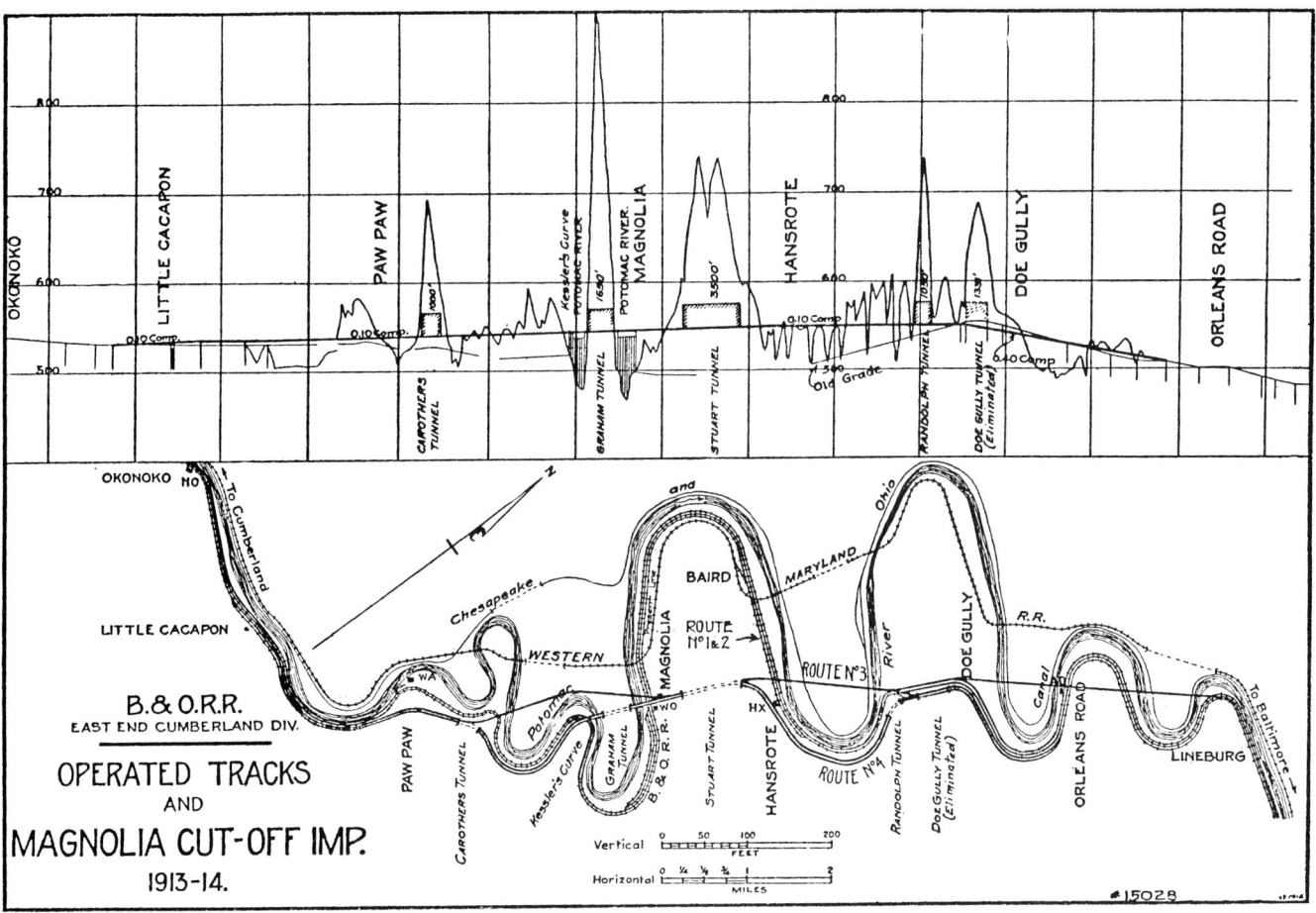

FOUR BASIC PLANS, plus 29 variants, were considered by B&O to solve the chokepoint problem. Plan One involved the construction of a third track along the old line while retaining the helper grade and Doe Gully Tunnel ... cost, $2,235,000. Plan Two raised the ante to four tracks, still keeping the helper grade and tunnel ... $3,375,000. Plan, or Route Three on the map, called for the construction of a super railroad, four tracks wide and running on an almost straight line from Paw Paw past Orleans Road to Lineburg. The old line would be abandoned. The estimated cost was breathtaking ... $15,575,000. Actually, as early as 1902-03, the Potomac Railroad was chartered by B&O to lay claim to this route. Plan Four, for $6,000,000, was the one chosen. With all the advantages of hindsight, we must say that this decision was a wise one. Other urgent projects on B&O needed large chunks of money in the turbulent 1910-15 era and the ten million dollar difference was important. Also, motive power development was in a dramatic upcurve in the first two decades of this century and B&O was a leader in taking advantage of all the benefits ... mallets, trailing trucks,

EAST END

superheaters, larger boilers and so on. B&O probably reasoned that power improvements would negate the disadvantages to Plan Four and they were right. The diesel revolution, not even a dream at this time, would be such a dramatic leap forward that even the Low Line would become redundant. Plan Four provided tunnel clearance, track centers and vertical curves for mallets, although B&O's early experience with this mode of power was unhappy until 1916 as detailed in the book *West End*. In the event, mallets would not be seen on the East End in any numbers until late in the steam era. Curiously, passenger comfort also played a role in the final selection ... remember that the East End was a chokepoint for such movements. Before the air conditioning and diesel eras, tunnels were bad news for passenger comfort ... in the summer passengers would be gassed through windows and in the winter showered with cinders through ventilators. By retaining the Low Line, passenger trains could and would take the scenic river route tunnel-free and the comedians would have one less subject on which to carp. One last tiny point ... note Baird on the map upper center. A tower was built here in 1893 and apparently it was a telegraph station earlier ... we believe it was supplanted by Hansrote. Baird was also the location of a connecting track with Western Maryland as shown and was retained as such until the Low Line was abandoned.

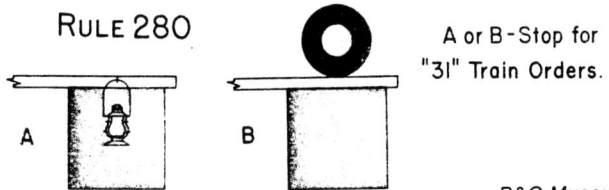

B&O Museum

WE WILL NOW proceed from east to west on the Magnolia Cutoff, pointing out that the reader should go to the frontispiece on page two for a superb view of the Orleans Road complex. This location just west of Orleans Road is very familiar to B&O historians because it was used for many posed publicity shots like this one. In this case in the early 1950s, Alco DF7s 806 and 815 were the stars with coal drags ... the 815 in the distance apparently managed to get a drag up the Low Line, quite an accomplishment with this class of power and probably accompanied by some sparkling language on the part of the engineer. Alcos were not, to say the least, popular ... handsome, yes. These trains rest on a deep fill as we shall see.

THE MAGNOLIA CUTOFF

THIS C. 1950 view looks east toward Orleans Road ... the signal bridge at far left center is the one from which the preceding photo was taken. This location is known as Rockwell Run Water Station ... note the penstocks and the roof of the water jug barely seen to the right.

The fill here is quite deep and apparent ... the photographer is standing on Hillside Cut. The two tracks on the right are the High Line although obviously still at grade with the Low Line tracks on the left.

THIS IS FAMOUS Hillside Cut just west of Rockwell Run Water Station, which appears at center left. Taken during the winter 1912-14 just after a snowstorm, this view begins to give the reader an appreciation for just how much blasting and digging was necessary to build the High Line. The hillside was benched at roughly fifty foot intervals to avoid fouling the old mainline and the material removed was placed in the fill. The old line was raised in this area and the curvature eased from 6 degrees to 4 degrees. As we will see, fill from this cut was nowhere near enough to raise the line.

EAST END

ROCKWELL RUN FILL under construction, receiving what would end up as one million cubic yards of fill, most of which came from Doe Gully to the west. The method of filling is apparent ... the height of the enbankment is indicated by the size of the workmen.

A PANORAMIC VIEW, looking east c. 1950 at Rockwell Run Fill. Note Hillside Cut center left and the terraces left in place to protect the railroad from landslides ... the rock in this area turned out to be unstable. Raising the old line to match grade with cutoff tracks had several advantages ... getting the line away from the Potomac, avoiding the need for a wall between the two lines and easing the westward grade on the old line to a range of .26 to .33 percent. Four construction camps for workers were built for the project ... one was located to the left of the fill in this scene, others at Hansrote, Magnolia and Kesslers. These camps were comfortable, enjoying electric lighting and modern fixtures.

THE MAGNOLIA CUTOFF

THE FIRST of many major obstacles facing the builders of the Magnolia Cutoff was the mountain squatting on the Doe Gully Tunnel. B&O decided to dig for a new double track line to the north of the bore while using the old line for traffic ... in the process, the overburden on the tunnel would be removed to the arch. This scene, looking westward, shows the east portal of the tunnel and burden removal well underway. Unfortunately, the surface strata indications and the actual strata turned out to be quite different ... the rock underneath was rotten and decomposed when exposed to air, forcing the engineers to widen the cut and deepen benches to be sure slides did not close the old main. Keep in mind that, in the end, *four* tracks would penetrate Doe Gully and those four would be 12 feet *lower* than the original line to ease the Hansrote grade. The maximum depth was 200 feet, equivalent to a twenty story building. Oddly, the mountain has never had a name and B&O chose not to apply one. Some of the nearby peaks rise to 800 and 900 feet at their crests, but by the standards of the Potomac Valley must have been regarded as mere foothills. *B&OHS*

AGAIN LOOKING WESTWARD, the removal process is advanced and the tunnel is almost uncovered to the arch. The hole on the right would become the location of the old line and the new line would replace the old one on the left. The authors have found no depictions of the Doe Gully Tunnel portals dating before construction, which means the viewer is seeing them for the first time just before they would be destroyed. Again, the reader should be reminded that the final location of the old line would be twelve feet *below* its original level and would be at the same height as the new line. *B&OHS*

EAST END

NOW AT THE WEST END of Doe Gully looking east, we can see the west portal of the tunnel, the old line diverging to the left and the new line taking shape in the center. Right in the middle of this photo is where the grade would change ... both lines were at the same height to this point from Orleans Road, but would follow different profiles from here west to Okonoko. Note the men walking along the bench right center. In addition to normal construction hazards, much of the activity took place on and around a very busy railroad which posed serious safety hazards. Footpaths were built along all such rights of way and track walking was prohibited. Employees were required to read and sign safety instructions and rules ... special uniformed and plainclothed railroad police enforced the regulations with such vigor that reports indicate casualties were surprisingly low.

B&OHS

AGAIN LOOKING eastward at Doe Gully, the tunnel portal shows signs of a mishap. Of course, such incidents are inevitable ... the amazing thing about the whole project is that there were so few and the restoration of traffic so swift. All in all, 1,400,000 cubic yards of material (mostly rock) were removed from Doe Gully, almost half of the total removed on the entire cutoff. As reported earlier, most of the burden was used to create Rockwell Run Fill.

THE MAGNOLIA CUTOFF

DOE GULLY CUT about a third of a century after completion from the east portal of Randolph Tunnel, the first one on the High Line. The grade profile changes at the point of the rocky arrow ... just .04% against eastward tonnage on the Cutoff and reduced from .8% to .48% on the Low Line diverging to the left. From here to west of Paw Paw, the Magnolia Cutoff will always be at a higher elevation than the original line. Irregular and unstable strata in this area haunted the engineers, but they mastered this problem along with all others ... note the rockfall detritus just this side of the "arrow" point.

THE EAST PORTAL OF Randolph Tunnel on the High Line, from which the last photo was taken. This c. 1950 shot, not surprisingly, shows the carbon stains of countless steam locomotives which had pounded through here in the prior third of a century. This tunnel is on a four degree curve, is 1,014 feet in length and has ample dimensions ... 14 foot track centers, 15½ foot arch radius and 24½ feet from the top of the rail to the keystone. Rotten rock complicated construction, but B&O engineers refused to submit and solved the problem. The final roof course on all High Line tunnels was of brick because B&O had learned that exhaust gases had little effect on that versatile material.

B&OHS

EAST END

THE WEST PORTAL of Randolph Tunnel, nearing completion and as pristine as it will ever be ... the arch was first timber lined, which was left in place when the permanent lining was added. B&O lineside industries provided much of the material for the Cutoff ... limestone from Kearneysville, sand from the Potomac near Washington and brick from Thornton WV on the West End. Speed of construction of this tunnel apparently exceeded a previous world record set at the new Sand Patch Tunnel on what was then the Connellsville Division.

B&OHS

TWO POWER PLANTS were built to service the project ... one at Magnolia and the one seen here just west of the rocky "arrow" in Doe Gully on the old line. This plant housed four 100 and two 75 horsepower boilers, two air compressors and one 50 kilowatt generator. Evidence of the severity of winter 1913-14 is obvious, but B&O engineers gave the finger to Mother Nature and got on with the job.

THE MAGNOLIA CUTOFF

THE TWO LINES ARE slowly parting in this easterly view of the west portal of Randolph Tunnel and the west exit from Murray's Cut on the old line. This photo was taken in the early 1950s and, on the left, gives a glimpse of the scenic grandeur for which the Potomac River is famous.

HERE IS A CLOSER view of Murray's Cut on the old line, seen at a distance in the last photo and vaguely seen circa 1880 in the last chapter. While minor in the saga of the East End, there has been a much repeated legend that this was once a tunnel ... the late Raymond Hicks reported seeing concrete blocks in this area and told of a conversation with a signal maintainer that there had once been a tunnel at this location. We find the story unlikely and unimportant if true. Unlike most of this ridgeline, the rocks here appear quite stable and there would be no reason to tunnel such a short distance ... in addition, there is no written record of a tunnel.

HOTSPOT FOR YEARS, Hansrote became a mere place name after completion of the Cutoff. In this early 1950s easterly view, we see a westbound QD train on the High Line with an EM1 on the point, the connecting track between the lines in the foreground, a telephone booth and the majestic Potomac. The grade profile difference is quite apparent. The two lines paralleled each other to this point, but the High Line then turns to cut through the river "loop" and plunge into Stuart Tunnel ... the old line continues to follow the river. The photographer is standing on the new line.

EAST END

STUART TUNNEL was, of course, named for the hero of this chapter, but a more appropriate name would have been Murphy Tunnel . . . it was number two in line, number one in difficulty and number four (last) to be completed. Not only was the strata broken, rotten and unpredictable, it was also interlaced with clay. The original intent was to work headings from each end plus two roof shafts and end up with a 3,355 foot tunnel. In short order, the approach cuts started collapsing and, in the end, the eastern heading could not be opened. The roof caved-in at three places early in the drama . . . timber linings were replaced with steel forms and arches, but even they didn't hold and I-beams had to be woven into place. This c. 1952 photo shows the east portal with some maintenance equipment on the westbound track . . . the entrance is slightly spiraled, but most of the bore is tangent.

THE ORIGINAL PLAN called for this, the west end of Stuart Tunnel, to be a tunnel with the portal about 160 feet closer to the viewer. The roof collapsed early on and the decision was made to make this section a cut. Even then, as the viewer can see in this c. 1950 photo, a wall had to be built above the portal to hold back the fluid terrain. Compare the composition of the sub-strata on each side of the tracks . . . each is completely different. Some of the layers were almost vertical in the tunnel and under the roadbed. In the end, about 400,000 cubic yards of goop had to be excavated from this mile of railroad. The only redeeming feature to all this heartburn was that the location was well away from the Old Line and there was no risk of traffic interruption.

HAVING GOTTEN FREE from Stuart Tunnel, the High Line soared above the town of Magnolia, across the Potomac and the old line almost at a right angle and headed straight for a mountain on the other side. Here, in April 1914, we see the reinforced concrete piers under construction and the gaggle of support facilities in the Magnolia area . . . this view is easterly toward Stuart Tunnel. The High Line cleared the original tracks by fifty feet and the river by 80 feet above low water . . . the bridge is about 1,000 feet long. The piers rest on bedrock about five feet below the river bottom . . . cofferdams were of plain sheathing and clay puddling and the foundations were poured without incident. The forms seen here were of ordinary wood and were raised by derricks.

THE MAGNOLIA CUTOFF

Smithsonian Institution

BY EARLY SUMMER OF 1914, the piers were being capped and a saw mill was turning out ties by the thousands for the new line as Magnolia Tower surveyed a bustling scene.

BY AUGUST 1914, the steel was in place on the Magnolia Bridge and the giant fill on the east end was near capacity ... in fact, probably *over* as the material taken from Stuart Tunnel far exceeded original estimates. Just to the left of the fill can be seen the second power plant, and it was a big one with two 6100 hp boilers and two DC generators pumping out 200 kilowatts for lighting as well as running two saw mills and a forging/blacksmith shop ... a construction camp was also squeezed into Magnolia. The bridge boasts six 100', three 80' and two 75' deck plate girder spans ... the easterly spans were floored to deflect exhaust gases from the Low Line. It will take "forty days and forty nights" for the Potomac to reach this bridge and, if it should happen, a lot more than B&O will be in trouble. The grade from a quarter mile east of the bridge, over the bridge and through Graham Tunnel (out of sight to the west at lower left) was .10% ... a total of about a mile and the steepest climb on the Cutoff. Even that puny rise was ameliorated by a .02% eastbound mile-long *dip* on the other side of Graham Tunnel which allowed some momentum.

EAST END

THE SCENE is peaceful at Magnolia in the late 1950s and the low line has been reduced to one track, all a measure of success.

THE MAGNOLIA BRIDGE at an unusual angle in the late 1950s. At far left notice the black hole marking the east portal of Graham Tunnel and the height of the overburden, which introduces a question of definition. Is that a mountain, ridge or hill? It has no name and B&O called it a ridge, but to us it looks like a mountain and we submit if you had to climb it, you would call it that when you got to the top.

MURPHY apparently could not be in two places at one time because B&O got lucky at Graham Tunnel, the east portal of which we see here in the 1950s ... the rock was solid and stable, so this tangent 1580 foot bore was constructed without incident. But it was a near run thing ... study the tailings over the right edge of the portal and left side of the cut. A few feet one way or the other and B&O would have had another Doe Gully or Stuart Tunnel.

THE MAGNOLIA CUTOFF

WE ARE LOOKING at what would become the west portal of Graham Tunnel, a bore unusual in two respects. First, it is the only Cutoff tunnel in Maryland (or perhaps we should say *under* Maryland) and, second, it is located between two large, high bridges ... Magnolia on the east and Kesslers on the west. Again B&O had a near miss ... note the solid strata above the tunnel and the glob of rotten rock just to the right.

KESSLER BRIDGE, from the west portal of Graham Tunnel and under construction during the summer of 1914. Note the spindly footbridge on the right and the high trestle at upper left ... the latter was used to move concrete to the piers. The old line appears, very vaguely, behind the trestle and curves off to the right of the far pier.

EAST END

FROM THE West Virginia shore, Kessler Bridge was well advanced in July 1914 . . . the Graham Tunnel hole can be seen as well as the old line tracks in the foreground. Magnolia and Kessler Bridges combined consumed about 26,000 cubic yards of concrete and 3,000 tons of steel.

ABOUT 1,052 FEET LONG, Kessler Bridge presented this appearance in the middle of this century. The structure spans consist of four 100 foot and six 75 foot deck plate girders plus three skewed girders totaling 202 feet over the old line . . . the latter spans were floored for protection from gases as at Magnolia. Note how wide the flood plain at this point . . . the river is barely visible at the far eastern edge of the bridge.

THE MAGNOLIA CUTOFF

LOOKING WEST from the side of the ridge over Graham Tunnel, Kessler Bridge and the Potomac Valley gave this visage in 1946 as Train 23 *West Virginian* passes under the skewed spans. No trace of the construction facilities that made it all possible can be seen.

EXTRA WEST 7607, trailing 139 coal cars, drifts over Kessler Bridge on 27 May 1951 and is about to douse several eager photographers with a sniff of coal gas, carbon and cinders.

B&OHS/E. L. Thompson Collection

EAST END

OF ALL THE MAJOR projects on the Cutoff, the most impressive and stunning in visual impact turned out to be Concrete Wall. The ridge towers almost one thousand feet high and originally ran sheer to the river, allowing only a slight embankment on which the original line was placed. To build the cutoff, B&O had to slice into this ridge for almost a half mile and remove a staggering 80,000 cubic yards of rock. At the same time these intrepid engineers had to build an 1800 foot long retaining wall to provide a path for the cutoff without allowing *any* interference with low line traffic. With an eastbound passenger train on the low line giving a size reference, this c. 1950 photo gives the reader some appreciation for the magnitude of the accomplishment. The site is about a mile west of Kessler Bridge. Note the separation in the wall just behind the train . . . the wall was staggered to allow room for steps.

INGENUITY WAS THE watchword at Concrete Wall . . . Stuart and his compatriots developed this "traveler" which spanned the two low line tracks and moved on two side rails which were mounted on timber blocking. Equipped with two derricks with 50 foot booms and two boilers to power two hoisting engines on the upper deck, this futuristic device managed to place 22,000 cubic yards of concrete into the wall without hindering traffic and without moving materials across the operated tracks at grade. The Wall above the footings is 31 feet high with a width at the top of 2½ feet and at the bottom of 15 feet.

THE MAGNOLIA CUTOFF

THIS VIEW OF THE inside of the Wall was taken in December 1913, only *nine months* after the whole project was approved... Stuart didn't waste time. Footing construction "caused considerable trouble and was extremely difficult at places where it was necessary to excavate to a maximum depth of 14 feet below the top of the footing in order to secure a firm foundation." As seen in this photo, the sidehill cut was benched to prevent slides, protect the low line and provide room for a tramway to move material. The traveler, in this photo in the distance at the east end of the Wall, used one derrick to handle footing excavation and the other deposited concrete. A concrete plant was built about a half mile west of here and material delivered in small cars which were picked up and emptied into the forms. The Wall was built in fifty foot sections and about two sections were completed per week... at each joint a bond was made into the rock face. The preceding photo was taken in July 1914, so the reader can see the progress made in the interim.
B&OHS

THE STEPS at Concrete Wall in a scene that conveys the massiveness of the structure ... this photo was taken 9 May 1973 after, of course, the low line was no more.

EAST END

THE ORIGINAL operational plan for the cutoff was to use the old line for all westbound traffic and the new line for all eastbound movements. Most evidence indicates that this procedure, if in effect at all, did not last long and both routes were bidirectional. Passenger traffic was kept on the old line for reasons given earlier and this policy lasted until deep into the twentieth century ... one exception was the *Cincinnatian* which used the high line in the late 1940s to save a few minutes on a very tight schedule, but of course this train was completely air conditioned. Promotionally, the cutoff was tagged the "Fast Freight Line" and this title was actually painted on Kessler Bridge for many years. The advent of diesel power made the Hansrote grade less of an annoyance (one can overload traction motors for brief periods), thus on 27 May 1951, New York 94 Engine 291 with 93 cars was dispatched on the low line as we see here. The little building on the high line above the engine is a telephone booth.

B&OHS/E. L. Thompson Collection

ON 27 MAY 1951, we see Train 21 Engine 5090 *The Washingtonian* with seven cars laying into a curve below Concrete Wall on the low line. For all its scenic majesty, the East End was unappreciated by most B&O passengers simply because many feature trains went over it at dusk or night ... *The Washingtonian* was an exception and consequently was probably the most photographed train in history on Cumberland East and Pittsburgh East. A Baltimore-Cleveland daily, this train took the PL&E from east of Pittsburgh to Youngstown and the Erie from there to Cleveland.

B&OHS/E. L. Thompson Collection

THE MAGNOLIA CUTOFF

TRUE TO FORM, Train 22 also rolls by Concrete Wall led by the 5319 trailing five cars on 27 May 1951. The 5300s were designed for Washington-New York service and were rarely seen on the East End until diesel displacement made them excess... in the last days of steam, at least one was reduced to freight helper service out of Benwood far away in space and time from the glories of the Royal Blue Line.

B&OHS/E. L. Thompson

CSD 97 Engines 7615-7612 and 59 cars added to the scene on 27 May 1951. The EM1 7600s, of course, were built for West End service but dieselization pushed them into Keyser-Brunswick dispatchment in the early 1950s. That this train is doubleheaded has nothing to do with the need for power... because most tonnage was and is eastbound, power and cabooses would accumulate to the east and had to be returned as quickly as possible. The East End was a "double up" subdivision for the movement of coal, which of course was most of the tonnage. Drags off the West End would be weighed and classed at Keyser, then pushed east in doubled train length over the Patterson Creek Cutoff ... to some extent, the same procedure was employed at Cumberland for Pittsburgh East coal.

B&OHS/E. L. Thompson Collection

EAST END

FOR THE BENEFIT of those readers who are still skeptical about the power of flood waters, we present these two photographs of the low line at Concrete Wall after the 1936 deluge.

B&OHS

JUST WEST of Concrete Wall and looking west circa 1950, the low line swings away to the right to avoid the ridge and the high line turns left to pierce it. The original low line cut off a loop of the Potomac through Paw Paw Tunnel, deroofed early in this century. Both lines are now slowly coming together in terms of height.

THE MAGNOLIA CUTOFF

THE LAST TUNNEL on the cutoff is Carothers, about 993 feet long and on a gentle curve. The bore is through sandstone, slate and shale ledge ... since early records and reports do not decry this drift tunnel, we assume no unusual problems were faced. Still, 8,000 cubic yards of concrete were required for the lining. This is the east portal.

THIS westerly view toward Paw Paw from the top of the ridge tunneled by the Carothers bore clearly shows the original line approaching the town on the right and the new line sweeping west on the left. The two lines are now slowly closing on each other in height ... note, at extreme left, two road bridges over the new line. The nearest was constructed when the cutoff was built ... the farthest in more modern times. This photo dates to the late 1940s and does not give any impression of the depth of the cut necessary to get out of Carothers Tunnel which is located to the rear of the photographer.

PROMINENT IN the center of this easterly c. 1950 view is Paw Paw Cut, one of the least remarked yet largest on the cutoff ... over 500,000 cubic yards of material, mostly dirt, was removed and the cut reaches a maximum depth of 96 feet. In order to avoid extensive hillside cutting on the right, this dirt was hauled west to this area and used to raise the old line (the two tracks on the left) about seven feet, which was also shifted left toward the river. The town of Paw Paw can be barely seen center left.

EAST END

RIVER WALL was the last structure of consequence on the cutoff and it was small only in comparison to Concrete Wall. With an average height of 24 feet and 3100 feet long, River Wall was built to contain the dirt from Paw Paw Cut and allow the movement of the two tracks of the original line toward the river. The idea was to avoid "encroachment on the stream" and move both lines "above high water." The Potomac River was not amused nor mollified by this strategy and felt insulted by being called a "stream." The reader has already seen the river's reaction on occasion. River Wall required about 23,000 cubic yards of concrete and at least has never been washed away. It is at about this point that the new and old lines met at the same level ... the four tracks continued west to the Okonoko interlocker as reported and shown in the last chapter.

BLOCK SIGNAL RULES.

TWO-POSITION BLOCK SIGNALS.

502. The following signals will appear where conditions require their use:

502 AA.

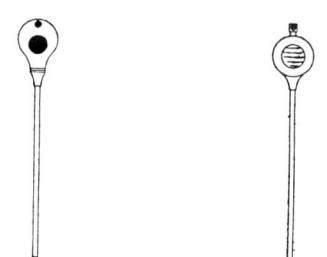

Indication—Stop; then proceed.
Name—Stop and proceed-signal.

THE MAGNOLIA CUTOFF

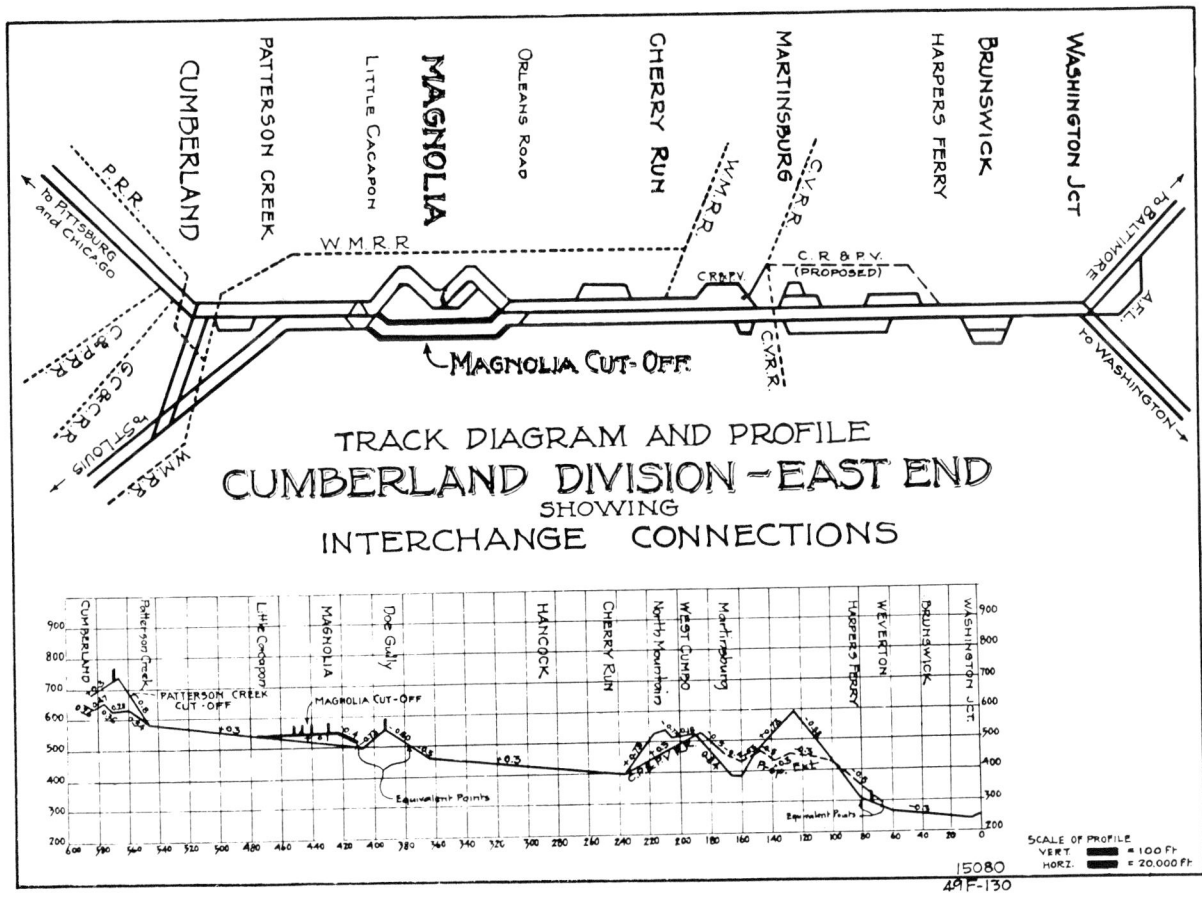

THE ABOVE SCHEMATIC, published by B&O in 1914, succinctly shows the relationship of the Magnolia Cutoff to the lines east and west of the project. Parenthetically, "Washington Junction" on the right would become Point of Rocks and the proposed CR&PV line was never built. Everything about this monumental project excites admiration, even after three quarters of a century. Seven contractors, with 2500 workmen, took just two months to place their equipment and only seventeen months to complete their jobs. They *all* finished simultaneously and *ahead* of schedule. The completion of Randolph Tunnel in eleven months beat the previous world's record at Sand Patch on Pittsburgh East. While there were casualties, there were less than on any comparable work to that time. The new line is eleven miles long with compensated eastbound ruling grade of just .1%, westbound only .4%. Degrees of curvature were only 803, which was 877 less than on the old line. Equipment employed totaled 22 power shovels, 55 locomotives, 2 locomotive cranes, 550 dump cars, 6 concrete plants, 1 traveler and 116 air and steam drills. One track for eastbound use was in service almost two months before final completion. Even B&O's final report to the public was done with style, class and cool modesty ... "The Magnolia Cutoff is one of the examples of the effort on the part of the management of the Baltimore and Ohio to maintain the reputation as the 'line of service.' The entire work from the standpoints of cost, hindrance to traffic and time of completion has been successfully carried out, and to the satisfaction of the management." No hype, no bluster, just a calm "we got the job done." Oh, and by the way, at less than estimated cost. Try that one on for size, Vaudeville. The original line continued in service until January of 1957 when work began to remove almost all of track 2, leaving only a 200 car siding at Magnolia. Track 1 remained in service signaled for westbound movements and track 3 on the cutoff was signaled for bidirectional movement. Finally, in November 1961, track 1 was pulled leaving only a siding from Okonoko to Paw Paw, later shortened to a switch closer to the town. Well done, Mr. Stuart.

EAST END

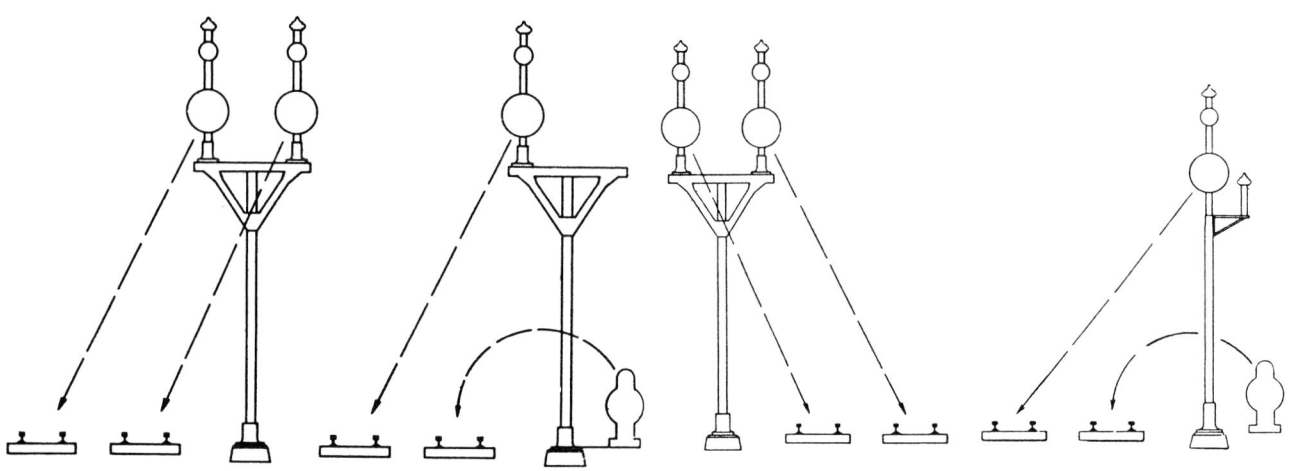

B&OHS

A FEW OF THE STALWARTS who built the cutoff are seen here at the portal of one of the tunnels, complete with dobbin. The upper arch would first be opened with air drills and dynamite, then the refuse would be loaded in dump cars and wasted. Some of the dump cars were electrically operated. The arch would be cribbed and then slowly deepened until a shovel could be fitted in to speed removal.

THE MAGNOLIA CUTOFF

B&OHS

MANY OF THE shovels were air operated for use inside tunnels, as in this scene. Note the two track gauges and the dump car . . . each of the latter held about four cubic yards of material.

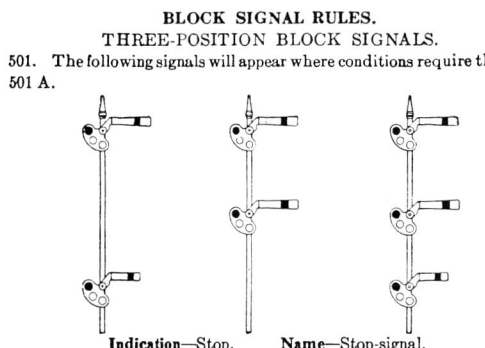

BLOCK SIGNAL RULES.
THREE-POSITION BLOCK SIGNALS.
501. The following signals will appear where conditions require their use:
501 A.

Indication—Stop.   Name—Stop-signal.

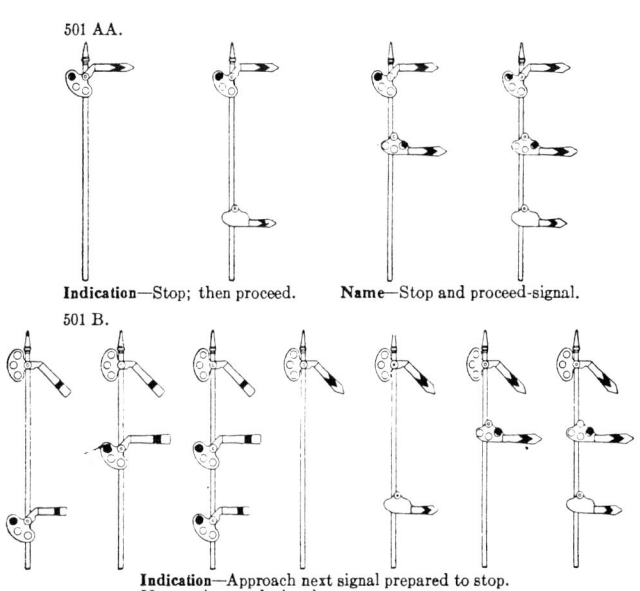

501 AA.

Indication—Stop; then proceed.   Name—Stop and proceed-signal.
501 B.

Indication—Approach next signal prepared to stop.
Name—Approach-signal.

135

EAST END

B&OHS

A BEVY OF dinky tank narrow-gauge locomotives used on the cutoff. Apparently there were two cylinder sizes: 10 by 16 inch and 12 by 18 inch. The contractors left their locomotives on site at the completion of the job and years later a firm bought them for scrap.

B&OHS

OF THE TWENTY-TWO shovels used on the project, all but one were Marion or Marion Osgood . . . as reported, a number were air powered for tunnel work. This one is steam powered. Incidentally, all six revolving concrete mixers were air powered and had a one cubic yard capacity.

THE MAGNOLIA CUTOFF

B&OHS

THE ONLY BUCYRUS used in cutoff construction was this behemoth. One cannot help but wonder where all these heavy steam and air shovels had been or were about to go. Perhaps there are steam shovel historians who can trace these molders of our destiny.

WE WOULD not want the reader to think that determined B&O cutoff engineers were without a sense of humor . . . this delightful cartoon appeared in the B&O employee magazine during the construction era. The levelman is demanding that the rodman hold the rod straight up with the bottom on the mark and that is not going to be easy.

Chapter 8

Easy Passage

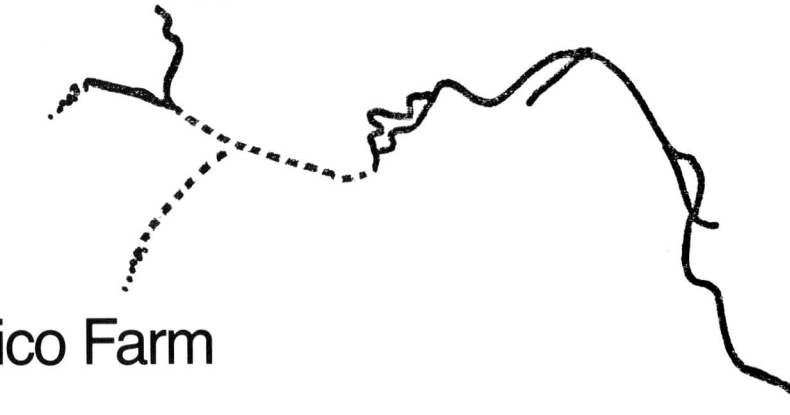

Okonoko to Mexico Farm

FREE OF THE FUNNEL at Okonoko, B&O lines sweep west over the South Branch of the Potomac, through Green Spring and its junction with the South Branch Railroad, over Patterson Creek and then over the North Branch of the Potomac at, appropriately, North Branch ... now back in Maryland (and a junction with the Western Maryland), the line of road approaches the outskirts of Cumberland, originally at Evitts Creek and today at Mexico Farm. The Patterson Creek Cutoff is seen between P Creek and McKenzie at upper left, piercing Knobly Mountain en route. The P Creek Cutoff was originally called the Pinto Cutoff because its western end connected with the West End of the Cumberland Division near that tiny town, but that name did not last long ... Pinto became a point on the WM. The SBRR was a B&O entity until recent years and can be seen here running southwesterly from Green Spring to Romney along (except near Green Spring) the South Branch of the Potomac ... this line continues off this map for many more miles to Moorefield and Petersburg for a total length half as long as the entire East End. While subject to floods of water and traffic, this section of the East End runs along broad and fertile bottomlands with no significant constrictions and has always been an easy passage for B&O.

While just as subject to the whims of nature and waves of traffic as the line of road east of Okonoko, B&O rails west of Okonoko to the front door of Cumberland run through terrain both gentle and scenic. Constrictions are minor and the route against prevailing tonnage is downhill all the way.

The entire route was double-tracked quite early. The opening of the Patterson Creek Cutoff in 1904, of course, relieved congestion at Cumberland and put tonnage on the East End at Patterson Creek . . . traffic growth made a third track from P Creek to Green Spring necessary and it was completed in July 1912. A third track from Green Spring to Okonoko had been provided prior to 1904. From P Creek to Okonoko remains triple-tracked with a long eastward passing siding at Green Spring.

From P Creek to North Branch, the railroad was double-tracked in the Civil War era and has remained in that configuration to this day . . . the P Creek Cutoff diversion removed any need for widening this stretch.

From North Branch to Evitts Creek three tracks were in place as early as 1904 . . . for years two tracks have been ample. The reader should note that Evitts Creek was the entrance point to the Cumberland Yard complex until a new westbound yard was opened in 1960 and the entrance moved about two miles east to Mexico Farm.

Aside from natural beauty, the only eye-catching object along this part of the East End is the tie treatment plant at Green Spring which opened in March 1913 and is quite active to this day. But more of that later.

Of course, William Prescott Smith toured the line in the 1850s and reported as follows:

> "Sixteen miles east of Cumberland, the south branch of the Potomac is crossed on a bridge 400 feet long. This is, in fact, the main Potomac and would have been so treated, it is said, by the commissioners who determined the boundary of Maryland and Virginia, but that the north branch has the appearance, at the confluence, of being the larger stream. (Maryland, and by extension the B&O, was touched still again by the fickle finger of fate.) The river bottoms are here wide and exceedingly fertile, and the scenery very beautiful. The arching of the strata in the section of the South Branch Mountain, just above the junction (of the two rivers), is most remarkable and grand."

> "Some two miles above is a fine straight line, over the widely expanded flats opposite the ancient village of Old Town, in Maryland. These are the finest bottom lands on the river, and from the upper end of them is obtained the first view of the Knobly Mountain, a remarkable elevation, which lies in a line with the town of Cumberland, and is singularly diversified by a profile which appears like a succession of huge artificial mounds. Dan's Mountain towers over it, forming a fine background to the view."

> "Patterson's Creek, eight miles from Cumberland, is next reached. Immediately below this stream is a lofty mural precipice of limestone and sandstone rock, singularly perforated in some of the ledges by openings which look like Gothic loopholes. The valley of this creek is very straight and bordered by beautiful flats. The viaduct over the stream is 150 feet long."

> "Less than two miles above, and six miles from Cumberland, the north branch of the Potomac is crossed by an iron viaduct 700 feet long, rising in a succession of steps—embracing also a crossing of the Chesapeake and Ohio Canal. This extensive bridge carries us out of Virginia and lands us once more in old Maryland, which we left at Harper's Ferry, and kept out of for a distance of 91 miles. The route thence to Cumberland is across two bends of the river, between which the stream of Evert's Creek [sic] is crossed by a viaduct of 100 feet span."

The original builders of the B&O, reaching for their immediate goal of Cumberland through this meek and lovely territory and with the worst of the East End behind them, must have gazed at those mountains in the distance with a mixture of pleasure and apprehension. Sooner or later, they would have to *cross* those majestic heights to get to the Ohio River and *that* passage would not prove to be easy.

But that is another story.

EAST END

ONE WOULD THINK that if the water in a spring was green, it would be something less than potable ... yet it didn't seem to bother the people who named Green Spring. Whatever the quality of the water, Green Spring was and is an active place on the East End. Here, c. 1914, we see the station, water jug, waiting shed and a clutch of other buildings as MOW men surface track. The famous tie plant is to the left rear of the photographer and the South Branch junction track can barely be seen curving off to the right ... this view, of course, is easterly. The locomotive taking water from a penstock in the distance is probably branch line power. The tower controlling this area was GI, in service February 1900, improved in 1914 and removed October 1951. According to track charts, it was located on the south side of the main about a half-mile east of the station. We can't find it on this photo ... perhaps the locomotive is blocking the view. In any event, the station still exists in 1992.

THE REAR of the Green Spring station is shown here in this c. 1914 photo. The tracks in the foreground, which do form a wye, mark the start of the South Branch to Romney and points south. Note the cattle chute at the boxcar to the right ... we *think* it's a boxcar, but it just might be a plug door reefer. Whatever, apparently the chute is being used to load something other than four-legged cargo.

AS THE SECOND DECADE of this century opened, B&O along with most other railroads faced a serious problem having to do with a rather mundane subject ... railroad ties. The forest cover was being cut over at an alarming rate, remaining timber resources were ever more distant from areas of use, regrowth to consumption rates were plummeting and the cost of wood was soaring as quality was dropping. B&O wisely decided to extend the life of ties by treatment and in March 1913 opened the famous tie treatment plant at Green Spring. The idea was to force creosote, zinc chloride and other chemicals into the wood under pressure in retorts and thus materially extend the life of ties on the line of road. In short, it worked. Tie life over the years was extended to fifteen and ultimately thirty years, at least in theory ... the process was so effective that tie wear was caused more by ballast undercutting than deterioration. Green Spring was chosen as the site for the plant because vast virgin timber tracts were to be found to the south along the South Branch Valley and also because large numbers of westbound empty cars could be used to transport ties to the rest of the system. Here, in 1928, we see the heart of the plant. On the left are piles of un- treated ties being seasoned by open air. They were then bundled, loaded on specially designed cars and placed in a retort ... at right center one can see both loaded cars as well as one empty one. Under pressure and heat, the ties were permeated with the chemicals and ready for long service.

THIS PHOTO, and the two to follow, are in a panoramic series starting with the preceding view ... that is, the photographer was standing in one place and moving his camera from left to right over the whole scene. The plant is on the north side of the B&O main and the first view was facing west ... this scene is facing north. The main plant is to the left and the coal cars are supplying fuel for the plant. Note the different size retort cars ... some single truck, some double. At first only ties were treated, but by the 1920s bridge timbers were also included in the program. At extreme right center an ancient coach is being used as an office and in the distance one can see still more ties being seasoned. The original plant consisted of two retorts 7 feet in diameter and 132 feet long ... a third one was added in the late 1920s.

EAST END

NOW LOOKING northeasterly, we see the other end of the coach/office, telegraph poles awaiting their turn, a narrow-gauge tank locomotive (more about this gem a little later), a regal engine house, a horse and still more retort cars. This operation is not small ... proper seasoning requires 6-8 months and most of the original 60 acre site was filled with aging wood in the early years. For example, in June 1927 there were over a million ties in various stages of seasoning and at that time B&O used two to three million ties annually. Prior to treatment, ties are sent to a woodworking plant on site to be properly sized and bored as no cutting should be done to the tie surface once it is treated. Fire retardance is also a benefit of treatment, although as we have reported in regard to the Harpers Ferry bridge fire the process apparently needed some refinement.

NOW LOOKING EASTERLY, the station and water jug at Green Spring can be seen in the distant center across a vast field of ties. Light colored wood is untreated, dark ready to use. On the far left, notice the sunken track with gondolas ready to receive ties from a string of retort cars. The woodworking shop is obvious with its sawdust tower. Above all, notice the dual-gauge track. The entire facility was laced with thirty-inch track and standard gauge was used only for ingress. When the tie plant was first opened, B&O enticed workers to this rural outpost by offering cabooses for rent as living quarters and constructing a commissary ... ultimately, of course, a town grew around the plant.

EASY PASSAGE

BY THE 1950s, narrow gauge was gone except for retort tracks and a sea of gondolas was required for handling. Each retort car could hold 43 ties and there were 15 cars to a "train," so 645 ties could be treated in one load . . . the plant rostered 130 of these cars. The two strings of treated and untreated ties are quite apparent in the middle of this scene. The Koppers Company (now Koppers Industries) began joint operation of the facility with B&O circa 1935 and bought the plant outright in 1973.

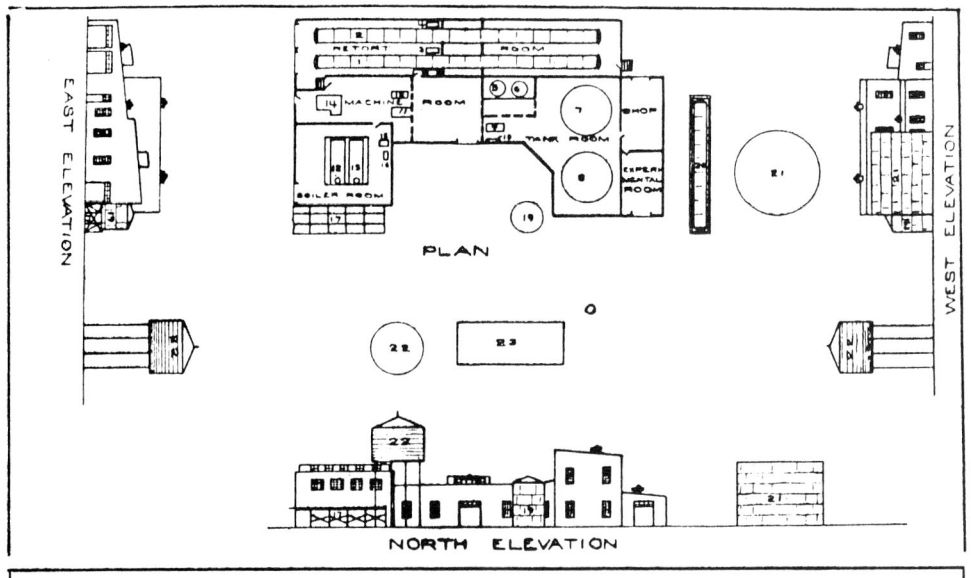

THIS FLOOR PLAN of the plant was published in 1914 and shows the facility as built. In the last six months of 1913, 3,354 cars of untreated ties were received and in all of 1913 (from opening in March) 1,490 cars of treated ties were shipped . . . it did not take B&O long to get up to speed considering that they started with green timber.

TIMBER TREATING PLANT FLOOR PLAN, ELEVATIONS AND LEGEND.

1-2 Retorts	11 Low Compressor, Clayton.	18 Vacuum Pump.
3-4 Centrifugal Pumps.	12-13 Boilers.	19 Zinc Chloride Tank.
5-6 Pressure Tanks.	14 Engine-Generator.	20 Underground Unloading Tank.
7-8 Working Tanks.	15 Feed Water Heater.	21 Creosote Storage Tank.
9 High Compressor, Clayton.	16 Feed Water Pump.	22 Water Tank.
10 High Compressor, Westinghouse.	17 Elevated Coal Trestle.	23 Settling Tank.

EAST END

ASK ANY B&O LOCOMOTIVE historian if the railroad had narrow-gauge power and the answer would be "no" except for a few acquired with Pittsburgh and Western in the last century ... those lasted only until B&O standard-gauged the line. Even the incomparable William D. Edson in his splendid 1992 all-time roster of B&O steam locomotives reported "no record" for class C15. Here is the 16, class C15, 30″ gauge, 12 × 16″ cylinders, weight 148,000 pounds, 10,080 pounds of tractive force and equipped with steam brakes. She was built by Vulcan Iron Works in Wilkes Barre, PA. Of course, we have seen her in action a few photos ago at the tie plant. We suspect B&O wanted to operate her at the plant with only an engineer and outfoxed the Brotherhood by slipping her in on the sly. Mt. Clare built a bumper car which was coupled to the rear of the 16 with two drums holding 300 feet of 5/8 inch wire cable ... the cable was used to pull the retort cars around the facility. Since the 16 did not exist, we cannot say what happened to her. *B&OHS*

IT WILL COME as no surprise to the reader to learn that wood floats. Here is the scene at Green Spring during the 1936 flood, which introduced B&O to the game of pick-up-sticks.

EASY PASSAGE

B&OHS

THE B&O SOUTH from Green Spring was long and, unfortunately, lean. The South Branch Railroad, a B&O creature, was completed from Green Spring to Romney in 1884 where it rested for many years. Finally, "independent" Hampshire Southern Railroad completed a line from Romney through Moorefield to Petersburg in 1910. It must not have prospered, for B&O subsidiary Moorefield and Virginia purchased the railroad in 1911 and brought it under B&O operation in 1914 obviously with an eye on vast virgin timberland in the area and the need for wood to feed the new tie plant. The first major metropolis along the line of road is Springfield, seen here c. 1914 awash in traffic and activity ... the harp switchstand was no doubt the main attraction in town.

THE SOUTH BRANCH RAILROAD boasted this interesting station at Romney, seen circa 1914. By the mid-1970s, B&O wanted to get rid of the entire 52 mile line and ended up donating it to the State of West Virginia in 1978, which promptly took over operations under the name South Branch Valley Railroad to provide service to a few local shippers. In 1985 a devastating flood took out most of the line ... restoration was not completed until late 1987. The SBV operates five days a week and its main customer is the Rockingham Poultry feed mill south of Moorefield, a fact that has earned the railroad the sobriquet West Virginia Chicken Line. The on-line scenery is lush and special excursions grace the rails several times a year.

B&O Museum

EAST END

WE WOULD NOT want the reader to suffer under the illusion that the North Branch of the Potomac was the only bad actor on the East End ... in 1936 South Branch flood waters did this number on Bridge 562 and its approaches. The viewer is looking west ... the bridge is at Sycamore, between Romney and Moorefield. The height of the waters is suggested by the amount of detritus on the bridge itself.

B&OHS

PATTERSON CREEK, about six miles west of Green Spring, is the next and one of the more prominent locations on the East End. This structure is probably the first bridge built over the stream and is shown here in the late 1840s ... we suspect the roof was added in the mid-1840s. A telegraph office and water station were created here when the line was first built and an additional tank was added in 1849. There is a bit of a bump in the roadbed approaching the span and the rails are something less than arrow-straight. Sadly, this bridge was one of the first burned by Rebels during the Civil War. This view is probably westerly.

PATTERSON CREEK (FN) marks the western end of the East End funnel and here is its first interlocker, built in 1893, improved in 1903 and 1913. The white line marks the crest of the 1924 flood. Oddly, flood waters never did quite take out this tower ... it was destroyed by a derailment circa 1957. P Creek's place in history is assured because it was the junction with the famed Patterson Creek Cutoff ... in this photo, the cutoff tracks run straight to and through the truss bridge in the left background ... East End rails to Cumberland curve to the right by the signal. The cutoff was chartered in March 1900 as the Patterson Creek and Potomac Railroad and was opened in 1904 ... it was built to bypass congestion at Cumberland and shovel West End volume out of Keyser to this point. The cutoff was always a West End line ... movements were handed over to the East End here. Incidentally, it has never been easy to get to this location ... the reader will recall that at least one operator rowed a boat across the river to get to work.

B&OHS

EASY PASSAGE

THIS HANDSOME AND modern interlocker was built to replace the old tower and B&O wisely decided to put it against the hill away from the river ... no sense pushing one's luck. Etched on a windowsill is the note "2/29/58 8:01 am operator D.L. Readd," so it is reasonable to assume that is the day the new tower went into operation. As to the cutoff, one of two tracks was closed in 1933 and reopened in 1939. The line was permanently reduced to one track signaled bidirectionally c. 1960 and completely closed c. 1974. The Great Coal Boom of the early 1980s almost caused a rebirth, but those plans passed with the boom. McKenzie (CO) at the west end of the cutoff was closed and interlocking handled remotely by FN at the same time this tower was put into service. The cutoff was upgraded for passenger service and in April 1924 the *National Limited* was the first feature train to be routed over it ... soon joined by the *Diplomat* and in the 1940s by the *Cincinnatian*. EM1 7600s couldn't use the cutoff until the Potomac bridge was strengthened in 1945. FN was closed 20 December 1991. Believe it or not, the interlocker is now handled remotely from the Great Round Bathtub in Jacksonville.

WITH SECOND CSD 97, KB1a 7707 leans into the first curve west of FN on the Cumberland line with 42 cars on 29 July 1949. The rugged ledges on the right are William Prescott Smith's "Gothic loopholes." The 7707 was one of ten examples purchased by B&O from Seaboard Air Line to alleviate a serious power shortage just after World War II ... they ran almost exclusively on the East End between Brunswick and Cumberland. Unlike earlier cousin EL6a mallets from SAL, which were superb, the KB1s were merely "OK" ... tested against Bix Sixes, the verdict was that they had too much "git" and not enough "dig." In addition to mediocrity in this service, they had a distressing tendency to develop back pressure in the smokebox which stalled the air compressors ... an event guaranteed to capture the attention of enginemen.

B&OHS/E. L. Thompson Collection

EAST END

B&OHS/E. L. Thompson Collection

FROM ATOP THE GOTHIC LOOPHOLES we see Second Train 8 Engine 5056 and 11 cars rolling into and over P Creek on 29 July 1949. Second 8 was a headend train out of Cumberland. As this photo attests, the Patterson Creek Valley is verdant, fecund and luxuriant.

EAST END RAILS cross the Potomac and the C&O Canal to reenter Maryland at North Branch. B&O was always public relations and party conscious ... during the summer of 1858 they sponsored an "artists" trip over the line of road and the guests drank and ate their way west. Here they paused on the North Branch Bridge in June of 1858 for a photograph. The period cars are interesting, but the Bollman deck truss more so ... it was installed in 1856 to replace a wooden trestle. Note the trestlework remaining on the left and the canal at the bottom ... we assume the trestle is typical of early construction and, if correct, this is the only known photo of such. Everything in sight was torched by Rebels early in the Civil War and replacement spans taken out time and time again. In 1901 a steel bridge was installed on new piers ... the old ones are still in the river.

B&O Museum

EASY PASSAGE

NORTH BRANCH, for all the charm it no doubt has for local residents, has never been an exciting point on the East End. This valuation photo probably dates to c. 1917 and looks west ... note the tower in the center and the WM overhead bridge. The tower appears to be boarded and that is logical as we shall see. An emergency connection with WM existed in this area for some years, but it left B&O rails well west of here on the south side and met WM to the left of the bridge ... the track on the right is a short siding.

B&O Museum

THE TOWER AT NORTH BRANCH (NB) sometime between 1906 and 1916, the former date because the WM bridge is in place and the latter because the tower was closed by 1916. This tower was opened in March 1901 and is one of the few "early" tower design examples of which we have found a photograph. For many years, a third track ran for about three miles from just west of the tower to Evitts Creek and was used as a departure track ... it is now an industrial lead track with no connection at NB.

B&O Museum

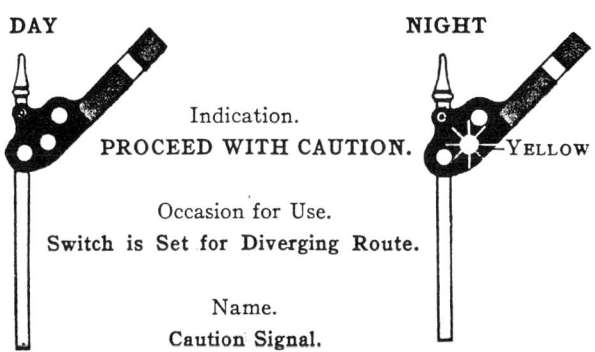

DISTANT SWITCH SIGNAL

DAY   NIGHT

Indication.
PROCEED WITH CAUTION.

Occasion for Use.
Switch is Set for Diverging Route.

Name.
Caution Signal.

EAST END

James Eells III

MEXICO (M) stands as guardian to the Cumberland Yards . . . here, on 31 July 1992 an eastbounder is beginning its trek on the East End. A little over two miles to the west of this location was Evitts Creek (GE) Tower, from 1892 to 1960 the entrance to the maze of tracks and structures which mark B&O's traffic focal point.

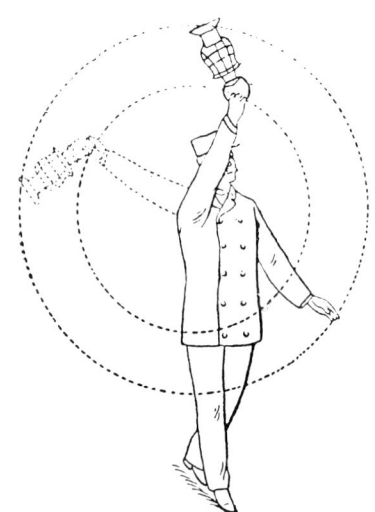

Train has Parted—Swung vertically in a circle at arm's length across the track.

Apply Air Brakes—Swung horizontally above the head.

Chapter 9

Cumberland

The Queen City

When William Prescott Smith first wrote about Cumberland in his 1853 work, he devoted exactly two short paragraphs to the town:

> "The entrance to the town of Cumberland is beautiful, and displays the noble amphitheatre in which it lies to great advantage—the gap of Will's Mountain, westward of the town, being a justly prominent feature of the view."
>
> "The Company's depot in Cumberland is in a central position at the intersection of the Rail Road and National Turnpike."

Ele Bowen, in 1854, committed himself to two somewhat longer paragraphs that concluded it was a very nice place and in a bowl.

Mr. Smith revisited Cumberland with prose in 1857, wrote two somewhat longer paragraphs, again alluded to "amphitheatre" this time with the adjective "grand" in front of it, called it a "Mountain City" and was pleased with the free meal-tickets supplied by B&O although he and all the other guests on this expedition had to suffer long after-dinner speeches in penance.

Both writers clearly gave the impression that they did not think Cumberland was very important in B&O's scheme of things and saw no point in elaborating on a place that was just another way station on the route to the Ohio River.

And, in the context of the times, they were quite correct. When the first celebratory passenger train arrived on 5 November 1842 with a distinguished party from Baltimore after a ten hour trip, all B&O eyes were focused on the next leap over the mountains to Pittsburg and thence to the Ohio at Wheeling. The gap made by a creek between Wills and Haystack Mountains just west of Cumberland (the Narrows) was far more important than the town because it provided an easy entrance approach to the main crossing of the mountains that loomed to the west.

There are vague insinuations that the "first" train broke down shortly before arrival and limped in a bit late. True or not, the incident would prove to be prophetic. B&O arrived haltingly with no intention of staying, eager only to divert traffic from the National Road, happy that they were now way ahead of rival C&O Canal (it would be eight more years before the canal reached Cumberland and it would end there) and content that Cumberland would play no permanent role in the future of the railroad.

Over one hundred and fifty years, of course, Cumberland and the lines east to Harpers Ferry would prove to be an unwanted pregnancy with no hope of abortion.

B&O sat in Cumberland for seven years before they could even begin to get out and then they had to reach Wheeling over the famed West End. The coal resources in the Cumberland area proved to be large and marketable with the consequence that volume poured into the town from branch lines. Of course, the Pittsburg line was completed in the early 1870s and Cumberland turned out to be the apex of the giant traffic "wye" from St. Louis and Chicago by the latter part of the last century. And then the vast coal deposits in Western Pennsylvania became a source of heavy eastward volume by early in this century.

All this growing volume dumped on Cumberland. B&O had to get it in and then get it out. And, from a terrain standpoint, the last place any sane person would select for a major in-transit yard would be that "amphitheater" in Cumberland.

B&O lines into Cumberland from the east were strung along a sinuous river and ended in a bowl. While there was ample room between the river and the surrounding hillsides for main line tracks, there was precious little width for the vast yards that would become necessary.

And, more than the physical limitations to the site, we have come away with the impression that for over a century and a half B&O has never really come to grips with the problem... each decision made appears to have been more on the order of providing temporary relief without any clear strategic goal. This conclusion may not be entirely fair, particularly in view of the unpredictable pattern of growth and financial limitations. After all, if hindsight were foresight beggars would be kings. Still, the thought lingers.

The first major relief was the creation of a major yard at Keyser in the 1870s to classify and "double up" eastbound tonnage coming off the West End... at least that tonnage could be run *through* Cumberland.

Then B&O made a decision that, in retrospect, was unfortunate... in the 1890s Brunswick Yard east of Harpers Ferry was conceived and built. Surely a major yard somewhere in the Cherry Run-Cumbo-Martinsburg area or even in the valley west of the Narrows and Hyndman would have been better, but that was not to be... perhaps because B&O did not pay taxes in Maryland and the alternate locations were in West Virginia and Pennsylvania.

Whatever the reasoning, there was little relief in Cumberland. Even the opening of the Patterson Creek Cutoff early in this century did little more than relieve Cumberland of through movements.

So the story of Cumberland Yards was one of constant growth and there was only one way to go ... east along the river. Ultimately, with the completion of a new westbound yard in 1960, the complex would reach a total length of about six miles from Viaduct Junction on the west to Mexico on the east.

Of course, Cumberland consisted of a lot more than yard trackage through history. Aside from the necessary engine servicing facilities, Cumberland became a focal point for heavy locomotive and car repairs... in fact, is so to this day. B&O even produced steel rail in a plant at Cumberland for many years as we shall see. And for many years Cumberland was home to many industrial shippers, adding to the confusing congestion.

In 1992, Cumberland remains a major and modern in-transit classification yard... Keyser, Brunswick and the P Creek Cutoff are extinct, lending at least some credence to our argument that B&O planning in the latter part of the last century was faulty.

We will make no attempt to detail 150 years of yard development in Cumberland, if for no other reason than yards are boring to rail historians and dull, expensive necessities to railroad management. We will confine ourselves to photos of interesting structures and overall scenes, moving as B&O did throughout history... east from the terminal area in downtown Cumberland where B&O first arrived in 1842.

For the benefit of those unfamiliar with classification yard layout, we would point out that every major yard must have, in *each* direction, a *receiving yard* where trains arrive and a *classification yard* downstream from the former where cars are reshuffled into new trains. Usually cars are pushed over a hump from the receiving yard and drift into the proper track as at Cumberland... these cars are braked by hand of riders or, more usually in modern times, retarders that press against wheel flanges to slow down the cars.

And finally there is a *departure yard* where trains are made whole and await mainline track space. All these movements require a lot of length as well as width as the reader will notice if he examines the rear end paper of this book where a circa 1960 schematic of the Cumberland Yard complex has been printed.

Also, we direct the reader to the Color Pictorial chapter later in this book for air views of Cumberland.

And now to Cumberland, the west end of the East End.

RULE 299

Fig. A
Temporary
Whistle Post

Fig. B
Permanent
Whistle Post

CUMBERLAND

CUMBERLAND in the mid-1850s through the eyes of William Prescott Smith's artist certainly would fit the description of small town complete with cows grazing by the main line. The Narrows, B&Os ultimate entryway to Pittsburg, appears at extreme center left. The C&O Canal can be vaguely seen on the right of the river. Only one smokestack appears to be darkening the sky, a situation that would soon change for the worse.

B&O Museum

BY THE EARLY 1870s, Cumberland had become a city complete with sprawl and haze. The B&O line of road runs straight across the center of this view ... note the original roundhouse at extreme center right. The railroad then loops around the town and meets the Potomac (upper left center) on its way to Viaduct Junction, the West End and Pittsburg. Coal and the B&O made Cumberland a "Queen City" ... massive deposits in the Georges Creek Valley in the mountains just west and southwest of the city poured black diamonds and gold into what had become by this time a boom town.

EAST END

![Revere House photograph]

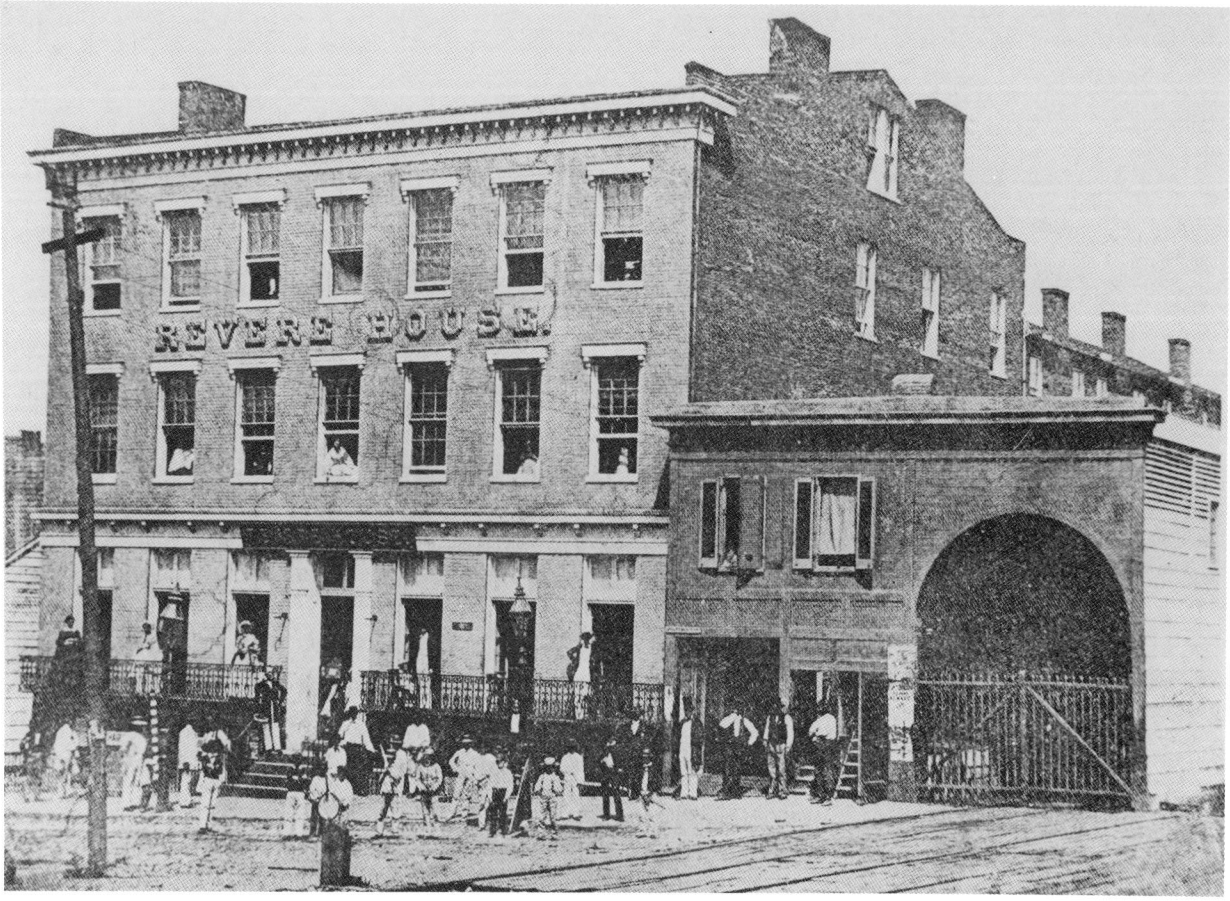

B&O's FIRST DEPOT in Cumberland was adjacent to the Revere House Hotel, convenient for arriving and departing passengers ... one assumes there was a bar as well as sleeping and dining rooms. Cumberland, the reader will recall, was at the eastern end of the National Road and in the early years B&O enjoyed passenger traffic from that connection. Bedford Springs, a resort area in nearby Pennsylvania, was also served by stage coaches from Cumberland.

A BROADER view of B&O's first terminal area in Cumberland with the Revere House and passenger shed on the left and various railroady structures on the right including what appears to be a crossing watchman's shanty. In the center is a Camel next to a pot hopper, from which it just might be coaling.

CUMBERLAND

B&OHS

OF ALL THE STRUCTURES on the East End throughout history, the Queen City Station-Hotel was the most magnificent, largest, expensive and mystifying. Located about three blocks east of the Revere House on the north side of the mainline, this architectural jewel lasted for almost exactly one hundred years. Construction was swift, starting 1 July 1871 with grand opening 11 November 1872 ... this photo shows the building on the verge of completion and alone attests to its splendor even without the benefit of the lush gardens and plantings that graced its three acre site. Described as "vaguely Italianate" (whatever that means), its visage strikes the authors as being almost unique ... indeed, even students of the subject report only two other similar structures in the United States. One was built at Altoona in 1854 and another somewhat earlier at nearby Cresson. While these two hotels were similar in general layout, they did not approach this building in grace and style. And probably didn't in cost ... the Queen City Station, a pet project of John W. Garrett, involved an outlay of over $350,000 which was a lot of bread in 1872. Shaped as an E, the station was 235 feet wide with two 48 by 84 foot, four story wings ... another three story 38 by 97 foot wing extended center/rear out of sight in this perspective. The two story front was 140 feet wide and was topped with a cupola complete with spiral staircase. As the viewer can see, the piazza envelopes the structure on three sides and is awash with cast iron floral trim. The inside was opulent, with about 150 guest rooms, a 400 seat dining/ballroom ... the center wing was devoted to kitchens, laundries and employee quarters. Even the basement was full and boasted game rooms. The building was heated by steam, although many of the rooms also enjoyed fireplaces. And, perhaps appropriately, the structure was wrapped in mystery. Who designed it? Latter day researchers believe it was a Thomas J. Heskett, a shadowy figure who was apparently on the engineering staff of the B&O Road Department and whose only other known accomplishment was to have his name appear on an 1864 trestle design installed at Harpers Ferry. And why such a sublime monument in, of all places, Cumberland? With all respects to Cumberland and its charms, no one has ever suggested that the town was a resort and indeed B&O never advertised the hotel as such. For feeding passengers? As late as 1886, only eight passenger trains each way stopped at Cumberland ... none paused more than twenty minutes and two of those were classed as "freights" which probably meant "express" and even they only stopped for 15-30 minutes. Of these trains, quite a few were through and arrived in the wee hours of the morning, so overnight lodging seems unlikely and certainly not enough to fill 150 rooms. The only thing the authors can advance is a theory ... coal was making many millionaires in Cumberland and Garrett may have envisioned this palace as a watering hole for the local *nouveau riche*. Even at that, 150 rooms can hold a lot of mistresses. The reader should note the duckbill passenger car, express car and, above all, what is probably an early caboose at lower right. The small building by the penstock was originally a baggage room.

EAST END

Herman and Stacia Miller Collection, City of Cumberland

THIS LATE NINETEENTH CENTURY view of the heroic station/hotel establishes that the original baggage house had been converted to a tower and a new frame baggage building constructed just to the west. By this time, B&O had obviously tired of maintaining white trim in a cindery atmosphere and had standardized on painting everything red, a practice that continued until the mid-1940s. And, of course, it would not be Cumberland without pot hoppers in sight.

ANOTHER VIEW, taken in 1884, of the tower and baggage/express house just west of the station. Actually, this "tower" was a dispatcher's office for the entire Cumberland Division. The whole Cumberland yard area was a maze of tracks, telegraph offices and communication systems. For example, on 1 July 1908 there were eight call letters in Cumberland: Evitts Creek (GE), Virginia Lane (GW), Cumberland (WC), Westbound Freight Yard (GW), Yardmaster's Office (DX), Queen City Hotel (CU), Dispatcher's Office (WC) and Trainmaster (V) ... the last five were in or near the station, so a lot of space in the building was used by the railroad. By 15 March 1924 the list had been reduced to two: Queen City Hotel (WC) and Dispatcher's Office (DU) ... these two lasted until the end. Incidentally, B&O's official name for the structure throughout recorded history was always "Queen City Hotel" with a mention that a station was located in it, which suggests that it was conceived and operated as a hostelry rather than just a depot.

B&O MATERIALLY improved the Queen City Hotel during 1912, adding a fourth story to the "kitchen" wing, umbrella sheds, a subway under the main tracks and general remodeling ... completion was in January 1913. The two enclosures under the sheds housed the subway stairs and provided protection to passengers from the weather. B&O reported that "passenger traffic is heavy, affected to a large extent by the great number of passengers transferring from one train to another." Garrett built three major station/hotels ... Queen City, Grafton and Relay near Baltimore and historians remain puzzled as to just what he had in mind because sleepers and dining cars were beginning to solve the feeding and lodging problem in that era. Two others, Deer Park and Oakland, were clearly resort facilities and were successful. Garrett is a controversial figure in B&O history, hero to some and bum to others. We have already advanced a theory to explain away the Queen City Hotel ... essentially we are postulating that local patronage in combination with visiting businessmen and lay people were the market to be served. We must admit, however, that none of these speculations explain Relay.

AFTER THE 1912 improvements, B&O took some interior photographs of the hotel ... unfortunately, this one of the waiting room is the only one publishable. While certainly the interior of the hotel was stately and dignified, it was in stark contrast to the exterior elegance. By the by, two other buildings served the hotel ... a 28 foot square ice house capable of holding 300 tons of ice and a 28 by 35 foot three story boiler house with two boilers.

EAST END

B&OHS

BY THE SPRING of 1953, the Queen City Hotel was still in good condition and about to receive an exterior renovation later in that year ... the trim would again be white. In the 1950s, the hotel was placed under the management of an independent contractor and was still offering services to patrons and B&O employees. This photo gives a particularly good view of the cast iron filigree which, some say, was cast at B&O's Mt. Clare Shops ... the 1953 restoration would not, however, restore this intricate iron work to white. Several views of the hotel appear in the Color Pictorial chapter and the reader should know that the incredibly talented Andrew Holzopfel is modeling not only the hotel but also Harpers Ferry station in HO scale ... while both models are well advanced, they could not be finished in time for this book.

BY THE LATE 1960s, the hotel was in poor condition but still in use as a station with B&O offices and a restaurant. Apparently some of the chemicals used in the 1953 cleaning had an adverse effect on exterior woodwork and, frankly, B&O was not making any real attempt to maintain the structure. A minor fire early in 1969 drew the attention of city inspectors and the building was declared a fire and safety hazard ... in addition, as one can see over the coaches in this photo, Interstate 48 (now 68) was constructed literally next to the building. Attempts by interested parties to save and restore the structure came to naught, in part because the building was so large and in such bad condition that it was difficult to develop an end use that would justify substantial investment. B&O continued to use parts of the hotel until February 1971, but finally as we see here demolition was under way in April of 1972. Subsequently, an Amtrak shack and Post Office facility were built on the site ... in the interim, tickets were sold from the B&O Medical Examiner's office west of the station. Another cause for tears on the East End.

B&OHS

CUMBERLAND

B&OHS

THE QUEEN CITY HOTEL dominates this c. 1890 view of Cumberland as well it should. The middle wing and power house are visible and just over the left (east) wing the original B&O roundhouse can barely be seen on the south side of the tracks. Also on the south side of the tracks to the right of the hotel one should note the two-story express building and one-story freight house. The bridge center right is vehicular. Yard trackage is already choking the area, extending far to the west (right) of the hotel and ballooning to the east ... this is the eastbound receiving yard then and now. Day and night activity just across from the hotel did not present a milieu conducive to a good night's sleep. And, to make matters worse, just out of sight at the extreme left was to be found a steel rail mill. Sweet dreams.

THESE TWO STRUCTURES across from the hotel and seen in the last photo were built in 1873 ... the nearest building is an express facility with various offices and the building on the left is a freight depot. The latter was replaced and enlarged in 1913. The whole area is now a Gee Bee parking lot.

B&O Museum

EAST END

STEEL RAIL was beginning to replace iron rail by the Civil War era and the transformation was well under way when B&O decided to make their own at Cumberland. Construction on this mill began 20 October 1869 and it rolled its first rail 30 January 1871 ... its annual capacity of about 25,000 tons was initially devoted to lay the Chicago and Pittsburg extensions. This photo was taken c. 1872 and visually understates the size of the facility as the reader will see. In 1887 a 110 by 75 foot shed was added ... by 1891 the mill was operated under contract with the Cambria Iron Company. It was located on the north side of the mainline just east of the hotel.

B&O Museum

THE ROLLING MILL was not a small affair ... here we see it in a westerly perspective c. 1897 with the hotel in sight over the right wing of the facility. The profusion of cars makes this photograph a treasure trove for nineteenth century car historians ... various sizes of pot hoppers, wooden coal cars, gondolas and box cars fill the scene which also includes, at lower left, livestock pens. A number of firms leased or operated the mill over the years ... we are not sure when rail rolling ceased. By 1966 the trackage on the west side was used by B&O for coach servicing and storage ... the buildings were torn down about a decade ago and a wye installed on the grounds to turn Amtrak equipment. Weeds now dominate the site. At extreme left center, it appears that the original roundhouse is gone although the angle of view may not be correct.

B&OHS

CUMBERLAND

B&OHS

THE FIRST B&O ROUNDHOUSE in Cumberland, seen here on an unknown date but probably in the 1870s, was constructed in 1854 on the same plan used at Martinsburg ... we have already located the facility in earlier photos. It did not suffer the fate of its twin and survived the Civil War ... in fact, Cumberland did not endure depredations during the war but was scared to death on a few occasions and suffered the indignity of having two Union generals captured in their beds by Rebel raiders. Apparently this roundhouse served deep into the last century before it was demolished.

B&OHS

B&O'S FIRST Cumberland roundhouse, seen in the background on the left, had the benefit of an office building as seen here on an unknown date. How many sides did the building boast? Four? Five?

161

EAST END

Smithsonian Institution

INCREASING TRAFFIC, train length and congestion forced B&O to build another, larger roundhouse in Cumberland and the only site available was over a mile east of the original one. So here we see B&O's second roundhouse in Cumberland, opened in November 1896 with 44 stalls and almost completely circular. A large machine shop was also built, vaguely seen right center with a clerestory roof. Incidentally, this photo has been published in the past and identified as being the Brunswick roundhouse ... we assembled a panel of B&O historians and all concluded that it is the Cumberland structure. This photo was probably taken in late 1897 and the Consolidation locomotive was still king. In this scene one will find E12 (Pittsburg October 1896) 1618, 1628, 1624 and 1627; E13 (Baldwin September 1896) 1634 and 1636; E14 (Baldwin June 1897) 1280; E15 (Pittsburg September 1897) 1502, 1513 and 1515. As will be shown, B&O built a third roundhouse just south of this one ... this structure, however, remained in service and was not razed until 1943. Note the coal trestle and water jug.

Herman and Stacia Miller Collection, City of Cumberland

THE BUILDING in the background of this blurry photo is probably the machine shop built alongside the second roundhouse, but is included here to give ecstasy to caboose historians. The caboose on the left is 1919 ... the number on the right caboose is too blurred to read. These cars are not of the same class ... note the dimensional differences. And the open-end gondola on the right is 50079. The caboose lettering reads "BALTo & OHIO," an early but not often seen styling. And the billboard "B&O," banished by Daniel Willard, was reborn in the 1950s.

CUMBERLAND

ONLY A DECADE AND A HALF after the second roundhouse was completed, traffic growth forced the construction of still another one which was completed in August 1913. Seen here in a westerly view from atop the coaling dock built at the same time (which we shall see), it was placed just to the south of the second one which can be seen at upper right. A new 70 by 140 foot machine shop was also built, seen here between the two roundhouses, along with a two story office building. The facility in the immediate forefront is the ash handling complex. Construction of this 31 stall roundhouse apparently solved the problem because no additional stalls were ever added. The turntable as built was 100 feet long and was later lengthened to 115 feet. We cannot pass this subject without pointing out that B&O set still another "first" on this table about ten or so years ago ... first woman engineer to put a locomotive into the pit, thus becoming a member of that distinguished fraternity. Or is it now a sorority? Incidentally, the house was built with wooden roller doors to facilitate repairs after they were smashed. We have no record as to how many locomotives were put through the outer walls. One reaches for the air and there is nothing there ... comes the awful sag or sound. Senior operating officials, of course, regard such events with stern displeasure and struggle to keep from laughing. Back to the photo, that stack is 150 feet high ... two fans, 190" and 200", were installed to change roundhouse air every fifteen minutes. This whole facility is on Virginia Avenue in South Cumberland ... the eastbound class yard begins off to the right and the huge backshop is to the left. Even today, the whole area throbs with activity. One other interesting "first" ... about a mile west of here on the mainline at Old Town Road was located the first interlocker on the East End (and fifth on the B&O). It was opened in November 1888 and improved in 1894. We do not think it survived yard expansion early in this century.

B&OHS

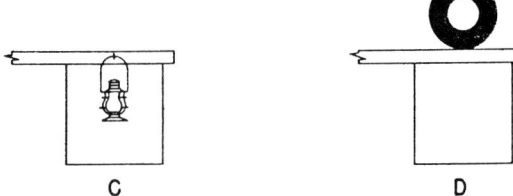

C or D-Reduce speed to pick up Clearance Card Form A.

INDICATION- Train Orders.   NAME- Train Order Board.

EAST END

B&OHS

THE LAST PHOTO was taken from atop this coaling dock, opened in 1913. This view is easterly and probably dates from c. 1915 . . . note the crows nest headlight on the locomotive.

THERE WAS STILL plenty of steam at Cumberland on 19 February 1950 . . . this scene shows power between the coaling dock and the third roundhouse. The ashpit traveling crane can be seen over the tender of the locomotive on the left, which is the 5501 Class T. Well, actually she was built as Class Ta and carried the "a" on her builder's plate until extinction. One of two Mountains (4-8-2) built by B&O in the twenties as passenger locomotives, the 5501 spent most of her declining years in helper and freight service. Note the brakeman's box and overfire jets. The engine on the right is the 6102, one of the famous Big Sixes. We have always been amused that the Big Sixes were officially described as "redesigned Class S" locomotives, which quite correctly relegates S power to the "dustbin of history" as the saying goes.

B&OHS/E. L. Thompson Collection

CUMBERLAND

B&OHS

THE 4533 gets a ride on the "new" turntable circa 1958 in a mood photo ... the huge Cumberland backshop looms on the right and the eastbound yard fills the scene to the horizon. As the roundhouse doors are no longer roller type, we assume that theory did not work out in practice.

B&O WAS BEGINNING to add longer tanks to mallet power and that, in turn, made it necessary to add to the roundhouse ... here, on 6 December 1940, we see the new outer wall under construction. It can be quite cold in Cumberland during the winter months and the capability of closing the doors was a real asset. And automobile fans would surely love to go back in a time capsule and scoop up those vintage cars.

B&OHS

EAST END

THE YMCA was a familiar home away from home for railroaders everywhere... here is the one in Cumberland c. 1912 in the Virginia Avenue complex. In 1944 this Y served 3,000 meals on a typical day, many at a canteen in the roundhouse and from food wagons traveling the yard areas. Believed built in 1910, this particular structure has been replaced by a newer one.

THE CAVERNOUS BACKSHOP at Cumberland, seen here in the late 1950s, is located just southeast of the roundhouse area. Opened in 1919, this facility was a major class repair operation on the B&O system (and even rebuilt some steam locomotives) and remains so today in the CSX scheme of things. Conversion to diesel servicing and repair began in 1957 and was completed in 1960. A disastrous fire at Mt. Clare Shops in Baltimore in 1962 severely damaged diesel facilities and B&O made the decision not to rebuild, transferring the work to this shop in Cumberland. By the by, it should be mentioned that the famous B&O engineers' school is located in the Virginia Avenue complex, although not in this building.

CUMBERLAND

B&OHS
GAZING AT THE ERECTING FLOOR of the Cumberland Backshop on 28 May 1919, the observer could be pardoned for believing the steam locomotive would be eternal.

B&OHS
EVEN AT REST and in a state of dishabille, this Big Six still projects an aura of power. For a third of a century this class of engine was the backbone of East End operations and Cumberland Backshop was the primary maintenance facility.

EAST END

BY THE DATE of this photo on 28 March 1961, the Backshop was devoted solely to diesel repair and maintenance ... it was now a "Progressive Diesel Shop." There were seven work stations in the shop at this time. Number 1, outside to protect workers from exhaust fumes, handled inbound running inspections. Number 2 was for ICC inspection and examination of crankcases and air equipment. Number 3 handled truck repair, lubrication and electrical running repairs. Number 4 was fitted for drop pit work and included coupler, draft gear and car body maintenance. Number 5 was assigned the tasks of replacing car bodies, engine intake filters and electrical running repairs. Number 6 was devoted to final ICC inspection, both electrical and mechanical, and Number 7 (again outside) cleaned the engines inside and out. In this era, six locomotives were processed every eight hours. Here the 4614, in a spotless milieu devoid of cinders, carbon and grime, is being brought up to snuff.

B&OHS

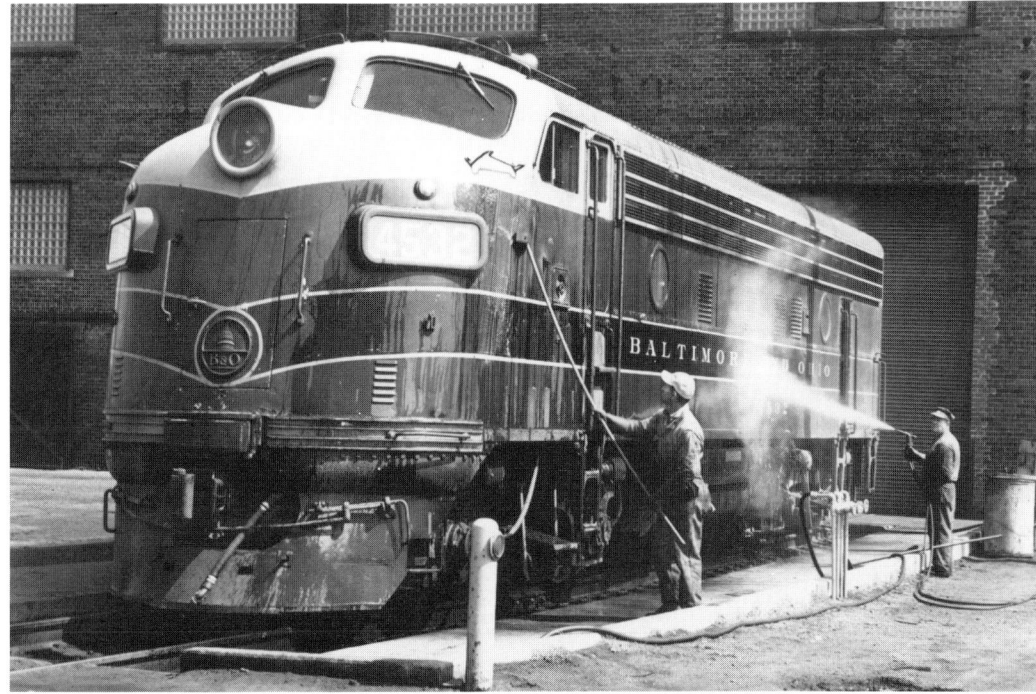

EVEN IN THE MIDST of financial strain in the early 1960s, B&O still made an effort to keep its power clean ... here, on 28 March 1961, we see the 4532 being scrubbed.

CUMBERLAND

B&OHS

A SEA OF CARS and cabooses fill this early 1960s scene overlooked by the Shop and the skeleton of the old and roofless coaling dock no doubt opining for a return to the good old days which will never come again.

CUMBERLAND has become a major car repair center in the CSX era ... this is the Cumberland Car Maintenance Facility opened 17 May 1989.

James F. Eells III

AS EARLY AS 1893, B&O was finding it necessary to move mainline tracks in a northerly direction to make room for expansion of Cumberland yard facilities. This photo, looking easterly at the eastbound yard, was probably taken in the late teens of this century and shows, on the left, the mainline tracks and the hump left center ... the building is a combination scale house and yard office. Apparently the Cumberland yards were flat until circa 1905 when humps were installed. *B&OHS*

AGAIN LOOKING easterly at the eastbound yard but probably in the mid 1920s, this photo provides a closer view of the scale house and yard office. While humping speeded up classification of cars, it was by no means a problem-free method. Switch tenders were needed to align turnouts and swift communication was necessary to minimize misplacement of cars ... when the latter occurred an engine had to be sent in to shift the miscreant cars to the correct track, slowing up the works. And, of course, cars all too often coupled with excessive force and increased car and lading damage. Many shippers plastered their cars with prominent "Do Not Hump" signs because of this problem, which we recall with some amusement as we spent several days at the Brunswick Yard in the 1950s watching scores of such cars sail over the hump with abandon. And a classification has to do more things than just rearrange cars in trains ... each car must be inspected for defects (and put on the Repair In Progress track when found) and, above all, weighed. Railroads sell their services on the basis of distance, class and *weight*. Here we see the gauntlet scale track ... the cars go over the scales *while moving* and weight is recorded in the office. The gauntlet tracks provide for the inevitable need to send a locomotive into the yard ... all that weight would prang the scales. The top of the hump is to the right in this view.

B&OHS

HERE IS A WESTERLY view of the eastbound hump in the twenties, probably on the same day as the last photo. One can see the hump engine on the right, a car going over the scales, a crowd of riders awaiting cars, a switchtender, a cut of two cars with a rider by the brake and, in the left distance, the Cumberland icing facility ... the latter still another chore for yard personnel. Glance at that rider again. He and his compatriots had what was probably the most hazardous job in railroading. It looks and sounds easy on this dry and sunny day, but imagine it at night, in rain, with ice on all handrails and platforms, or fog or snow ... in blazing heat or bitter cold. One misstep and you're under the wheels. But even worse was coupling ... a bad braking car or a misjudgement of speed results in a slamdunk collision that will flip the rider off and under the car. Gondolas and flat cars already on the class track were still another peril ... at night they did not throw a looming shadow and many a rider thought he had two car lengths to go when in fact there were two flat cars waiting to kill him. The rules said put a white lantern on the ends of such cars at night to warn the rider, but lanterns go out and men forget. This particular rider has a geared brakewheel and he can easily adjust braking power ... if it is working. It was another story with older horizontal brakewheels ... he had to use a club to get leverage and if the cog slipped or he lost control while trying to release, the wheel would spin and the club would knock him off. And, of course, management wants all the cars to couple the first time ... they didn't want to send an engine in to close up the new train. The rider is under pressure to do it right the first time ... don't stop short, don't hit too hard, but do hit hard enough to couple. And then go back and do it again and again and again, day in and day out, year in and year out. The cinders in all railroad yards soaked up a lot of blood and tears.

CUMBERLAND

AGAIN WE ARE LOOKING easterly at the eastbound yard, but now it is July of 1946 and a new two-story scale house and yard office has replaced the one-story affair seen in the preceding photos. We do not know when this improvement was completed, but suspect it was in the early 1940s. The yard still has handthrown turnouts and remains a rider hump. The man atop the stock car is burdened with an old horizontal brakewheel. Here it appears that riders are walking back to the hump ... some yards devoted a clear central track and MOW speeder to return riders more swiftly.

B&OHS

RARE IS THE LOCOMOTIVE that spends its entire life in just one duty, but that was the case with Class U 950 seen here in the mid-1930s ... she was always the hump engine for the Cumberland eastbound yard. The reader will recall Class T and Ta Mountains which were built with boilers from Class S engines ... the frames and running gear from the latter were used as a basis for the 950 and her near-twin the 951. With an 0-10-0 wheel arrangement and 58" drivers, the 950 boasted a tractive effort of 95,000 pounds ... ample to shove long trains over the hump. The 950 was built at Mt. Clare in 1926, renumbered to 1950 in 1951 and was sold for scrap in March 1953. Sister 951 spent her life in similar service at New Castle PA but with a booster until 1942. All the men in this scene are proud of something, but we are not sure just what.

B&OHS

171

EAST END

B&OHS/Barnard-Wolford Collection

JUST AFTER WORLD WAR II, B&O modernized the eastbound yard by installing retarders, power turnouts and controlling it all from this modernistic retarder control tower which opened in August 1947 and is seen here on 1 January 1966 ... a rendition also appears in the Color Pictorial chapter. Yard and tower operations were divided into alternating batches. From 6 a.m. to 2 p.m. QD trains were classified ... from 2 p.m. to 6 p.m. coal drags weighed and classified ... from 6 p.m. to midnight back to QD and then coal until 6 a.m.

B&OHS

TO MODERNIZE A YARD is not cheap and that is only an estimate. This impressive six-story Control Tower is the brain of B&O's new westbound Cumberland Yard opened in 1960, seen here on 16 August 1961. While there was always a westbound yard in Cumberland, B&O did most westbound classification work at Brunswick east of the Ferry ... in other words, did the same type of work at two locations rather than one. We have already treated this question earlier in this chapter and, by 1952, B&O began planning to correct this awkward and expensive arrangement. A detailed plan was finished by August of 1954, placing a new yard north of the mainline, a sensible but very expensive proposition ... in the event the yard was built south of the main. Even this modern and efficient installation was overwhelmed by traffic and much class work drifted back to Brunswick for some years after opening. This tower is located about 700 feet west of the crest of the hump ... the top floor housed yardmaster operations, the fifth car retarder operator, the fourth communications equipment, the third was reserved for expansion and the first two for offices, signal equipment and lunch/locker rooms.

CUMBERLAND

WE MUST CONFESS we are not sure whether this early 1960s photo portrays the fifth or sixth floor of the westbound control tower, but whichever it is the view is magnificent. B&OHS

MUNDANE OR NOT, weighing still has to be done ... here is the spanking new westbound scale house on 16 August 1961.

THE HEART of a modern classification yard is the retarder, the device that saved riders' lives and limbs and cost them their jobs. Here in the early 1960s are a group of westbound retarders ... the operation is simple in concept, difficult in operation. The retarders between the rails squeeze against car wheels to slow (but not stop) the car. In this scene, out of sight to the right is a "master retarder" through which all cars must pass ... a system of relays and appliances measure the weight, speed and rollability of the car and the retarder automatically slows the car to a pre-determined speed. The car is then automatically shunted to the correct group of class tracks and passes through another non-automatic retarder (those seen here) which are manually controlled by the retarder operator from the control tower. The car then drifts into a class track and hopefully couples up without destroying itself and the cars in front of it. Shippers have long since surrendered to the inevitable ... "Do Not Hump" signs are history. Needless to say, the whole process is hard on wheels, cars and retarders. The new westbound yard consumed 95 acres and pushed the entrance to Cumberland back to Mexico. Cumberland yard trackage, from the eastbound receiving yard just west of the Queen City Hotel to Mexico, now formed a giant S configuration five miles long. Cumberland did not turn out to be just another station stop on the way to the Ohio River.

EAST END

B&OHS

MOVING WESTWARD AGAIN, we could not resist this interesting twenties scene taken from Evitts Creek Tower and looking westerly at the eastbound yard. Engine 6107, the eighth S1 built, is shown here "doubling" New York 94 and Philadelphia 94 as another train waits in the distance. Increasing train length throughout history has continually made yards obsolete soon after expansion and this is merely another example. The 6107, incidentally, was built by Baldwin Locomotive Works in October 1923 and was sold for scrap in June 1954.

A BIT OVER a half-mile west of the site of the old Queen City Hotel is Viaduct Junction (ND), the western boundary of the East End and the beginning of B&O's leap over the mountains to the Midwest. The tracks to the left are on the fabled West End and to the right on the equally historic Pittsburgh line... here is where it all comes together. The tower, built in 1901, is still quite active and sports the Stars and Stripes on 3 May 1991 to welcome home the veterans of Desert Storm.

Chapter 10

The Uncivil Civil War

The East End Becomes the Meat in the Sandwich

Whatever else may be said about events leading to the explosion of war in the Spring of 1861, and the four years of bloody convulsions that followed, it must be remarked that there were very few "slow news days," the bane of editors, journalists and historians. On the East End, there were none at all.

It should be noted that the existence of this chapter was a subject of some debate between the co-authors, one wishing to treat the topic in the "running chapters" and the other arguing that the war had such an impact upon the history of the B&O and, indeed, all the great trunkline railroads that it would be better to explore it in some depth as a separate entity. Roberts agreed, with some reluctance, to undertake the task. The reluctance stems from his conviction of long standing that the Civil War was the most unnecessary war ever fought, that rarely in history were the issues that caused a war more susceptible to reasoned compromise, that the hotheads on both sides ultimately took control of events (but rarely were to be found in the line where loud noises are heard) and that hundreds of thousands of fine American soldiers were turned to smash as a result. And, not incidentally, his favorite railroad was gutted and its future prospects seriously set back.

It is also true that war is very exciting and a lot of fun for those who survive unmaimed . . . we have yet to find a way to communicate with the dead for their views. Robert E. Lee summarized it neatly when he observed that it is good that war is so horrible else we would grow fond of it.

To adequately explore just what happened to the East End, we must step back and review the situation, the terrain and the key personalities as events unfolded in the Spring of 1861.

Abraham Lincoln took office in March and publicly proclaimed that he had taken an oath to preserve the Union. Many Southern States (but not Virginia) had seceded and formed the Confederate States of America with a temporary capital in Montgomery, Alabama. Fort Sumter in South Carolina was attacked and surrendered 13 April 1861. Lincoln called for volunteer troops to put down the rebellion by force and that act pushed Virginia over the edge. Lincoln then made his first (and last for three years) brilliant choice of subordinates by offering Robert E. Lee command of the Union armies. Lee decided he could not fight against his own people and became the *de facto* Rebel Commander-in-Chief as the Confederate capital was transferred to Richmond. The fat was in the fire.

Lincoln and Lee took to their maps, started forming armies, selecting subordinate leaders and weighing the politics of the moment. Frankly, Lee was better at all these things, particularly map reading.

For the first time in the history of war, railroad lines appeared on those maps.

And the State of Maryland was awkwardly situated between the Federal capital at Washington and the rest of the Union.

What would Maryland do? And what would that vast area of Virginia (which would become West Virginia in 1863), awash in pro-Union sentiment, do when push came to shove?

There had been a mindboggling proliferation of railroads in the United States during the 1850s.

In the East, four major east-west trunklines were in full flower. Moving from South to North, they were the B&O in Maryland and (West) Virginia; the Pennsylvania (PRR); the Erie and the lines that would become the New York Central. The Midwest was awash in railroads connecting with these trunklines.

Running from North to South in the East, there were only a few railroads and they were located between the major seaport cities along the coast . . . pertinent to this story there were just three. The B&O ran from Baltimore to Washington; the Northern Central (controlled by PRR) from a connection with PRR at Harrisburg to Baltimore; the Philadelphia, Wilmington and Baltimore, at this time in history independently owned and running between the cities in its name.

The mere existence of railroads added a whole new dimension to the conduct of war and the Civil War would prove to be the first conflagration to experience the effects. Railroads dramatically changed Supply and Space/Time dynamics.

First, let's take Supply. Armies consume vast tonnages of materiel . . . food, ammunition, fuel, weapons, *et al* . . . and these supplies must be delivered to the troops in a constant, unending stream. Until the Civil War, the animal-drawn wagon was the only overland means available. Animals must eat. Thus one must haul fodder to feed, or fuel if you will, the animals. At a certain range, this process becomes self-defeating because the entire payload is taken up by fodder. So bases must be created and supplies forwarded by leaps and bounds.

The railroad swept away this problem. A locomotive can haul a vast tonnage with very little relative fuel consumption and at far greater speed, thus the range and mobility of the army in the field was dramatically increased.

And the railroad can also carry the *army itself*. Old Space/Time calculations went out the window. An army could be moved from here to there in a fraction of the time previously required, with all that implies.

There are nine principles of war . . . one of those is Mass. If we may quote from Field Service Regulations/Operations, Mass is "the concentration of superior forces . . . at the decisive place and time, and their employment in a decisive direction" to create the conditions essential to victory.

Units could now be farther apart in *space*, but much closer in *time*. The very first significant battle of the Civil War at Bull Run demonstrated this new math perfectly . . . the Rebel Army was scattered, the Union Army condensed and the Rebels were able to quickly mass by rail at the decisive point and win the battle. As we shall see, this example would be far from the last one.

Incidentally, it didn't take imaginative soldiers long to figure out a sort of flip-side arithmetic with the new formula. General William Sherman took Atlanta and was supplied by a long, tenuous railroad link to the midwest. He packed up, started his famous "march to the sea," lived off the land, wrote off his railroad tail, resupplied by sea when he reached the coast and let his Rebel opponent flounder around cutting a railroad he no longer needed. Of course, this was later in the war when Lincoln had finally improved his skills at picking subordinates.

Now the reader must bear with us as we set the stage for our story by explaining the difference between exterior and interior lines. Please study the little sketch and follow the bouncing balls.

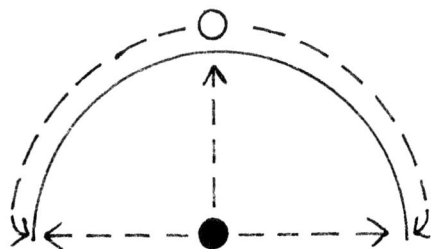

The semicircle is the dividing line between opposing forces. The solid ball is on "interior lines." The hollow ball is on "exterior lines."

The solid ball (Lee) has it made in the shade because a straight line is the shortest distance between two points and it can bounce around with alacrity to thwart the poor hollow ball (Lincoln), which has a long way to go to get anywhere. Lincoln's mission was to crush Lee, so he had to move. Lee was happy with things the way they were, so all he had to do was counter Lincoln's moves.

Now imagine that the semicircle is the B&O from Baltimore/Washington to Cumberland and the midwest. Lee does not need the B&O because it runs across his front, but he has a vested interest in cutting it because it is vital to Lincoln. Lincoln desperately needs the B&O, not only because it facilitates movement but also because it is a major supply route from the midwest.

It took Lee about two minutes to figure it out. It took Lincoln and his host of myopic subordinates a long, long time . . . in fact, one wonders if they ever really did get a good grip on it.

Now the reader will recall that there was some question whether Maryland would stay in the Union. (Actually, all the talk of Maryland seceding was more smoke than flame . . . a Marylander's heart may be South, but his head is North.)

Lincoln's lack of skill in map reading had some limits. As the Federal capital was *south* of Maryland, *ipso facto* Lincoln *had* to have Maryland. Since he had to sneak through Maryland into Washington to take office because of an alleged assassination plot and there was a bit of a bloody riot in Baltimore when a mob clashed with a Yankee Regiment moving through the city, the situation in the Free State attracted his eye.

To be fair to Lincoln, he had some reason to be alarmed. Now Lincoln had political skills (and was a great prose writer), so he grasped the nettle and practiced what the Germans like to call *realpolitik*. He sent troops in, seized the B&O lines leading to Washington, clapped the secessionists into gaol, suspended *habeus corpus* so they couldn't get out and even went so far as to mount cannon aimed at downtown Baltimore, admonishing the citizens that if he heard one more word he would blow the town to Kingdom Come. Since he was now using language Marylanders could understand, all talk went "poof" and Maryland became a loyal Union State.

While Lincoln was concentrating on eastern Maryland, Lee was surveying the scene with a cool gaze. He did not want to irritate Marylanders if there was a chance they would secede, and he was uncomfortable about the situation in western Virginia. There was no way he was going to allow Federal troops and supplies from the midwest to move across his front, but at least there was a chance Maryland would join the Confederacy in which event *he* would desperately need John W. Garrett's B&O.

So, as soldiers would say, he put some of his forces into a "switch position." He moved units forward to B&O lines between Harpers Ferry and Cherry Run, but with orders to do nothing except gut the Federal Arsenal at Harpers Ferry. In the process, Lee made one of many important subordinate appointments by selecting a Virginia Military Institute professor to take command in this area. The name was Thomas J. Jackson. Jackson was, by all accounts, a bit of a squirrel. It was bad enough that he was a professor . . . he was also a religious fanatic and hypochondriac utterly lacking a sense of humor. Sadly for B&O, he would prove to be one of the greatest battlefield commanders of all time and gain the sobriquet "Stonewall." That nickname, incidentally, was a contradiction in terms . . . he earned it at Bull Run in a defensive action, of all things. Jackson's status as a Great Captain in history had little to do with defense. And, as it turned out, he did have a rather sardonic sense of humor.

As the Spring of 1861 wore on, Lee found the situation on both of his flanks deteriorating. His motley campaign along B&O lines west of Cumberland to Wheeling did not go well and in eastern Maryland Lincoln had forestalled secession. The East End, solidly in his hands at the moment, was really at the point of a salient. So Lee told Jackson to take out B&O and withdraw.

Jackson, of course, always carried out his orders. It was the "how" of it that laid the groundwork for his reputation as a genius.

Squatting at Harpers Ferry, Jackson calmly wired B&O's Garrett that the constant movement of trains through his encampments was disturbing the sleep of his men and he wished that future movements be confined to daylight hours. Garrett had little choice but to instantly obey.

Then Jackson informed Garrett that even daylight movements were interrupting the training of his men and "requested" that all movements be confined to midday hours. Again, Garrett fell all over himself complying.

Having gotten the Pavlovian reaction he wanted, on 22 May 1861 Jackson stopped up the railroad at Martinsburg and Point of Rocks east of the Ferry, allowing all trains to enter but none to leave. When he judged that the net contained as much fish as it would hold, Jackson blew down rocks on the railroad to the east, burned bridges on the west and then proceeded to harvest a very large haul of B&O motive power, cars, rails, telegraph wire and so forth in an orgy of theft and destruction that boggles the imagination. We do not know if Garrett burst into tears, but one could hardly blame him for doing so.

Jackson's party lasted for some weeks . . . for example, the bridges at the Ferry were not destroyed until the middle of June. Early on, Jackson took four locomotives and some cars down the W&P to Winchester and then hauled them overland with teams to the Staunton railhead. Most of the loot, however, was too heavy for W&P rail and bridges, so it was set afire or dumped into rivers and streams.

The Rebels discovered that iron coal cars loaded with coal burned very nicely, but locomotives did not. So, at Martinsburg, teams of forty horses (four wide and ten deep) were employed to haul locomotives and tenders south to serve on Rebel railroads. The Martinsburg depot and shops were burned, but the turntable was borrowed and sent south. All together, fourteen B&O engines went south . . . that all but one were returned at the end of the war was small solace.

The final tab was 42 locomotives stolen or destroyed, 386 cars (mostly pot hoppers), 17 bridges on the East End, 36½ miles of rail, 102 miles of telegraph wire and all the shop machinery at Martinsburg. On 30 September 1860 B&O rostered 3453 freight cars and 236 locomotives, so they lost 11% of the former and 18% of the latter in just a few weeks.

As bad as all this appears to be, Jackson did not turn out to be B&O's worst enemy. *No through trains ran from Wheeling to Baltimore from 14 June 1861 to 28 March 1862.* The Union's most important trunkline was closed down for over *nine* months in spite of heroic attempts on the part of B&O to reopen it. Why? For the answer to that question, we must leave the East End and return to Baltimore and Washington to contemplate one of the ugliest episodes in the nation's history.

The cast of villains numbered but two, by name Simon Cameron and Thomas A. Scott, Secretary of War and Assistant Secretary respectively . . . both, we point out, appointees of Abraham Lincoln upon whose head ultimate responsibility must rest.

Cameron was a director of the Northern Central, controlled by PRR, and Scott was a PRR vice-president. Both were self-professed Union patriots and quick to point at Garrett as a suspected traitor to the Cause. As we shall see, the scenario that followed perhaps gave rise to the axiom that patriotism is the last refuge of the scoundrel.

First, this duo seized B&O lines entering Washington "in the name of the Republic's emergency." They then took action to insure that the vast flood of war traffic pouring into Baltimore would only travel over PRR and NC lines, even to the extent of diverting southbound traffic, which normally would have flowed over the short PW&B link, to the roundabout route over PRR lines from Philadelphia to Harrisburg and thence the NC to Baltimore. They jacked rates for this business sky high.

The reader must also remember that the Civil War closed the Mississippi River, forcing all export freight from the midwest (mostly flour and grain) to flow over eastern trunklines and canals. Further, European crops were poor in this time frame and this traffic soared almost beyond belief . . . all in *addition* to ballooning war traffic.

And the Cameron/Scott cabal refused to lift a finger to help B&O reopen its lines. Federal troops stood idle in Hagerstown and Frederick while Jackson and his cohorts laid waste to the East End. For tactical reasons, Rebel forces withdrew as we have shown but still Cameron refused to order Federal troops to protect B&O workmen attempting to repair the line.

To be sure, traffic jammed onto B&O's Washington Branch, going from a prewar average of eight cars a day to over four hundred. But almost two hundred B&O locomotives and two thousand B&O cars were underemployed as traffic overwhelmed the PRR, Erie and NYC to the extent that shipments were embargoed. As winter approached and the spectre of canal freezing loomed, the Union transportation situation reached crisis proportions. In the face of all this, Cameron and Scott increased rates on *all* traffic to levels that gave avarice a bad name. A tidal wave of treasure poured into PRR/NC coffers and the overflow enriched Erie and NYC.

Lee must have contemplated this picture with disbelief, finding it hard to accept that the Secretary of War for the United States would be such an ally. Acting with his usual dispatch, he began issuing orders for raiding parties to slash at the East End, a practice that continued to the end of the war.

The stench finally reached Lincoln's nostrils and by early in 1862, he sent Cameron to Russia as Minister (about as far away as he could send him), Scott back to PRR and appointed Edwin M. Stanton as Secretary of War. Skillful as always with prose, Lincoln stated that Cameron was so corrupt that he would steal everything in sight except for a red-hot stove.

The Russians must have tired of Cameron, for he returned, went to the Senate in 1867, continued to assault rival B&O in a series of incidents beyond the ken of this story and left his mark on history by defining an Honest Politician as one who "once bought, stays bought."

In the introduction to this book, we made reference to the views of the late Julian Barnard that the Civil War was the fundamental reason behind B&O's relegation to third place in the eastern trunkline race. It is not the purpose of this history to explore this contention in depth, although we feel that there is much evidence to support Barnard's theory. We will leave it to some future historian to digest this story, but cannot leave the subject without noting that at the end of the war PRR was very rich and very powerful and the best that could be said for B&O was that it survived.

The tribulations of the East End did not pass after the line was reopened in the Spring of 1862, even with an honest Secretary of War. Sadly, the East End crossed the Great Valley and this would prove to be unfortunate.

This Valley runs from southwest to northeast. To the Rebels, it was an arrow pointing to Federal vitals with nice flank protection in the form of mountains. To the Union side, it went nowhere, disappearing into mountain fastnesses far from Richmond.

Thousands of military histories have treated the fascinating campaigns that swept up and down this Valley . . . every single one of them washed over the East End. Twice Lee used this Valley in an attempt to reach Harrisburg, destroy the railroad bridges at that point, sweep east in a giant enveloping movement to cut Northern Central and conquer the Baltimore/Washington complex. He failed . . . first at Antietam in 1862 and again at Gettysburg in 1863, although in the latter case he came close. Both times Lee had switched to exterior lines and both times even the bumbling Union commanders managed to stave him off. Both times the East End was devastated.

Stanton at least tried to protect B&O lines, but the task was hopeless. Jackson and other Rebel commanders were of such a quality that they outwitted, outfought and outmarched every Union commander so bold as to venture forth against them. Only in the last year of the war did a desperate Lincoln finally rise above his weakness for selecting donkeys as subordinates and find three soldiers who would bring him final victory . . . Grant, Sherman and Sheridan.

Grant took one look at the Valley, told Sheridan to take it out to the extent that a crow could fly over it without finding sustenance and Sheridan did so. At long last, the East End got some peace.

The long and short of it is that, throughout the war, B&O had to look out for itself. In and of itself, that story is fascinating. Most incidents were reported in detail in B&O Annual Reports, although those reports were usually issued two years after the event. Page after page of actions great and small were reported . . . the sheer volume is so great that we decided not to reprint them.

The most significant fact to arise from a study of these actions is that a railroad is almost impossible to destroy. Once repair teams were organized and equipped, reaction was swift and effective. In one case the Rebels burned a bridge and B&O had replaced it *thirty minutes later*. This was not an isolated incident. The whole story is replete with astonishing feats of repair and improvisation.

The Union had an urgent need for steam coal to fuel Navy warships. When the East End was cut, coal was loaded in C&O Canalboats at Cumberland and floated to Sandy Hook (just east of the Ferry) and transloaded into rail cars. When the Ferry bridges were out, pontoon bridges and rope ferrys were employed. Those bridges, incidentally, were destroyed and rebuilt *nine* times during the war at a total cost to B&O of $169,337.

Replacement trestling, rails and ties were preprepared and sited at numerous locations along the line of road . . . time after time the Rebel raiders were not out of earshot before the damage had been repaired and trains were moving.

One of Stonewall's staff officers cried that it was all a waste of time and energy . . . four times, he said, he saw the futility in trying to stop the B&O teams. Even Lee lamented that "the system of repair is so perfect that destruction will only cause a delay of a few days."

It was all very expensive and frustrating, of course, but the point is that B&O could not be broken by the Rebels or floods or ice or rain or snow. Ice and "freshets" probably took out more B&O trestling than the Rebels, but B&O merely shrugged and persevered.

The strategic value of the B&O was demonstrated on several occasions during the war. In the Fall of 1863, the Union had suffered a nasty defeat at Chickamauga and its army was trapped in Chattanooga in desperate need of reinforcement. Within seven days, an entire Federal Army Corps of 20,000 men complete with impedimenta was transferred by rail from Washington to the scene, a trip of about 1200 miles, 400 of which took place over B&O lines.

In January 1865, a similar movement took place, but in reverse. A 15,000 man Federal Corps was moved from Tennessee to Washington in eleven days, a trip of 1400 miles.

B&O even tried armored trains and cars to surprise Rebel raiders, although we do not come away with the impression that this gambit was very successful.

We have, however, come away with the impression that the real heroes of the saga were unsung as usual. Every B&O employee, whether moving or stationary, was in the front line in an active combat zone. The normal hazards of railroad operations were magnified by the eternal threat of military action . . . or, more bluntly, every employee could be shot and killed at any time. Item: 18 January 1865, "Watchman captured and rail taken up 1½ miles east of Duffield's; engine, tender and one car thrown off the track; the contents of three cars carried off." Just another minor annoyance.

Actually, the first B&O casualties fell before the war began . . . at Harpers Ferry on 17 October 1859. A bloodthirsty abolitionist named John Brown, who had a taste for hacking his opponents into little pieces with a broadsword, arrived with an armed band at the Ferry and promptly killed stationmaster Fontaine Beckham and porter Hayward Sheppard. The latter was a freed black man, but Brown saw to it that he was freed a second time. The end of the John Brown story is well known so will not be repeated here, but we must say that in all our research we did not find a clue as to the status of his soul.

War is not an amusing subject, but we must confess that the odd act of comedy does occasionally occur.

Rebel Colonel John Mosby and his merry band, favorites of Lee, regularly raided the East End. One time they derailed a passenger train and commenced a looting spree. One car was full of German immigrants who could speak little English. Mosby motioned them to leave the car, but they refused to do so on the sound reasoning that they had paid for their transportation and were not about to be stiffed out of it. So Mosby simply set fire to the car and laughed as they scrambled to the doors.

Welcome to America.

THE UNCIVIL CIVIL WAR

STONEWALL wasn't in any great hurry to blow the Ferry bridges... after all, Federal troops weren't stirring and it was more convenient to use a bridge than wade the Potomac. But finally Lee told him to come South and down they came. Actually, the bridges were torched and blown on the night of 14 June 1861, but this illustration made at the time will suffice.
B&O Museum

WHILE IT IS TRUE that Jackson found locomotives hard to burn, this view of a Winans Camel clearly shows that such action did little to improve the appearance of an iron horse. This photo was probably taken at Martinsburg during the summer of 1861.
B&O Museum

EAST END

B&O Museum

ON 13-14 OCTOBER 1864, Rebel Colonel John Mosby hauled in a lush prize ... a B&O passenger train complete with Federal payroll car. Known forever after as the "Greenback Raid," Mosby took off with almost $200,000 and expressed his gratitude by burning the train. Here we see the remnants on B&O flat cars being removed to Baltimore for scrap. The incident took place near Kearneysville.

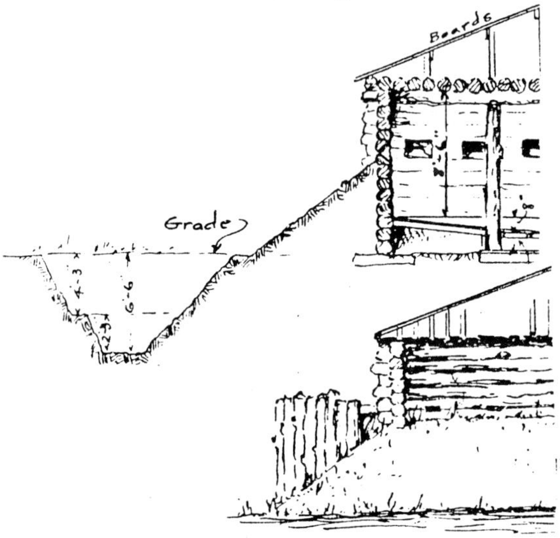

IN EARLY 1863, the War Department tried to help B&O by building and staffing blockhouses along the line of road ... they were located at Duffields, Kearneysville, Vanclevesville, Opequon, North Mountain, Back Creek, Sleepy Creek, Sir Johns Run, Great Cacapon (2), Paw Paw, Little Cacapon, South Branch, Green Spring (2), Oldtown, Patterson Creek and North Branch. The one at Oldtown was located on Alum Hill on the opposite side of the Potomac from Green Spring between the river and the C&O Canal. The drawings that accompany this caption were actually made in 1929 by B&O building engineers from plans supplied from War Department files. In 1929, B&O made an extensive study

B&O Museum

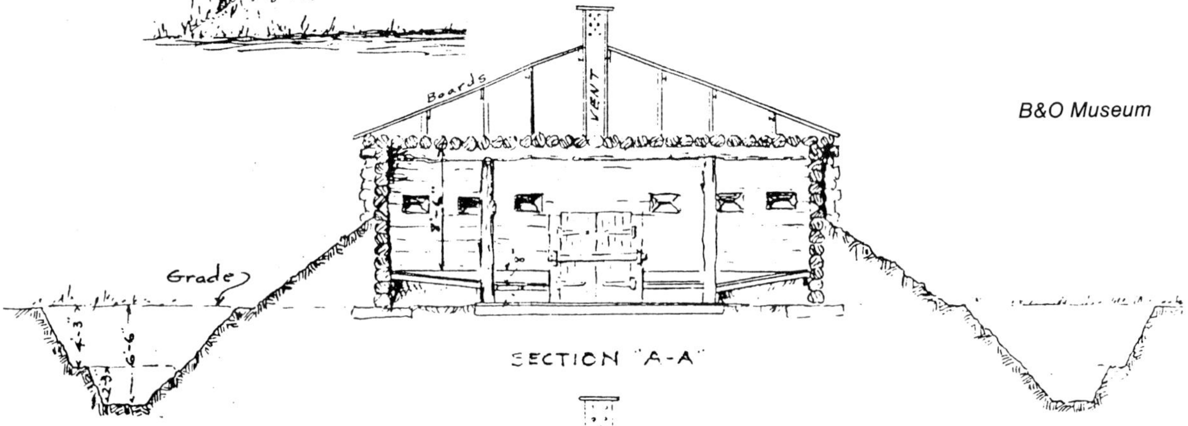

SECTION A-A

SIDE ELEVATION.

THE UNCIVIL CIVIL WAR

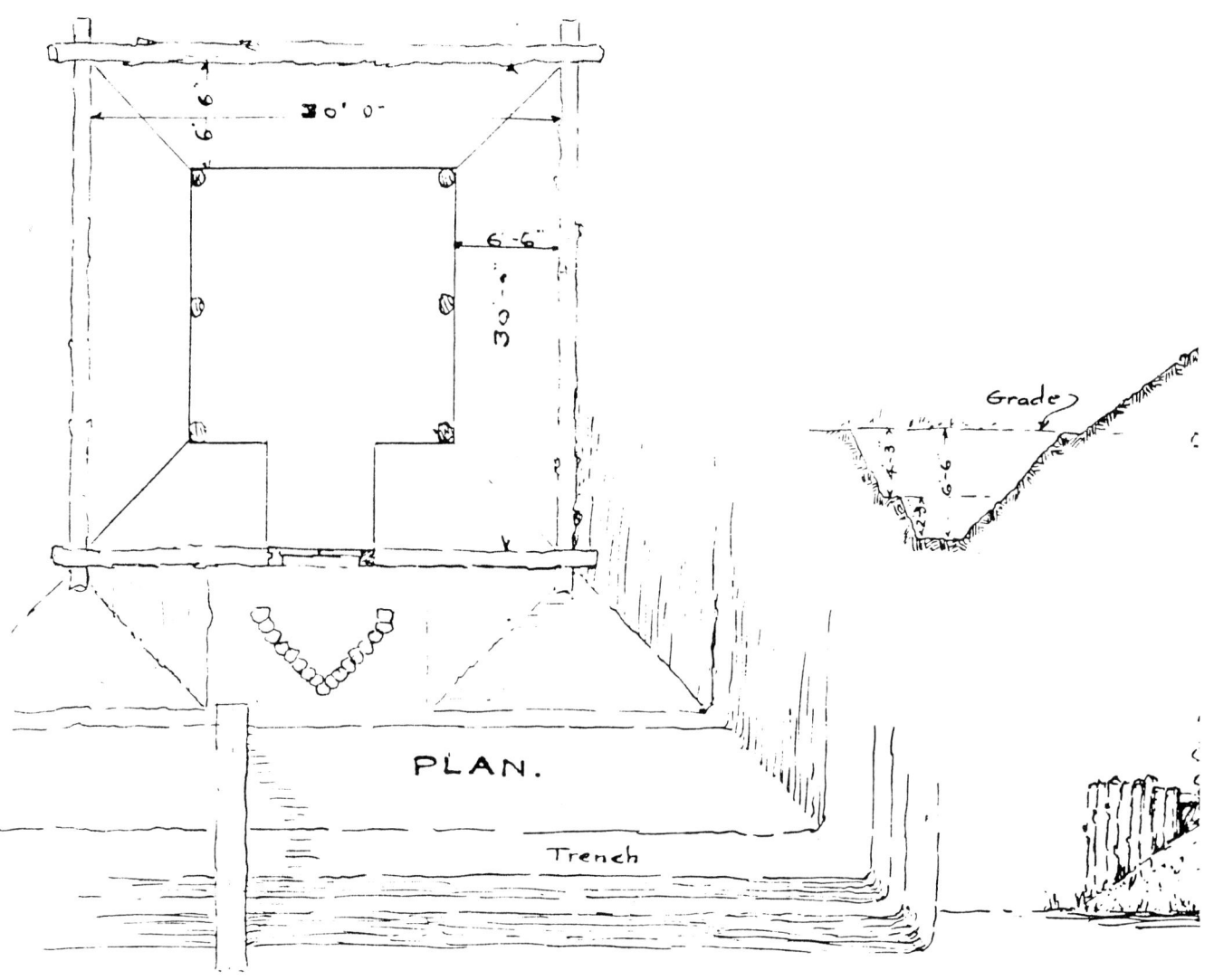

of blockhouse location on the East End with the intent of rebuilding some as tourist attractions for passing passengers and they pinpointed the sites of quite a few. The Great Depression ended the project. There were several east of the Ferry and quite a few west of Cumberland. Militarily, such fortifications are of questionable value ... the idea is to protect, say, a bridge by fire and while that is very nice in theory, veteran soldiers would point out that if you make it impossible for the enemy to get in, you also make it impossible for you to get out. There are reports that blockhouses were attacked on the East End and elsewhere, with and without success. On balance, they probably did more good than harm and at least served as outposts, giving warning of Rebel forays.

WESTWARD

East End Cumberland Division.
TIME-TABLE No. 16.
April 28, 1929.

Distance from Weverton	Train Order Stations	Station	Passing Siding Capacity in Cars	3 DAILY A.M.	17 DAILY A.M.	29 DAILY Ex. Monday A.M.	13 DAILY Ex. Monday A.M.	53 DAILY Ex. Sunday A.M.	33 DAILY Ex. Sunday A.M.	55 DAILY Ex. Sunday A.M.	21 DAILY A.M.	15 DAILY P.M.	51 DAILY Ex. Sunday P.M.	5 DAILY P.M.	31 DAILY P.M.
	DN	WEVERTON.		1.18	1.55	5.36	6.15	S 6.28	S 7.17	S10.26	S10.48	12.23	S 4.13	4.27	S 4.27
2.0		SANDY HOOK.		.....	.....	.....	.....	F 6.32	F 7.20	F10.30	.....	.....	F 4.18	.....	.....
2.9	DN	HARPER'S FERRY.		1.22	S 2.01	5.40	6.19	A 6.35	S 7.26	A10.33	S10.55	S12.29	A 4.21	4.31	S 4.36
6.2	DN	ENGLE.		1.27	2.06	5.46	6.24	.....	S 7.32	.....	11.00	12.35	.....	4.36	S 4.42
9.3		DUFFIELDS.		.....	.....	.....	.....	.....	F 7.37	.....	.....	.....	.....	.....	F 4.46
10.2		SHENDNDOAH JCT.		S 1.37	S 2.15	.....	.....	.....	S 7.42	.....	S11.11	.....	.....	.....	S 4.53
12.0	DN	HOBBS.		1.42	2.19	5.56	6.34	.....	7.48	.....	11.15	12.44	.....	4.44	4.58
13.7		KEARNEYSVILLE.		.....	.....	.....	.....	.....	F 7.51	.....	.....	.....	.....	.....	F 5.04
16.6		VANCLEVESVILLE.		.....	.....	.....	.....	.....	F 7.56	.....	.....	.....	.....	.....	F 5.08
21.1	DN	MARTINSBURG.	238	S 2.00	S 2.36	6.10	S 6.53	.....	S 8.07	.....	S11.32	S 1.01	.....	Y 4.55	S 5.19
23.5		FAWVER.		.....	.....	.....	.....	.....	.....	.....	.....	.....	.....	.....	.....
26.3	DN	WEST CUMBO.		2.12	2.46	6.19	7.03	.....	F 8.19	.....	11.42	1.12	.....	5.02	F 5.28
28.7		NORTH MOUNTAIN.		.....	.....	.....	.....	.....	S 8.24	.....	U11.45	.....	.....	.....	S 5.32
34.8		CHERRY RUN.		.....	.....	.....	.....	.....	S 8.35	.....	.....	.....	.....	.....	F 5.42
35.8	DN	MILLER.		2.24	2.58	6.31	7.16	.....	8.38	.....	11.55	1.24	.....	5.18	5.45
39.8	DN	SLEEPY CREEK TOWER.		2.29	3.03	6.36	7.21	.....	8.45	.....	12.00	1.29	.....	5.23	5.57
44.2	DN	HANCOCK.		2.35	3.08	6.41	7.27	.....	S 8.54	.....	S12.07	1.34	.....	5.28	S 6.06
47.3		ROUND TOP.		.....	.....	.....	.....	.....	F 8.59	.....	.....	.....	.....	.....	.....
49.8	DN	SIR JOHN'S RUN.		2.42	3.15	6.49	7.35	.....	F 9.04	.....	12.16	1.42	.....	5.35	F 6.15
53.9	DN	GREAT CACAPON.		2.48	3.20	6.55	7.41	.....	S 9.10	.....	12.22	1.47	.....	5.40	S 6.22
55.0		WOODMONT.		.....	.....	.....	.....	.....	F 9.13	.....	.....	.....	.....	.....	.....
57.0		LINEBURG.		.....	.....	.....	.....	.....	F 9.18	.....	.....	.....	.....	.....	F 6.28
60.1	DN	ORLEANS ROAD.		2.57	3.28	7.04	7.50	.....	F 9.24	.....	12.30	1.56	.....	5.48	F 6.34
62.3		DOE GULLY.		.....	.....	.....	.....	.....	F 9.30	.....	.....	.....	.....	.....	F 6.38
64.8		HANSROTE.		.....	.....	.....	.....	.....	F 9.35	.....	.....	.....	.....	.....	.....
66.8		GREEN RIDGE.		.....	.....	.....	.....	.....	F 9.39	.....	.....	.....	.....	.....	F 6.45
70.3		MAGNOLIA.	115	.....	.....	.....	.....	.....	S 9.45	.....	.....	.....	.....	.....	F 6.53
75.2		PAW PAW.		.....	.....	.....	.....	.....	S 9.54	.....	S12.50	.....	.....	.....	S 7.03
77.8		LITTLE CACAPON.		.....	.....	.....	.....	.....	F 9.59	.....	.....	.....	.....	.....	F 7.08
79.9	DN	OKONOKO.		3.23	3.52	7.29	8.16	.....	F10.04	.....	12.56	2.20	.....	6.11	F 7.13
82.7		FRENCH.		.....	.....	.....	.....	.....	F10.10	.....	.....	.....	.....	.....	F 7.18
84.8	DN	GREEN SPRING.	171	3.30	3.59	7.36	8.23	.....	S10.15	.....	S 1.07	2.27	.....	6.17	S 7.27
91.6	DN	PATTERSON CREEK.		3.40	4.08	7.48	8.32	.....	F10.30	.....	1.16	2.36	.....	6.26	F 7.37
93.7		NORTH BRANCH.		.....	.....	.....	.....	.....	F10.35	.....	.....	.....	.....	.....	B 7.40
97.1	DN	EVITTS CREEK.		3.49	4.16	.....	8 39	.....	10.44	.....	1.24	2.44	.....	6.33	7.45
99.5	DN	CUMBERLAND.		A 3.55	A 4.23	.....	A 8.45	.....	A10.50	.....	A 1.30	A 2.50	.....	A 6.38	A 7.50
				A.M.	A.M.	A.M.	A.M.	A.M.	A.M.	A.M.	P.M.	P.M.	P.M.	P.M.	P.M.
		Time over Division		2.37	2.28	2.12	2.30	0.7	3.33	.07	2.42	2 27	0 8	2.11	3.23
		Average speed per hour		38.0	40.3	41.5	39.8	24.8	28.0	24.8	36.8	40.6	21.7	45.5	29.4

Passenger trains will not exceed a speed of 55 miles per hour.
Speed as shown in Special Instruction 5, and such other restrictions as may be in effect, will not be exceeded.

WESTWARD

Distance from Weverton.	Train Order Stations.	East End Cumberland Division. TIME-TABLE No. 16. April 28, 1929.	Passing Sidings. Capacity in Cars.	FIRST CLASS.							SECOND CLASS.				
				19	11	1	407	707	7	9	97	97	97	97	97
				DAILY	DAILY	DAILY	DAILY Ex. Sunday	Sunday ONLY	DAILY	DAILY	Chicago DAILY	St.Louis DAILY	Pittsb'g DAILY	Cin. DAILY	Clev'd DAILY
				P. M.	P. M.	P. M.	P. M.	P. M.	P. M.	P. M.	A. M.	A. M.	P. M.	P. M.	P. M.
	DN	WEVERTON.		4.57	5.46	7.42	S 8.12	S 8.25	8.48	11.35	5.00	5.20	2.30	7.00	8.10
2.0		SANDY HOOK. 2.0		.....	.....	.....	F 8.16	S 8.29	.....	.....					
2.9	DN	HARPER'S FERRY. 0.9		5.01	E 5.50	7.46	S 8.20	A 8.32	S 8.54	11.40					
6.2	DN	ENGLE. 3.3		5.06	5.55	7.51	.....	.....	9.00	11.45					
9.3		DUFFIELDS. 3.1													
10.2		SHENDNDOAH JCT. 0.9		M 5.11	.....	.....	.....	.....	.....	C11.55					
12.0	DN	HOBBS. 1.8		5.14	6.04	7.58	.....	.....	9.09	12.00					
13.7		KEARNEYSVILLE. 1.7													
16.6		VANCLEVESVILLE. 2.9													
21.1	DN	MARTINSBURG. 4.5	238	S 5.30	S 6.20	L 8.09	.....	.....	S 9.26	S12.19					
23.5		FAWVER. 2.4													
26.3	DN	WEST CUMBO. 2.8		5.38	6.30	8.16	.....	.....	9.37	12.29					
28.7		NORTH MOUNTAIN. 2.4													
34.8		CHERRY RUN. 6.1													
35.8	DN	MILLER. 1.0		5.50	6.43	8.33	.....	.....	9.49	12.42					
39.8	DN	SLEEPY CREEK TOWER. 4.0		5.55	6.48	8.38	.....	.....	9.54	12.47					
44.2	DN	HANCOCK. 4.4		6.00	6.53	8.43	.....	.....	9.59	12.53					
47.3		ROUND TOP. 3.1													
49.8	DN	SIR JOHN'S RUN. 2.5		6.07	7.00	8.50	.....	.....	10.06	1.01					
53.9	DN	GREAT CACAPON. 4.1		6.12	7.05	8.55	.....	.....	10.11	1.07					
55.0		WOODMONT. 1.1													
57.0		LINEBURG. 2.0													
60.1	DN	ORLEANS ROAD. 3.1		6.20	7.13	9.03	.....	.....	10.19	1.16					
62.3		DOE GULLY. 2.2													
64.8		HANSROTE. 2.5													
66.8		GREEN RIDGE. 2.0													
70.3		MAGNOLIA. 3.5	115												
75.2		PAW PAW. 4.9													
77.8		LITTLE CACAPON. 2.6													
79.8	DN	OKONOKO. 2.1		6.43	7.37	9.26	.....	.....	10.43	1.42					
82.7		FRENCH. 2.8													
84.8	DN	GREEN SPRING. 2.1	171	6.49	7.44	9.32	.....	.....	10.50	1.49					
91.6	DN	PATTERSON CREEK. 6.8		6.57	7.53	9.41	.....	.....	10.59	1.59	.....	9.20	.....	11.30	.....
93.7		NORTH BRANCH. 2.1													
97.1	DN	EVITTS CREEK. 3.4		7.04	8.00	.....	.....	.....	11.07	2.07					
99.5	DN	**CUMBERLAND.** 2.4		A 7.09	A 8.06	.....	.....	.....	A11.12	A 2.15	A 9 40	.....	A 7.10	.....	A 1.40
				P. M.	P. M.	P. M.	P. M.	P. M.	P. M.	A. M.	A. M.	A. M.	P. M.	P. M.	A. M.
		Time over Division........ Average speed per hour........		2.12 45.2	2.20 42.6	1.59 46.1	.08 21.7	.07 24.8	2.24 41.5	2.40 37.3	4.40 21.8	4.00 22.9	4.40 21.8	4.30 20.4	5 30 18.1

Passenger trains will not exceed a speed of 55 miles per hour.
Speed as shown in Special Instruction 5, and such other restrictions as may be in effect, will not be exceeded.

EASTWARD

East End Cumberland Division.
TIME-TABLE No. 16.
April 28, 1929.

Distance from Cumberland	Train Order Stations	Station	Passing Sidings Capacity in Cars	18 DAILY A.M.	10 DAILY A.M.	6 DAILY A.M.	20 DAILY A.M.	406 DAILY A.M.	4 DAILY A.M.	32 DAILY A.M.	52 DAILY Ex. Sunday A.M.	2 DAILY A.M.	56 DAILY Ex. Sunday P.M.	22 DAILY A.M.
	DN	CUMBERLAND.		S 3.50	S 4.22	S 4.53	S 5.11	.....		S 6.15	.....	.....	.....	S10.54
2.4	DN	EVITTS CREEK. 3.4	419	3.55	4.28	4.58	5.16	.....		6.21	.....	.....	.....	11.00
5.8		NORTH BRANCH. 2.1		.....	.....	.....	.....	.....		F 6.26				
7.9	DN	PATTERSON CREEK. 6.8		4.03	4.36	5.05	5.23	.....	6.04	F 6.30	.....	8.24	.....	11.07
14.7	DN	GREEN SPRING. 2.1		4.11	4.46	5.14	5.32	.....	6.13	S 6.45	.....	8.32	.....	11.16
16.8		FRENCH. 2.8		.....	.....	.....	.....	.....		F 6.50				
19.6	DN	OKONOKO. 2.1		4.17	4.53	5.20	5.38	.....	6.20	F 6.56	.....	8.38	.....	11.23
21.7		LITTLE CACAPON. 2.6								F 7.00				
24.3		PAW PAW. 4.9								S 7.07				
29.2		MAGNOLIA. 3.5								F 7.16				
32.7		GREEN RIDGE. 2.0								F 7.22				
34.7		HANSROTE. 2.5												
37.2		DOE GULLY. 2.2								F 7.30				
39.4	DN	ORLEANS ROAD. 3.1		4.40	5.18	5.44	6.02	.....	6.43	F 7.35	.....	9.00	.....	11.46
42.5		LINEBURG. 2.0								F 7.41				
44.5		WOODMONT. 1.1								F 7.45				
45.6	DN	GREAT CACAPON. 4.1		4.48	5.26	5.52	6.10	.....	6.51	S 7.49	.....	9.08	.....	11.54
49.7	DN	SIR JOHN'S RUN. 2.5		4.53	5.32	5.57	6.15	.....	6.56	F 7.56	.....	9.13	.....	11.59
52.2		ROUND TOP. 3.1												
55.3	DN	HANCOCK. 4.4		5.00	5.40	6.04	6.22	.....	7.03	S 8.07	.....	9.20	.....	S12.08
59.7	DN	SLEEPY CREEK TOWER. 4.0		5.05	5.46	6.09	6.27	.....	7.08	8.13		9.25		12.14
63.7	DN	MILLER. 1.0		5.10	5.52	6.14	6.32	.....	7.13	8.19		9.30		12.19
64.7		CHERRY RUN. 6.1								F 8.22				
70.8		NORTH MOUNTAIN. 2.4								S 8.32				
73.2	DN	WEST CUMBO. 2.8		5.22	6.05	6.27	6.43	.....	7.25	S 8.37	.....	9.42	.....	12.31
76.0		FAWVER. 2.4												
78.4	DN	MARTINSBURG. 4.5		S 5.33	S 6.18	G 6.41	S 6.55	.....	S 7.36	S 8.50	.....	S 9.53	.....	S12.42
82.9		VANCLEVESVILLE. 2.9								F 9.00				
85.8		KEARNEYSVILLE. 1.7								F 9.08				
87.5	DN	HOBBS. 1.8	223	5.47	6.34	6.55	7.10	.....	7.52	9.13	.....	10.07	.....	12.57
89.3		SHENANDOAH JCT. 0.9		Q 5.50	Q 6.37	.....	.....	.....		S 9.21				S 1.02
90.2		DUFFIELDS. 3.1								F 9.25				
93.3	DN	ENGLE. 3.3		5.57	6.43	7.03	7.18	.....	8.01	S 9.30	.....	10.15	.....	1.07
96.6	DN	HARPER'S FERRY. 0.9		Q 6.04	S 6.50	7.08	7.25	S 7.28	V 8.09	S 9.42	S 9.47	10.20	S12.28	S 1.15
97.5		SANDY HOOK. 2.0						F 7.30	.....	K 9.44	F 9.50		F12.32	
99.5	DN	WEVERTON.		6.10	6.57	7.13	J 7.30	S 7.35	8.15	S 9.49	S 9.54	10.25	F12.35	1.21

				A.M.	A.M.	A.M.	A.M.	A.M.	A.M.	A.M.	A.M.	A.M.	P.M.	P.M.
		Time over Division		2.20	2.35	2.20	2.19	.07	2.11	3.34	.07	2.01	.07	2.27
		Average speed per hour		42.6	38.5	42.6	43.7	24.8	41.9	27.7	24.8	45.4	24.8	40.6

Passenger trains will not exceed a speed of 55 miles per hour.
Speed as shown in Special Instruction 5, and such other restrictions as may be in effect, will not be exceeded.

EASTWARD

East End Cumberland Division.
TIME-TABLE No. 16.
April 28, 1929.

Distance from Cumberland.	Train Order Stations.	Station	Passing Sidings. Capacity in Cars.	FIRST CLASS. 8 DAILY P.M.	30 DAILY Ex. Monday P.M.	54 DAILY Ex. Sunday P.M.	34 DAILY P.M.	16 DAILY P.M.	14 DAILY Ex. Monday P.M.	12 DAILY P.M.		SECOND CLASS. 94 Cumb. Valley DAILY A.M.	94 DAILY A.M.	96 DAILY P.M.
	DN	CUMBERLAND.		S12.45	S12.50	......	S 3.45	S 5.30	S 6.50	S10.25				
		2.4												
2.4	DN	EVITTS CREEK.	419	12.50	12.56	......	3.51	5.36	6.55	10.30		8.30	8.45	9.30
		3.4												
5.8		NORTH BRANCH.		......	......	......	F 3.56	......	......	......				
		2.1												
7.9	DN	PATTERSON CREEK.		12.57	1.04	......	F 4.01	5.44	7.02	10.37				
		6.8												
14.7	DN	GREEN SPRING.		S 1.06	1.13	......	S 4.14	S 5.57	7.21	10.47				
		2.1												
16.8		FRENCH.		......	......	......	F 4.19	......	......	......				
		2.8												
19.6	DN	OKONOKO.		1.14	1.20	......	F 4.25	6.05	7.28	10.54				
		2.1												
21.7		LITTLE CACAPON.		......	......	......	F 4.30	......	......	......				
		2.6												
24.3		PAW PAW.		......	......	......	S 4.37	F 6.12	......	......				
		4.9												
29.2		MAGNOLIA.		......	......	......	F 4.45	......	......	......				
		3.5												
32.7		GREEN RIDGE.		......	......	......	F 4.51	......	......	......				
		2.0												
34.7		HANSROTE.		......	......	......	F 4.55	......	......	......				
		2.5												
37.2		DOE GULLY.		......	......	......	F 5.00	......	......	......				
		2.2												
39.4	DN	ORLEANS ROAD.		1.38	1.44	......	F 5.05	6.33	7.53	11.22				
		3.1												
42.5		LINEBURG.		......	......	......	F 5.11	......	......	......				
		2.0												
44.5		WOODMONT.		......	......	......	F 5.14	......	......	......				
		1.1												
45.6	DN	GREAT CACAPON.		1.46	1.52	......	S 5.17	6.41	8.01	11.31				
		4.1												
49.7	DN	SIR JOHN'S RUN.		1.51	1.58	......	F 5.24	6.46	8.07	11.38				
		2.5												
52.2		ROUND TOP.		......	......	......	F 5.29	......	......	......				
		3.1												
55.3	DN	HANCOCK.		S 2.00	2.06	......	S 5.37	S 6.56	8.15	11.45				
		4.4												
59.7	DN	SLEEPY CREEK TOWER.		2.06	2.12	......	5.44	7.02	8.21	11.51				
		4.0												
63.7	DN	MILLER.		2.11	2.17	......	5.52	7.07	8.26	11.57				
		1.0												
64.7		CHERRY RUN.		......	......	......	S 5.56	......	......	......				
		6.1												
70.8		NORTH MOUNTAIN.		......	......	......	S 6.07	......	......	......				
		2.4												
73.2	DN	WEST CUMBO.		2.24	2.30	......	S 6.12	7.21	8.38	12.12		11.10		
		2.8												
76.0		FAWVER.		......	......	......	......	......	......	......				
		2.4												
78.4	DN	MARTINSBURG.		S 2.35	S 2.43	......	S 6.25	S 7.35	S 8.52	S12.24				
		4.5												
82.9		VANCLEVESVILLE.		......	......	......	F 6.35	......	......	......				
		2.9												
85.8		KEARNEYSVILLE.		......	......	......	F 6.43	......	......	......				
		1.7												
87.5	DN	HOBBS.	223	2.50	2.59	......	6.47	7.52	9.08	12.42				
		1.8												
89.3		SHENANDOAH JCT.		H 2.54	......	......	S 6.55	S 7.56	......	H12.46				
		0.9												
90.2		DUFFIELDS.		......	......	......	F 6.59	......	......	......				
		3.1												
93.3	DN	ENGLE.		2.59	3.08	......	S 7.06	8.02	9.17	12.54				
		3.3												
96.6	DN	HARPER'S FERRY.		S 3.06	3.14	S 7.03	S 7.20	S 8.09	9.23	1.02				
		0.9												
97.5		SANDY HOOK.		......	......	F 7.06	F 7.24	......	......	......				
		2.0												
99.5	DN	WEVERTON.		3.12	3.20	S 7.10	S 7.30	8.15	9.30	1.08			12.50	2.30
				P.M.	P.M.	P.M.	P.M.	P.M.	P.M.	A.M.		A.M.	P.M.	A.M.
		Time over Division		2.27	2.30	.08	3.45	2.45	2.40	2.43		2.40	4.05	5.00
		Average speed per hour		40.6	39.8	21.7	26.6	36.2	37.3	36.5		27.4	24.4	19.6

Passenger trains will not exceed a speed of 55 miles per hour.

Speed as shown in Special Instruction 5, and such other restrictions as may be in effect, will not be exceeded.

WESTWARD

East End Cumberland Division.
TIME-TABLE No. 53.
April 25, 1948.

FIRST CLASS.

Distance from Weverton.	Train Order Stations.	Station	Passing Sidings. Capacity in Cars.	7 DAILY A.M.	79 DAILY A.M.	29 DAILY Ex. Monday A.M.	11 DAILY A.M.	75 DAILY A.M.	55 DAILY Ex. Sunday A.M.	21 DAILY A.M.	31 DAILY Ex. Monday A.M.	9 DAILY P.M.			
	DN	**WEVERTON.**		12.02	12.53	5.30	8.03	8.58	P 9.40	11.07	11.35	2.07	.....		
1.8		SANDY HOOK. 1.8		.....	.....	.....	.....	.....	F 9.42	.....	.....	.....			
2.8	DN	HARPER'S FERRY. 1.0		12.06	12.57	5.34	S 8.07	9.01	A 9.45	S11.11	11.39	S 2.11			
6.0		ENGLE. 3.2		.....	.....	.....	.....	.....	.....	.....	.....	.....			
9.2		DUFFIELDS. 3.2		.....	.....	.....	.....	.....	.....	.....	.....	.....			
10.1		SHENANDOAH JCT. 0.9		S12.16	S 1.07	.....	S 8.25	.....	.....	.....	.....	S 2.22			
11.9	DN	HOBBS. 1.8		12.20	1.12	5.48	8.30	9.11	.....	11.23	11.52	2.26			
13.5		KEARNEYSVILLE. 1.6		.....	.....	.....	.....	.....	.....	.....	.....	.....			
16.5		VANCLEVESVILLE. 3.0		.....	.....	.....	.....	.....	.....	.....	.....	.....			
21.1	DN	MARTINSBURG. 4.6	191	S12.34	S 1.27	S 6.05	S 8.47	S 9.23	.....	S11.36	S12.09	S 2.43			
23.4		FAWVER. 2.3		.....	.....	.....	.....	.....	.....	.....	.....	.....			
26.4	DN	WEST CUMBO. 3.0		12.42	1.36	6.15	8.57	9.30	.....	11.44	12.19	2.51			
28.7		NORTH MOUNTAIN. 2.3		.....	.....	.....	.....	.....	.....	.....	.....	.....			
34.8		CHERRY RUN. 6.1		.....	.....	.....	.....	.....	.....	.....	.....	.....			
35.6	DN	MILLER. 0.8		12.52	1.47	6.26	9.08	9.40	.....	11.55	12.31	3.02			
38.7		SLEEPY CREEK. 3.1		.....	.....	.....	.....	.....	.....	.....	.....	.....			
44.2	DN	HANCOCK. 5.5		1.01	1.56	6.35	S 9.23	9.48	.....	12.04	12.40	S 3.13			
49.8		SIR JOHN'S RUN. 5.6		.....	.....	.....	.....	.....	.....	.....	.....	.....			
53.9		GREAT CACAPON. 4.1		.....	.....	.....	.....	.....	.....	.....	.....	.....			
55.0		WOODMONT. 1.1		.....	.....	.....	.....	.....	.....	.....	.....	.....			
57.1		LINEBURG. 2.1		.....	.....	.....	.....	.....	.....	.....	.....	.....			
60.2	DN	ORLEANS ROAD. 3.1		1.18	2.14	6.53	9.41	10.06	.....	12.22	1.00	3.31			
62.0		DOE GULLY. 1.8		.....	.....	.....	.....	.....	.....	.....	.....	.....			
64.7		HANSROTE. 2.7		.....	.....	.....	.....	.....	.....	.....	.....	.....			
66.7		GREEN RIDGE. 2.0		.....	.....	.....	.....	.....	.....	.....	.....	.....			
70.3		MAGNOLIA. 3.6		.....	.....	.....	.....	.....	.....	.....	.....	.....			
75.3		PAW PAW. 5.0		.....	.....	.....	S10.01	.....	.....	.....	.....	S 3.50			
78.3		LITTLE CACAPON. 3.0		.....	.....	.....	.....	.....	.....	.....	.....	.....			
80.0	DN	OKONOKO. 1.7		1.40	2.37	7.15	10.07	10.20	.....	12.44	1.23	3.57			
82.8		FRENCH. 2.8		.....	.....	.....	.....	.....	.....	.....	.....	.....			
85.4		GREEN SPRING. 2.6	159	.....	.....	.....	E10.14	.....	.....	.....	.....	.....			
92.0	DN	PATTERSON CREEK. 6.6		1.54	2.51	7.29	10.22	10.33	.....	12.58	1.39	4.11			
93.8		NORTH BRANCH. 1.8		.....	.....	.....	.....	.....	.....	.....	.....	.....			
97.1	DN	EVITTS CREEK. 3.3		2.01	2.58	7.36	10.30	.....	.....	1.05	1.47	4.18			
99.5	DN	CUMBERLAND. 2.4		S 2.08 / 2.13	S 3.05 / 3.10	S 7.42 / 8.09	S10.38 / 10.48	.....	.....	S 1.10 / 1.15	S 1.55 / 2.10	S 4.26 / 4.31			
100.1	DN	**VIADUCT JCT.** 0.6		2.15	3.12	8.11	10.50	.....	.....	1.17	2.12	4.33			
				A.M.	A.M.	A.M.	A.M.	A.M.	A.M.	P.M.	P.M.	P.M.			
		Time over Division Average speed per hour		2.13 / 45.2	2.19 / 43.2	2.41 / 37.3	2.47 / 36.0	1.35 / 54.5	.05 / 33.6	2.10 / 46.2	2.37 / 38.3	2.26 / 41.1			

Passenger trains will not exceed a speed of 60 miles per hour.

Speed as shown in Special instruction 5, and such other restrictions as may be in effect, will not be exceeded.

WESTWARD

Distance from Weverton.	Train Order Stations.	East End Cumberland Division. TIME-TABLE No. 53. April 25, 1948.	Passing Sidings. Capacity in Cars.	FIRST CLASS.											
				5	25	19	1	15	17	3	23				
				DAILY	DAILY	DAILY	DAILY	DAILY	DAILY	DAILY	DAILY				
				P. M.	P. M.	P. M.	P. M.	P. M.	P. M.	P. M.	P. M.				
	DN	**WEVERTON.**		5.33	5.42	6.54	7.35	8.21	9.37	10.33	11.15	.....	.....	.....	.....
1.8		1.8 SANDY HOOK.		.....	.....	.....	.....	.....	.....	.....	.....				
2.8	DN	1.0 HARPER'S FERRY.		5.37	5.46	F 6.58	7.39	8.25	9.41	10.37	11.19				
6.0		3.2 ENGLE.		.....	.....	.....	.....	.....	.....	.....	.....				
9.2		3.2 DUFFIELDS.		.....	.....	.....	.....	.....	.....	.....	.....				
10.1		0.9 SHENANDOAH JCT.		.....	.....	.....	.....	.....	.....	.....	S11.42				
11.9	DN	1.8 HOBBS.		5.49	5.58	7.10	7.51	8.37	9.53	10.49	11.47				
13.5		1.6 KEARNEYSVILLE.		.....	.....	.....	.....	.....	.....	.....	.....				
16.5		3.0 VANCLEVESVILLE.		.....	.....	.....	.....	.....	.....	.....	.....				
21.1	DN	4.6 MARTINSBURG.	191	S 6.00	S 6.10	S 7.24	S 8.04	S 8.51	S10.07	S11.01	S12.07				
23.4		2.3 FAWVER.		.....	.....	.....	.....	.....	.....	.....	.....				
26.4	DN	3.0 WEST CUMBO.		6.07	6.17	7.31	8.12	9.00	10.15	11.09	12.17				
28.7		2.3 NORTH MOUNTAIN.		.....	.....	.....	.....	.....	.....	.....	.....				
34.8		6.1 CHERRY RUN.		.....	.....	.....	.....	.....	.....	.....	.....				
35.6	DN	0.8 MILLER.		6.17	6.27	7.41	8.22	9.11	10.25	11.19	12.28				
38.7		3.1 SLEEPY CREEK.		.....	.....	.....	.....	.....	.....	.....	.....				
44.2	DN	5.5 HANCOCK.		6.25	6.35	7.50	8.31	9.20	10.34	11.27	12.37				
49.8		6.6 SIR JOHN'S RUN.		.....	.....	.....	.....	.....	.....	.....	.....				
53.0		4.1 GREAT CACAPON.		.....	.....	.....	.....	.....	.....	.....	.....				
55.0		1.1 WOODMONT.		.....	.....	.....	.....	.....	.....	.....	.....				
57.1		2.1 LINEBURG.		.....	.....	.....	.....	.....	.....	.....	.....				
60.2	DN	3.1 ORLEANS ROAD.		6.42	6.53	8.08	8.49	9.39	10.52	11.44	12.55				
62.0		1.8 DOE GULLY.		.....	.....	.....	.....	.....	.....	.....	.....				
64.7		2.7 HANSROTE.		.....	.....	.....	.....	.....	.....	.....	.....				
66.7		2.0 GREEN RIDGE.		.....	.....	.....	.....	.....	.....	.....	.....				
70.3		3.6 MAGNOLIA.		.....	.....	.....	.....	.....	.....	.....	.....				
75.3		5.0 PAW PAW.		.....	.....	.....	.....	.....	.....	.....	.....				
78.3		3.0 LITTLE CACAPON.		.....	.....	.....	.....	.....	.....	.....	.....				
80.0	DN	1.7 OKONOKO.		7.04	7.15	8.30	9.11	10.02	11.14	12.05	1.18				
82.8		2.8 FRENCH.		.....	.....	.....	.....	.....	.....	.....	.....				
85.4		2.6 GREEN SPRING.	159	.....	.....	.....	.....	.....	.....	.....	.....				
92.0	DN	6.6 PATTERSON CREEK.		7.17	7.28	8.44	9.25	10.17	11.28	12.19	1.32				
93.8		1.8 NORTH BRANCH.		.....	.....	.....	.....	.....	.....	.....	.....				
97.1	DN	3.3 EVITTS CREEK.		7.24	7.35	8.51	.....	10.25	11.35	.....	1.40				
99.5	DN	2.4 CUMBERLAND.		S 7.31 / 7.36	S 7.42 / 7.47	S 8.58 / 9.03	.....	S10.33 / 10.38	S11.40 / 11.45	.....	S 1.48 / 1.58				
100.1	DN	0.6 **VIADUCT JCT.**		7.38	7.49	9.05	.....	10.40	11.47	.....	2.00				
				P. M.	P. M.	P. M.	P. M.	P. M.	P. M.	A. M.	A. M.				
		Time over Division Average speed per hour		2.05 48.0	2.07 47.3	2.11 45.8	1.50 50.2	2.19 43.2	2.10 46.2	1.46 52.1	2.45 36.4				

Passenger trains will not exceed a speed of 60 miles per hour.

Speed as shown in Special Instruction 5, and such other restrictions as may be in effect, will not be exceeded.

EASTWARD

East End Cumberland Division.
TIME-TABLE No. 53.
April 25, 1948.

Distance from Viaduct Jct.	Train Order Stations	Station	Passing Siding Capacity in Cars	FIRST CLASS								
				10	80	18	2	20	26	6	34	734
				DAILY	DAILY	DAILY	DAILY	DAILY	DAILY	DAILY	DAILY Ex. Sunday	Sunday ONLY
				A.M.	A.M.	A.M.	A.M.	A.M.	A.M.	A.M.	A.M.	A.M.
	DN	VIADUCT JCT.		2.48	3.48	4.01	.....	4.53	5.15	5.27	.....	.....
0.6	DN	CUMBERLAND.		S 2.50 / 2.57	S 3.50 / 3.55	S 4.03 / 4.08	.....	S 4.55 / 5.00	S 5.17 / 5.22	S 5.29 / 5.34	S 5.45	S 6.30
3.0	DN	EVITTS CREEK.		3.02	4.01	4.14	.....	5.05	5.26	5.38	5.50	6.35
6.3		NORTH BRANCH.										
8.1	DN	PATTERSON CREEK.		3.09	4.09	4.21	4.32	5.12	5.33	5.45	5.59	6.42
14.7		GREEN SPRING.									S 6.08	
17.3		FRENCH.									F 6.13	
20.1	DN	OKONOKO.		3.22	4.23	4.35	4.46	5.25	5.46	5.58	S 6.19	6.56
21.8		LITTLE CACAPON.									F 6.22	
24.8		PAW PAW.									S 6.29	
29.8		MAGNOLIA.									F 6.36	
33.4		GREEN RIDGE.										
35.4		HANSROTE.										
38.1		DOE GULLY.									F 6.46	
39.9	DN	ORLEANS ROAD.		3.43	4.46	4.58	5.09	5.47	6.07	6.20	F 6.50	7.19
43.0		LINEBURG.									F 6.54	
45.1		WOODMONT.										
46.2		GREAT CACAPON.									F 7.01	
50.3		SIR JOHN'S RUN.									F 7.08	
55.9	DN	HANCOCK.		4.00	5.05	5.17	5.28	6.05	6.24	6.38	S 7.20	S 7.40
61.4		SLEEPY CREEK.									S 7.27	
64.5	DN	MILLER.		4.09	5.15	5.27	5.38	6.14	6.32	6.46	7.33	7.50
65.3		CHERRY RUN.									F 7.35	
71.4		NORTH MOUNTAIN.									S 7.46	
73.7	DN	WEST CUMBO.		4.20	5.26	5.38	5.49	6.25	6.42	6.56	F 7.50	8.01
76.7		FAWVER.										
79.0	DN	MARTINSBURG.		S 4.31	S 5.38	S 5.50	S 6.00	S 6.37	S 6.51	G 7.05	S 8.04	S 8.12
83.6		VANCLEVESVILLE.									F 8.11	
86.6		KEARNEYSVILLE.									S 8.16	
88.2	DN	HOBBS.	165	4.44	5.51	6.03	6.13	6.49	7.03	7.18	8.20	8.25
90.0		SHENANDOAH JCT.		S 4.49							S 8.27	S 8.29
90.9		DUFFIELDS.										
94.1		ENGLE.									S 8.35	
97.3	DN	HARPER'S FERRY.		S 5.01	6.04	6.15	6.25	F 7.02	7.14	7.29	S 8.44	S 8.42
98.3		SANDY HOOK.										
100.1	DN	WEVERTON.		5.07	6.10	6.20	6.30	7.08	7.19	7.34	S 8.50	8.48
				A.M.	A.M.	A.M.	A.M.	A.M.	A.M.	A.M.	A.M.	A.M.
		Time over Division		2.19	2.22	2.19	1.58	2.15	2.04	2.07	3.05	2.18
		Average speed per hour		43.2	42.3	43.2	46.8	44.5	48.4	47.3	32.3	43.3

Passenger trains will not exceed a speed of 60 miles per hour.

Speed as shown in Special Instruction 5, and such other restrictions as may be in effect, will not be exceeded.

EASTWARD

East End Cumberland Division.
TIME-TABLE No. 53.
April 25, 1948.

Distance from Viaduct Jct.	Train Order Stations.	Stations	Passing Sidings. Capacity in Cars.	FIRST CLASS.											
				4 DAILY A.M.	**8** DAILY P.M.	**22** DAILY P.M.	**54** DAILY Ex. Sunday P.M.	**76** DAILY P.M.	**40** DAILY Ex. Monday P.M.	**32** DAILY P.M.	**12** DAILY P.M.				
	DN	VIADUCT JCT.		......	12.10	2.40	......	......	6.03	6.46	8.32				
0.6	DN	CUMBERLAND.		......	S 12.12 12.17	S 2.42 2.47	......	......	S 6.05 6.20	S 6.50 7.40	S 8.36 8.43				
3.0	DN	EVITTS CREEK.		......	12.22	2.52	......	......	6.25	7.45	8.48				
6.3		NORTH BRANCH.		......	......	......	......	......	......	......	......				
8.1	DN	PATTERSON CREEK.		7.27	12.29	2.59	......	5.36	6.32	7.52	8.55				
14.7		GREEN SPRING.		......	......	......	......	......	......	......	......				
17.3		FRENCH.		......	......	......	......	......	......	......	......				
20.1	DN	OKONOKO.		7.41	12.42	3.12	......	5.48	6.46	8.06	9.08				
21.8		LITTLE CACAPON.		......	......	......	......	......	......	......	......				
24.8		PAW PAW.		......	......	F 3.18	......	......	......	......	F 9.14				
29.8		MAGNOLIA.		......	......	......	......	......	......	......	......				
33.4		GREEN RIDGE.		......	......	......	......	......	......	......	......				
35.4		HANSROTE.		......	......	......	......	......	......	......	......				
38.1		DOE GULLY.		......	......	......	......	......	......	......	......				
39.9	DN	ORLEANS ROAD.		8.03	1.03	3.36	......	6.02	7.08	8.28	9.31				
43.0		LINEBURG.		......	......	......	......	......	......	......	......				
45.1		WOODMONT.		......	......	......	......	......	......	......	......				
46.2		GREAT CACAPON.		......	......	......	......	......	......	......	......				
50.3		SIR JOHN'S RUN.		......	......	......	......	......	......	......	......				
55.9	DN	HANCOCK.		8.21	1.20	S 3.55	......	6.19	7.27	8.46	S 9.51				
61.4		SLEEPY CREEK.		......	......	......	......	......	......	......	......				
64.5	DN	MILLER.		8.30	1.29	4.04	......	6.27	7.36	8.55	10.00				
65.3		CHERRY RUN.		......	......	......	......	......	......	......	......				
71.4		NORTH MOUNTAIN.		......	......	......	......	......	......	......	......				
73.7	DN	WEST CUMBO.		8.41	1.40	4.15	......	6.37	7.47	9.06	10.11				
76.7		FAWVER.		......	......	......	......	......	......	......	......				
79.0	DN	MARTINSBURG.		S 8.51	S 1.50	S 4.26	......	S 6.51	7.58	S 9.17	S10.25				
83.6		VANCLEVESVILLE.		......	......	......	......	......	......	......	......				
86.6		KEARNEYSVILLE.		......	......	......	......	......	......	......	......				
88.2	DN	HOBBS.	165	9.04	2.02	4.39	......	7.02	8.12	9.31	10.38				
90.0		SHENANDOAH JCT.		......	S 2.07	......	......	......	......	......	......				
90.9		DUFFIELDS.		......	......	......	......	......	......	......	......				
94.1		ENGLE.		......	......	......	......	......	......	......	......				
97.3	DN	HARPER'S FERRY.		V 9.17	S 2.20	S 4.52	S 6.44	7.13	8.25	9.44	S10.51				
98.3		SANDY HOOK.		......	......	......	F 6.46	......	......	......	......				
100.1	DN	WEVERTON.		9.22	2.25	4.57	F 6.49	7.17	8.30	9.50	10.57				
				A.M.	P.M.	P.M.	P.M.	P.M.	P.M.	P.M.	P.M.				
		Time over Division		1.55	2.15	2.17	.05	1.41	2.27	3.04	2.25				
		Average speed per hour		48.0	44.5	43.8	33.6	51.3	40.9	32.6	41.4				

Passenger trains will not exceed a speed of 60 miles per hour.

Speed as shown in Special Instruction 5, and such other restrictions as may be in effect, will not be exceeded.

WESTWARD

SouthBranch—Sub-Division.
TIME-TABLE No. 16.
April 28, 1929.

Distance from Green Spring.	Train Order Stations.	STATIONS	Length of Sidings in Cars.	FIRST CLASS		SECOND CLASS
				67	**61**	**65**
				DAILY Ex. Sunday	DAILY Ex. Sunday	DAILY
				A. M.	P. M.	P. M.
	DN	GREEN SPRING.		S 7.05	S 7.40	S 1.20
1.8		MILLEN.	2	F 7.11	F 7.46	F 1.25
3.5		DONALDSON.	3	F 7.17	F 7.52	F 1.29
7.5		SPRINGFIELD.	4	S 7.27	S 8.05	S 1.39
9.2		GRACE.	13	F 7.32	F 8.11	F 1.44
9.9		RITTER.		F 7.34	F 8.13	F 1.46
10.8		RIDGEDALE.	2	F 7.37	F 8.16	F 1.49
12.5		ROCKS.	4	F 7.43	F 8.22	F 1.54
13.5		VANCE.	2	F 7.46	F 8.26	F 1.57
15.2		WAPOCOMO.		F 7.51	F 8.31	F 2.01
15.4		ROMNEY JCT.	20	7.52 / 8.30	8.32	2.02 / 2.12
17.8		WEST ROMNEY.	35	S 8.45		F 2.17
20.8		HAMPSHIRE CLUB.		F 8.55		F 2.23
22.8		JOHNSON.	3	F 9.02		F 2.28
24.1		PANCAKE.	4	F 9.06		F 2.32
26.8		GLEBE.	23	S 9.13		F 2.38
27.8		CAMP WICKHAM.		F 9.16		F 2.41
28.7		TROUGH CLUB.		F 9.18		F 2.43
32.8		SYCAMORE.	3	F 9.32		F 2.54
33.8		McNEILL.	17	F 9.36		F 3.03
35.8		MAPLETON.	2	F 9.42		61 F 3.08
37.2		CUNNINGHAM.	20	F 9.47		S 3.11
38.2		MEADOW.		F 9.50		F 3.13
39.8		MOOREFIELD.	42	S 10.00		S 3.18
41.7		TAYLOR.		62 F 10.20		F 3.23
44.4		BROOK HILL.		F 10.28		F 3.29
46.8		SPRING BROOK.		F 10.36		F 3.34
47.8		DURGON.	10	F 10.40		F 3.37
49.8		WELTON.	4	F 10.45		F 3.42
52.8		PETERSBURG.	48	A 10.55		A 3.50
				A. M.	P. M.	P. M.
		Time over Division		3.50	.52	2 30
		Average speed per hour		13.7	17.7	21.0

WESTWARD

Romney and Romney Junction Sub-Division.
TIME-TABLE No. 16.
April 28, 1929.

Distance from Romney Junction.	Train Order Stations.	STATIONS	Length of Sidings in Cars.	FIRST CLASS			SECOND CLASS		
				367	**369**	**361**	**467**	**469**	**465**
				DAILY Ex. Sunday	DAILY Ex. Sunday	DAILY Ex. Sunday	DAILY Ex. Sunday	Sunday ONLY	DAILY
				A. M.	P. M.	P. M.	A. M.	A. M.	P. M.
		ROMNEY JUNCTION.		7.53	4.15	8.33	11.05	11.49	2.03
0.6	D	ROMNEY.	51	A 7.56	A 4.18	A 8.36	A 11.08	A 11.52	A 2.05
				A. M.	P. M.	P. M.	A. M.	A. M.	P. M.
		Time over Sub-Division		.03	.03	.03	.03	.03	.03
		Average speed per hour		12.0	12.0	12.0	12.0	12.0	12.0

No. 467 is superior to No. 462, No. 465 is superior to No. 466, No. 469 is superior to No. 464, No. 369 is superior to No. 364, No. 367 is superior to No. 368, Romney Junction to Romney.

Trains shown as second class will carry passengers.

Trains will not exceed a speed of 25 miles per hour between Green Spring and Petersburg, except speed for motor train as shown in Special Instruction 5.

Speed as shown in Special Instruction 5, and such other restrictions as may be in effect, will not be exceeded.

Chapter 11

Color Pictorial

OVER A CENTURY AGO, Harpers Ferry was a great tourist attraction as evidenced by this spread in an album published by the Union News Company for sale on trains and in stations. In the two bottom pictures, note the B&O trestle/bridge on Arsenal Island.

Jeff Madden

CINDERS REVISITED the 1930 Harpers Ferry Bridge in September 1978 as the Chessie Steam Special raced westbound. No fire resulted.

Jeff Madden

BY JULY OF 1972, F units in this painting scheme were quite rare on B&O lines ... the train is westbound on the "new" bridge heading literally and figuratively toward the sunset.

193

EAST END

Michael P. Welsh

"C-C-C-OLD" was the caption written by Mike Welsh for this splendid view of the Harpers Ferry station taken 11 December 1989, looking toward the North Pole.

IN SEPTEMBER OF 1981, century and half-century met at Milepost 100 in Martinsburg as General Motors 50 led the way.

Jeff Madden

POWER NOT OFTEN photographed is MARC (Maryland Rail Commuter) 7183 approaching the "station" at Martinsburg in October 1984 with the ancient freight house in the background.

COLOR PICTORIAL

THE EASTBOUND TURBO made it as far as Martinsburg on this spring day in 1972, framed by the station and east roundhouse. To be more precise, photographer Hollis *says* she was eastbound ... you cannot tell by looking.

THE 6955 and at least two mates, resplendent in spanking new Chessie System paint, pauses on the Frog Hollow Branch switch on a July night in 1977 with NA Tower in the background in one of the nicest night scenes we have ever seen.

ANOTHER EAST END cause for tears ... the east roundhouse in hot ruin on 14 May 1990. The vandals who caused this atrocity were "no Stonewall Jackson," to paraphrase a current expression.

EAST END

APRIL FOOLS DAY in 1979 produced a bit of a surprise as WM 7596 leads a westbounder through North Mountain Cut. Far from the deepest cut on B&O lines, the steep sides indicate that the rock formations in this area are stable.

AN EASTBOUNDER approaches West Cumbo on the Low Grade line at 1:45 p.m. on April Fools Day in 1990 as Operator M. D. Duvall surveys the scene. W has a spiral staircase, somewhat unusual in B&O towers. Reportedly only QN at Washington DC and Sand Patch on Pittsburgh East have similar arrangements.

Michael P. Welsh

R396 with 2104, 6513 and 4252 at the sharp end roars by W at 11:56 a.m. 29 October 1989 apparently destined to stay on the old main.

Michael P. Welsh

COLOR PICTORIAL

Gary Schlerf

Brian Paulus

MILLER (R) at Cherry Run, active today and when this photo was taken in September of 1973.

R342 (Cumberland-Conrail/Enola Yard) has completed its duties at Hancock yard and is enroute east for Hagerstown via Cherry Run and Big Pool on 31 August 1988, passing the B&O Hancock station with engine 8382 in the lead. Engine 6146 is being held with a westbounder. The track on the left is the branch to Berkeley Springs.

LED BY GP40-2 6010, R137 has passed HO Tower at Milepost 123 in Hancock and is speeding to Cumberland and eventually Chicago on 5 October 1988.

Brian Paulus

EAST END

Michael P. Welsh

ON BRIDGE 5 on the Berkeley Springs Branch, B853 Engine 2073 drags out a load of fine sand on 21 October 1991 and in the process gives hope for all model railroaders ... note the kink in the track at the bottom of the photo.

THERE IS A LITTLE more to the mining of sand than just digging it out of the ground ... Engine 6565 of B853 is switching at U.S. Silica's rather impressive plant near Berkeley Springs at noon on 31 October 1991. Now *that* would make an interesting model.

Michael P. Welsh

COLOR PICTORIAL

POSED AND hand colored, this magnificent publicity photo graced a B&O "Coals" book in the 1940s. The scene, of course, is looking westerly just west of Orleans Road with Magnolia Cutoff tracks on the left and original line tracks on the right, all on the same gradient and with a trio of Big Sixes starring in the show. There is truth in art . . . eastbound coal dominated the East End.

Michael P. Welsh

R217 ENGINES 7690 and 7676 has just left the west portal of Randolph Tunnel on cutoff tracks at 9:32 a.m. 22 October 1991, racing through vivid Fall splendour and hinting that auto rack cars may be pushing clearance limits. The trace of the original line can be seen between the train and the Potomac River.

EAST END

Brian Paulus

AN EASTBOUND grain train with an SD60-SD50-SD60 lashup crosses Kessler Bridge and is about to enter Graham Tunnel on 10 August 1991, a beautiful day in a beautiful valley. The low line passed under the bridge on the right and followed the river to Magnolia.

COAL CARS still roll on the East End ... here, on 21 September 1991, trio 8576, 8568 and 8251 keep 107 cars moving at 40 mph while exiting Stuart Tunnel.

FAMOUS 614 leans into the Concrete Wall curve in September 1980 with a tour train, bouncing her exhaust off the rock cutting and showering the long-gone low line with cinders.

Michael P. Welsh

Jeff Madden

CO-AUTHOR Roberts is so fascinated by the Magnolia Cutoff that he has modeled it in HO scale ... on this page we see various scenes between Graham and Carothers Tunnels on different days in the Fall of 1949. Coal cars, drags and the *Cincinnatian* on the high line and two passenger trains on the low line attract the eye. The *Cincinnatian*, incidentally, was scratchbuilt by Andy Holzopfel and was his first B&O modeling project.

EAST END

Brian Paulus

THE CAPITOL LIMITED, P030, stirs the heart as well as snow at 10:15 a.m. on 23 November 1989 as she sweeps east between Okonoko and Paw Paw on cutoff rails. We must say this is one of the finest railroad photographs we have ever seen.

WITH 6081 followed by the 6053 and about thirty cars, R347 pops out of the west portal of Carothers Tunnel on 22 October 1991 and is about to enter Paw Paw cut. The alert reader may have noticed that we did not show this portal in the Magnolia Cutoff chapter ... we knew this fine photo was coming.

Michael P. Welsh

COLOR PICTORIAL

COAL CARS on R343 (Enola Yard-Cumberland) pass beneath the signal bridge at MP 164 on 4 November 1989 ... the 8638 leads the way. This bridge was removed in 1991 in conjunction with installation of CTC and closure of FN at Patterson Creek ... the line to the right is the South Branch Valley Railroad.

Brian Paulus

GREEN SPRING and the tie plant were rather startled to see steam again in September 1980 as the 614 dashes westbound with a tour train. More than one observer feels that the 614 was the most handsome steam locomotive ever built.

Jeff Madden

CHICKEN FEATHERS OR NOT, good taste prevails on the SBVRR ... in May of 1992 they repainted the 6604 in full B&O passenger livery and here she is on 18 July 1992 north of Romney Junction. This GP9 was built in April 1955 and served B&O under three numbers ... 6604, 3411 and 751. We hope the rumor is true that she will be in Cumberland to help celebrate the 150th anniversary of B&O's arrival in that city.

David P. Lubic

EAST END

F40PH 263 leads the *Capitol Limited* westbound on No. 2 track past FN at Patterson Creek on 30 April 1991 ... in eight months, the tower would be out of service, but happily that would not be the case for the *Cap*.

Brian Paulus

Michael P. Welsh

OPERATOR Dave Findley tends shop in FN on 8 December 1991, one of the last few days of normal operation for this distinctive tower.

CW40-8 7731 pulls eastbound Q396 (Saginaw-Philadelphia) through the Mexico interlocker on 7 October 1991.

Brian Paulus

COLOR PICTORIAL

CUMBERLAND YARDS in the summer of 1972 stretch to the horizon. The new 1960 westbound yard is in the foreground on the right (note the train being humped). In the distance at upper left is the eastbound yard and shop area.

GP40 6573, in Western Maryland paint on 5 April 1988, leading R344 (Cumberland-Brunswick) past Mexico Tower. The 6573 was the last unit in WM colors and she was reportedly dropped from the CSX roster 25 June 1992 in Cincinnati ... still red and white.

Brian Paulus

EAST END

THE 255 with two mint Sentinel Service cars pose in front of the eastbound retarder control tower, bringing joy to more than one reader.

THE EASTBOUND yard in 1972, with the shop and servicing complex at lower right . . . this view is, of course, easterly. Note the truncated roundhouse . . . the hump is in the center of the photo and the westbound yard can be seen in the distance.

COLOR PICTORIAL

THE QUEEN CITY HOTEL on a hand-tinted postcard dated 8 October 1911 is mellowed by trees, gardens and ivy, but remains regal.

AN UNUSUAL angle on the hotel from the east, dated 27 December 1912, gives prominence to the fine gardens and pond while guiding the eye away from the power house on the right.

THE PAINT is new in 1953, at least some trees remain and while the gardens are gone, at least the lawn is well tended. Whatever the merits of economic argument, no one can see the photos on this page without coming away with the feeling that something very fine was lost.

EAST END

B&OHS

WHERE THE B&O WORLD all comes together ... an easterly view of Viaduct Junction in the early 1970s with the West End curving off to the right over the Wills Creek viaduct, the line to Pittsburgh departing at bottom and the East End wending off to downtown Cumberland in the distance.

Chapter 12

Operations

Throughout the preceding chapters, the reader has already received an insight into operations on the East End . . . the inherent problems of volume and terrain as well as the various solutions applied at different times by B&O management.

Traffic can be categorized into three broad groupings . . . First Class (passenger and express), Second Class (fast freight/Quick Dispatch) and Third Class (slow/tonnage/drags). The reader knows that the predominant traffic was eastbound, was heaviest in the third class category (principally coal) and that B&O practiced "doubling" train length and weight pouring off the mountain divisions . . . initially at Piedmont and later Keyser on the St. Louis line and at Cumberland on the Chicago line. "Doubling," incidentally, worked in both directions . . . westward slow freight (primarily empty coal cars) went over the East End in double-length and were "singled" at Piedmont/Keyser and Cumberland for mountain passage.

Yet there is evidence that for the first forty or so years the practice was to "triple." An 1863 report states that First Division freight trains (Baltimore to Martinsburg) averaged 25 sixteen-ton cars and Second Division (Martinsburg to Piedmont) averaged 30 . . . yet over the Third Division west from Piedmont the average was only 9 cars. This subject has been thoroughly explored in the book *West End* with the net conclusion that B&O did not begin helper operations until c. 1880, opting until then to balance power and car movements in each direction.

We have reported that there is some slight evidence that tonnage adjustments were made at Martinsburg for movement east over Nine Mile Grade in the 1850s, but that does not refute our principal conclusion.

We must admit that the same 1863 report alluded to helper engines being stationed on the First and Fourth (Grafton to Wheeling) Divisions at "80 foot grades" and, indeed, on the Third Division at "106 and 116 foot grades." We suspect these helpers were extra headend power and, in any event, no mention was made about the East End. Only in an 1889 Form 6 do we find reference to a "helper switch" and that was at North Mountain.

Whatever the validity of our reasoning, there is no question that the East End was awash in traffic and helpers in the 1890s and well into this century . . . the reader should study the train movement chart at the bottom of page 217 for a study of a 1914 bag of worms, keeping in mind that the volume was down about 5% from the preceding year because of the outbreak of World War I. The Magnolia Cutoff was opened just in time and even with that there were still problems . . . notice the westbound backup between Okonoko and Patterson Creek. Trains for Keyser still had to crossover to get on the P Creek Cutoff and that slowed up things in both directions.

As to first and second class trains, the reader should study the employee timetables on pages 184-192 for an insight into *that* problem . . . and the timetables don't include extra sections and plain old extras (B&O ran a lot of tour trains). Let alone MOW work extras and local switching runs. If a dispatcher could survive on Cumberland East, he could run any railroad anywhere under any conditions so long as he had enough antiacid pills.

And the reader should also study the 1949 Adjusted Tonnage Ratings for the East End on page 212 to gain some appreciation for the mental juggling a dispatcher had to endure. Diesels were beginning to arrive in that era, but we will spare

EAST END

the reader a glimpse into the complications this new development brought to operating people. For more turmoil, read the 1954 Form 6 extracts on pages 213 to 217 and count the number of shippers which had to be served along the East End.

Let the reader see if he can follow the events on 20 December 1926 between Hancock and Sleepy Creek. Extra East 4476 left Hancock at 4:02 p.m. on No. 1 track while Extra East 6110 left at 4:03 p.m. on the middle track . . . the latter arrived at Sleepy Creek at 4:10 p.m., two minutes ahead of EE4476. Both trains passed Extra West 6109 running on No. 3 track. At 1:47 p.m. Extra West 6135 arrived at Sleepy Creek and was diverted to the middle track to allow Train No. 15, passing Sleepy Creek at 1:53 p.m., to run around. Follow that? During the week ending 10 December 1926, a *daily* average of 102.2 trains traversed the East End just between Miller and Orleans Road. Which pod is the pea under?

And, of course, Murphy was alive and well on 30 January 1952. It was a nice day, clear and cold with temperatures ranging between 8 and 28 degrees. Following are the "unusual occurrences" listed on the Dispatcher's Record of Movement of Trains for that day:

W signal lights out; EW 7601 leaking steam; broken rail 3 track CK; broken rail 2 track Reedson; switch 4 to 2 track failing RN; No. 97 Engine 803 traction motor inoperative; EW 7623 leaking steam *bad*; No. 97-803 now has sticking brakes on 50th car; No. 94-941 Mexico yard reports sliding wheels; No. 94-7615 HO air pump failing; EE 7608 NA 4 track circuit out; No. 94-809 R steam generator shut down; EE 7628 engine slipping, sand low, had to scrape down; No. 96-805 CK set off car with hotbox; EE 4459-4471 WA brakes sticking two cars, cut out both; No. 96-7616 RN no water and did not clear stoker when filled in on 4 track and then starting light burning and call on phone to see if helper on. What did he say? And perhaps the reader has noticed that we have made snide remarks about Alco diesels . . . engines 803 and 809 were B&O Class DF7, made by guess who.

The day of 30 January 1952 was a typical one on the East End. Westward there were 13 passenger trains, 12 QD (including 3 CSD on at Cherry Run), 11 extras (including 3 on at Cumbo and 3 at Cherry Run) and 3 locals. Of the QDs, 6 were preblocked at or east of Brunswick for points west of Cumberland. The extras were almost all coal cars ranging from 140 to 150 cars.

Eastward there were 14 passenger, 8 QD (2 CSD off at Cherry Run), 9 extras (including 6 from the P Creek Cutoff, 2 off at Cherry Run and 1 at Cumbo) and 1 local. The extras were almost entirely coal in 120-130 car trains.

Martinsburg helpers that day were engines 6179 and 6190. Four extras in each direction passed the Harpers Ferry-Brunswick route off the "W&P." The Berkeley Springs Branch was busy, with Q7f 4835 and E60 3130 bringing out 90 loads and delivering 84 empties. The South Branch produced only 9 loads and 16 empties, powered by Alco DS9a switcher 227 . . . even an Alco could handle that tonnage. This day, incidentally, was a Wednesday . . . QD traffic is usually heavier in mid-week.

Of these movements, 27 west and 26 east passed Martinsburg. Fifty years later, on 10 July 1992, there were 24 west and 20 east past the same point. The traffic mix was different, but there was still a lot of it.

During the calendar year 1991, 53,320,571 Gross Ton Miles (GTM) passed between Viaduct Junction and North Branch, 66% of it eastbound.

Cumberland received 31,781,862 GTM from what is now known as the Keystone Subdivision (that name for Pittsburgh East makes a B&O student gag), 25,240,914 GTM from the Mountain Subdivision (the West End) and 1,285,500 GTM from the Hampshire Sub (ex WM). There is local traffic, so the numbers do not add up exactly.

Of the volume through North Branch, 7,714,000 GTM went through Cherry Run on the ex-WM to and from Hagerstown.

At Harpers Ferry, 47,661,557 GTM passed, again 66% of it eastbound.

So even today, the East End is alive and well and it is still B&O's "Neck of the Bottle." Long live the Queen.

POWER DEVELOPMENT on the B&O throughout history was primarily spurred by the needs of the mountain divisions, the reasoning being that if it worked on The Hill it would work anywhere ... the book *West End* provides insights into this aspect of B&O history as well as progress in car design. Yet the East End traffic problem inspired two very significant classes of B&O steam power ... the Mikado 2-8-2 and the Santa Fe 2-10-2. As to the former, this class was spawned as an emergency solution to East End traffic intensity as shown in the Magnolia Cutoff chapter. B&O purchased literally hundreds of Mikes in class Q ... the first 150 Q1 engines were built by Baldwin on a crash basis with the first fourteen being delivered 2 January 1911 and from then until March of 1923, when the last Q4b was completed, B&O was a Mikado railroad in non-mountain territory. Of course, many more of this wheel arrangement were acquired with the purchase of other railroads and there were still many Mikes on the roster at the end of the steam era. B&O pioneered massive use of this type of power ... even the mighty Pennsylvania Railroad did not build its first Mike until April of 1914. Here we see Q1c 4221 at Sir Johns Run with 63 loaded steel coal cars weighing 4,600 gross tons, photographed as part of B&O's report to the public on their conquest of the East End congestion problem. The 4221 was built in June of 1913, was improved many times and was finally buried at DuBois on 19 February 1952.

Howard N. Barr, Sr.

TO PRODUCE still another leap forward in efficiency on the East End, B&O ordered 125 "Big Six" engines from Baldwin and Alco in the years 1923-26 as classes S1 and S1a ... these giant locomotives boasted about a two-thirds increase in tractive power over the Mikado classes and became the backbone of East End motive power until the diesel. Here the Queen City Hotel and a seldom photographed penstock bridge overlook S1a 6194 about to help P1aa 5076 and Train 21 on 6 July 1947 ... yes, these splendid engines could perform in passenger as well as tonnage and QD service.

THE BALTIMORE AND OHIO RAILROAD COMPANY

CUMBERLAND DIVISION - EAST END

ADJUSTED TONNAGE RATINGS FOR STEAM LOCOMOTIVES

\multicolumn{6}{c}{WESTBOUND}	RUN	\multicolumn{6}{c}{EASTBOUND}
Routes	Remarks	KB-1	S-1	EM-1	Service		Service	EM-1	S-1	KB-1	Remarks	Routes
All	Single	3000	3200	4500	93	Cumberland - Brunswick	All Q.D.	5500	4000	3750	Single	All
"	"	3200	3400	4800	97	" - "	"	8000	6000	5600	Hlpr."A"	"X"
						" - "	"	9000	7000	6550	Hlpr."B"	"X"
						" - "	Tonnage	5700	4000	3650	Single	No. Mountain
All	Single	3350	3650	5175	Tonnage-Loads	" - "	"	6750	4750	4350	Single	C.Run Low Grade
"	"	3100	3400	4500	Ton.Mtys&R.T. 89	" - "	"	9750	7750	7350	Hlpr."A"	"X"
						" - "	"	11500	9500	8700	Hlpr."B"	"X"
All	Single	4200	4600	6500	Tonnage	Cumberland - Cumbo	Tonnage	7400	5200	4750	Single	"Y"
"	"	3350	3650	4500	Ton. All Mtys	" - "	"	11500	9500	8700	Single	"X"
"	"	3900	4200	6000	97	Cumbld.-C.Run-Hagerstown	94	6200	4500	4200	Single	All
						" - " - "	96	5800	4200	3900	Single	All
All	Single	4200	4600	6500	Tonnage-Loads	" - " - "	Q.D. Extra	11200	8200	7650	Single	"Z"
"	"	3350	3650	4500	Ton. All Mtys	" - " - "	Tonnage	12000	11300*	10500*	Single	"Z"
"	"	3200	3400	4800	97	Keyser - Brunswick						
"	"	3350	3650	5175	Tonnage-Loads	" - "	Tonnage	5700	4000	3650	Single	All
"	"	3100	3400	4500	Tonnage All Mtys & R.T.89	" - "	"	9750	7750	7350	Hlpr."A"	"X"
						" - "	"	11500	9500	8700	Hlpr."B"	"X"
All	Single	3750	4100	5700	Tonnage-Loads	Keyser - Cumbo	Tonnage	7400	5200	4750	Single	"Y"
"	"	3350	3650	4500	Tonnage-Mtys	" - "	"	11500	9500	8700	Single	"X"
"	"	3750	4100	5700	Tonnage-Loads	Keyser-C.Run-Hagerstown	Tonnage	11500	9500	8700	Single	"Z"
All	Single	3350	3650	4500	Ton. All Mtys	" - " - "						

Note: Doubleheaders will be rated at 90% of combined ratings of engines used
* - Limited by Western Maryland Railway Tonnage Rating.

FULL SLOW FREIGHT RATINGS FOR SINGLE LOCOMOTIVES OVER RULING GRADES

RATING DISTRICTS	Grade	EM-1	EL-5A	S-1	KB-1	Q-4	Q-1C
Keyser - Patterson Creek	0.30	11500	10000	9500	8700	6750	5500
Cumberland - Patterson Creek	0.25	12000	12000	12000	11000	9000	7500
Patterson Creek-C. Run via Magnolia Cut Off (High Line)	0.25	12000	12000	12000	11000	9000	7500
Patterson Creek-C. Run via Hansrote (Old Line)	0.70	7400	6250	5200	4750	3750	3300
Cherry Run-Martinsburg via Cherry Run Low Grade	0.30	11500	10000	9500	8700	6750	5500
Cherry Run-Martinsburg via North Mountain	1.00	5700	5000	4000	3650	3000	2500
Martinsburg - Brunswick	0.90	6750	5800	4750	4350	3600	3000
Brunswick - West Cumbo	1.00	5175	4500	3650	3350	2800	2300
West Cumbo or Cherry Run - Cumberland	0.50	7000	6350	5200	4750	3900	3150
Patterson Creek - Keyser	0.80	5700	5000	4100	3750	3000	2500

DESCRIPTION OF ROUTES

Route "X" - High Line and Low Grade
Route "Y" - Old Line and Low Grade
Route "Z" - High Line

DESCRIPTION OF HELPER SERVICE

"A" - 1-Q-1C Cherry Run or Martinsburg to Hobbs
"B" - 1-S-1 Cherry Run or Martinsburg to Hobbs

ADJUSTMENT IN TONS PER CAR

DISTRICTS	A Above 35°	B 20° to 35°	C 0° to 20°	D Below 0°
East End - Eastbound	15	25	35	45
East End - Westbound	7	11	14	18

R. A. J. Morrison
Superintendent

Office of Assistant to Vice President, Operation & Maintenance (J.H.H.),
Baltimore, Maryland - August 15, 1949.

EASTERN REGION
CUMBERLAND DIVISION

Form 6 Official List No. 30–1 Jan 1954

J. Edwards, Jr., General Manager
H. L. Exley, Asst. to General Manager
A. W. Conley, Superintendent
E. H. Riecks, General Passenger Agent
M. W. Grove, Division Passenger Agent
G. M. Gemmill, Division Freight Agent

LEGEND
- C— Coupon Ticket Office
- D— Derricks or Cranes
- G— Frog and Switch Removed
- K— Coaling Point
- L— Livestock Facilities
- M— Mine or Plant Closed
- P— Prepaid Order Book Agency
- S— Track Scales
- T— Turntable
- V— Third Track
- W— Water Tank
- Y— Wye Track

Index Reference	Siding Capacity (Cars 45 feet long)				Valuation Section	Telegraph Call	Station Number		Stations and Sidings with character references, population and additional index references	County	Miles from	Agents, Etc.	Foreign Lines and Track Connections
	Passing	Company	Joint	Private			For Engineering Dept. Use	For Reporting Car Movements					
									BALTIMORE AND OHIO R. R. **Main Line**		Park Junct.		
1685					1–MD–17.3				West End Baltimore Division.. Mile Post B–79 & Div. Marker (1186)......Md. Beginning of Cumberland Div..	Washington	173.2		
1686							268	268	Sandy Hook, P. 300.............. "		174.7		
1687									Harper's Ferry Tunnel {East Portal........ " / West Portal......... "		175.3 / 175.5		
1688									Shenandoah Sub-division Switch (1587).. "		175.6		
1689									Md.-West Va. State Line........Md.-W.Va.		175.7		
1690						HF	269	269	**Harpers Ferry**, P. 825—**CP** (1590)....W.Va.	Jefferson	175.7	L. D. Nichols....F. & T.	
1691		16					272A	272A	Kelly Siding.................. "		178.7		
1692						N			Beginning of Third Track....... "		178.9		
1693							272	272	**Englo**, P. 125................ "		179.0	L. W. Rodgers...F. & T.	
1694									Baker Branch Switch (1974)..... "		179.1		
1696		4					275A	275A	Baker Elevator Co............. "		182.0		
1697							275	275	Duffields, P. 40............... "		182.0		
1698		12					276	276	**Shenandoah Junction**, P. 250—**C**.... "		183.0	W. L. Fink....J. F. & T.	N.&W.—a,o.
1699		6					276B	276B	Bardane, P. 75—**L**............ "		181.5		
1700	223						277	277	Hobbs........................ "		184.7		
1701		5					278	278	Hobbs Siding—Back-off........ "		184.9		
1702		12					280C	280C	Quarry Track.................. "		185.8		
1703		17					280	280	Kearneysville, P. 350........... "		186.4		
1704				4			280A	280A	Hodges-Lemen Co.............. "		186.4		
A1704									County Line................... "		188.1		
1705									Yard Limit Board............... "		188.7		
A1705				110			281	281	U. S. Government (N. D. Baker Hospital). "		188.9		
1706							282	282	Vanclevesville, P. 50........... "		189.3		
1707		37					284	284	Blairton, P. 300................ "		191.4		
1708				204			284A	284A	Blair Limestone Co............. "		191.5		
							286A	286A	Continental Clay Products Corp...... "		192.9		
1710		2		211			286B	286B	Martinsburg Light & Heat Co..... "		193.5		
									R. M. Roach.................. "				
1711									End of Third Track............. "		193.8		
1712		3					286D	286D	Martinsburg Fruit Exchange..... "		193.8		
1713									Frog Hollow Branch Switch (1979)... "		193.9		
1714	62	271				NA	286	286	**Martinsburg**, P. 17,000—**CKPW** (1980).... "	Berkeley	193.9	D. A. Leonard.....F. / W. T. Bergdoll......T.	
1715							286C	286C	Martinsburg Shops............. "		193.9		
1716		11					286F	286F	Elevator Siding................ "		194.0		
1717		5					287B	287B	Consumer Fuel Co............. "		194.2		
1718		4		8	1–WV–36.1		287C	287C	J. W. Bishop Co............... "		194.3		
1719		15					287E	287E	National Fruit Products Co...... "		194.3		
1720							288F	288F	West Quarry Spur............. "		194.5		
1721				5			288E	288E	American Oil Co............... "		194.8		
1722		42					288A	288A	R. R. Fellows.................. "		195.1		
1723				24			288B	288B	Pennsylvania Crossing.......... "		194.5		P.R.R.—a,o.
1724		70					288C	288C	Pennsylvania Interchange....... "		194.9		P.R.R.—a,f.
1725							289	289	Fawver....................... "		196.2		
1726		8		4			290A	290A	Thorn-Porterfield Siding........ " / State Road Commission......... "		197.3		
1727						W	292A	292A	West Cumbo Tower—C. R. & P. Branch Conn. (1994)................. "		199.1 / 199.2		
1728							292	292	West Cumbo, P. 20............. "		200.8		
1729		65					293	293	Pullout Track-Cumbo Yard...... "		201.5		
1730		78					295	295	**North Mountain**, P. 110......... "		201.5	F. W. Kilmer....F. & T.	
1731		12					295E	295E	Eastern Fruit Growers, Inc....... "		202.1		
1732				25			295D	295D	United Clay Products Co....... "		202.4		
1733									Yard Limit Board............... "		207.0		
1734									County Line................... "				
1735							301	301	**Cherry Run**, P. 100—(1990)...... "		207.6	L. G. Shank....J. F. & T.	W.Md.—a,f.
1736		6					301A	301A	Peach Siding.................. "		207.6		
1737									Beginning of Third Track........ "		208.3		
1738									C. R. & P. Switch (1987)........ "		208.4		
1739						R	302	302	Miller (1988).................. "		208.4		
1740		20					305	305	Sleepy Creek, P. 200............ "		211.5		
A1740		4					307	307	West Bound Back-off Siding..... "		213.1		
1741		182					310	310	**Hancock**, P. 1,037—**CS** (see Note)....Md.-W.Va.		217.0	J. L. Brown......F. & T.	
1742							310B	310B	Berkeley Springs Branch Switch (2004).. "		217.0		
1743						HO			Hancock Tower—Beginning of Fourth Track.................... "	Morgan	217.2		
1744		19		7			311A	311A	Penna. Glass Sand Corp........ " / Penna. Pulverizing Co.......... "		218.1		
1745							313	313	Round Top.................... "		220.1		
1746		64					315B	315B	Sir Johns Run Coal Tipple—**KW**.. "		221.9		
1747		14					315A	315A	Company Siding............... "		222.4		
1748							316	316	Sir Johns Run, P. 150........... "		222.6		
1749									End of Fourth Track............ "		222.7		
1750		23					320	320	Great Cacapon, P. 1,052........ "		226.7		
1751		2					320B	320B	W. B.-Back-off................. "		227.2		

Note—Hancock, W. Va. (a local station on the Baltimore and Ohio R. R.) and Hancock, Md. (a local station on the W. Md. R'y), are located on opposite banks of the Potomac River and connected by an overhead bridge.

EASTERN REGION
CUMBERLAND DIVISION

Index Reference	\multicolumn{4}{c}{SIDING CAPACITY Cars 45 feet long}			Valuation Section	Telegraph Call	STATION NUMBER		STATIONS AND SIDINGS with character references, population and additional index references	County	Miles from	AGENTS, Etc.	Foreign Lines and Track Connections
	Passing	Company	Joint	Private				For Engineering Dept. Use	For Reporting Car Movements					
										Main Line—Con.		Park Junct.		
1752								321	321	Woodmont..............W.Va.		227.8		
1753								323	323	Lineburg, P. 25............ "		229.8		
1754								326	326	Orleans Road, P. 96........ "		232.9		
1755		2						326A	326A	East Bound Back-off Track.. "		233.1		
1756							AD	326B	326B	Orleans Road Tower (2009)—Magnolia Cut-off Switch......... "		233.3		
1757										End of Third Track......... "		233.3		
1758								327	327	Rockwell Run (Water Station)—**W** (2010)... "		233.8		
1759		2						328A	328A	West Bound Hot Box Track.. "		234.6		
1760								328	328	Doe Gully, P. 40, (2012)..... "		235.0		
1761										Magnolia Cut-off—Connection.. "		237.2		
1762								331	331	Hansrote, P. 200............ "		237.7		
1763								333	333	Green Ridge............... "		239.4		
1764								333A	333A	Emergency Detour Connection—W.M.R'y.. "		239.7		W.M Ry—a,o.
1765		4						336	336	Magnolia, P. 125........... "	Morgan	243.0		
1766		6						336A	336A	West Bound-Back-off....... "		243.5		
1767		15						341A	341A	Consolidated Orchard Co.... "		247.9		
1768				8				341D	341D	Appalachian Orchard Co.... "		247.9		
1769		52						341	341	**Paw Paw**, P. 990.......... "		248.0	B. M. Holliday.... F. & T.	
1770		5		51				341B	341B	H. Brock & Sons........... "		248.0		
1771										County Line.............. "		249.0		
1772		10						344	344	Little Cacapon, P. 20 (2022).. "		251.0		
1773						1—WV—36.1	NO	345	345	Okonoko Tower—(2023)—Switch to Magnolia Cut-off........ "		252.2		
1774										Beginning of Third Track.... "		252.5		
1775		11						347	347	Okonoko, P. 51............ "		252.9		
1776		9						349	349	French.................... "	Hampshire	255.5		
1777	153	10					GI	351	351	**Green Spring**, P. 300—**WY** (2025).. "		258.1	J. N. Friday..... F. & T.	
1778										South Branch Switch (2024).. "		258.2		
1779		616						352	352	Tie Treating Plant......... "		259.0		
1780										County Line............. "		260.5		
1781		4						355	355	Dans Run................. "		262.4		
1782							FN			Patterson Creek Tower (2081)—P. C. & P. Branch Conn.......... "		264.4		
1783										End of Third Track......... "		264.4		
1784		15						358	358	Patterson Creek, P. 150..... "	Mineral	264.7		W.Md.—b,o.
1785										West Va.-Md. State Line.....W.Va.-Md.		266.3		
1786										Yard Limit Board......... "		266.5		
1787		8						360	360	North Branch, P. 168.......Md.		266.5		
1788										Beginning of Third Track.... "		266.6		
1789								363C	363C	Emergency Detour Connection—W.M.R'y.. "		267.1		W.M R'y—a,o.
1790		4						363A	363A	Evitts Creek Water Station—**W**... "		269.5		
1791							GE	363	363	Evitts Creek............... "		269.8		
										Yard Masters Office....... "		270.3	R. W. Pitcher... T. T. M.	
								363D	363D	Virginia Lane-Inlet of Eastbound Yard..... "		270.8	L. E. Madden.. G. Y. M.	
1792										Locomotive Shop—**KTW**... "				
		386						363F	363F	Receiving Tracks.......... "				
		519						363F	363F	Classification—**S**—Tracks... "				
		1757					·	363G	363G	Miscellaneous Tracks—**L**—Team Track.... "				
1793										Beginning of Fourth Track... "		270.8		
1794		33						364A	364A	Taylor Lead............... "		270.8		
1795		4		13				364B	364B	Hiser Supply Co........... "				
1796		63		7				364C	364C	South Cumberland Planing Mill Co.. "				
1797		651						364D	364D	Hump-West-Bound Yard... "		271.5		
										Receiving & Classification.. "				
1798		1		1				364E	364E	Cumberland Macaroni Mfg. Co.. "		271.5		
1799				6				365B	365B	Cumberland Undergarment Co.. "		271.8		
1800		7		1	1—MD—40.1			365C	365C	Feldstein Iron & Metal Co... "	Allegany	271.8		
										Spur Distributing Co....... "				
1801		30						365D	365D	Western Md. Conn.—**Y**.... "		271.8		WMd.—a,f.
1802		6						365E	365E	Cumberland Steel Co....... "		272.0		
1803										Lead—Rolling Mill Yard.... "		272.1		
1804		266						365F	365F	Rolling Mill—**W**........... "				
1805		5		2				365G	365G	Cumberland Lumber Co.... "				
1806							WC			Queen City Hotel—Passenger Station..... "		272.2	L. B. Cross........... F.	
1807							DU			Dispatcher's Office........ "		272.2	R. G. Smith..... J. T.	W.Md.—a.
1808								365	365	**Cumberland**, P. 37,679—**CPWY**.... "		272.2	W. S. Beggs..... C. B.	P.R.R.—a,f.
1809										Storage Warehouse Track.. "		272.3		
1810		2						365H	365H	Farmers Feed & Supply Co... "				
										Sunshine Feed Store....... "				
1811		22						365J	365J	Tri-State Mill & Mine Supply Co.. "				
										Armour & Co............ "				
										Swift & Co............... "				
										Southern States Cooperative.. "				
1812										End of Fourth Track....... "		272.4		
1813		3						365L	365L	L. Bernstein & Co......... "		272.4		
										Merchants Wholesale Grocery.. "				
1814		6						365M	365M	The Kenneweg Co......... "		272.5		
1815		89						365P	365P	Cumberland Freight Station—**D**.. "		272.5		
1816		15		2				365Q	365Q	D. R. Kitzmiller Co........ "		272.6		
										Schriver & Sons........... "				
1317		1						365R	365R	Potomac Produce Co....... "		272.6		

EASTERN REGION
CUMBERLAND DIVISION

Index Reference	Siding Capacity - Passing	Siding Capacity - Company	Siding Capacity - Joint	Siding Capacity - Private	Valuation Section	Telegraph Call	Station Number - Engineering	Station Number - Reporting	Stations and Sidings	County	Miles from	Agents, Etc.	Foreign Lines and Track Connections
									Main Line—Con.		Park Junct.		
1818					1-MD-40.1				End of Third Track.................Md.		272.7		
1819						ND	366	366	Viaduct Junction (Junction with Pittsburgh Div.) (4950)		272.7		
1820					1-MD-40.2		366H	366H	Wharf Branch Connection........		273.1		
B1820				12	30-MD-67.1		367H	367H	Buchanan Lumber Co. (Wharf Branch)		273.2		
C1820			3				367N	367N	City of Cumberland..............		273.2		
D1820				8			367M	367M	Cumberland Contracting Co.....		273.5		
1821				15			367	367	Beall St. Siding.................		273.4		
1822				5			367A	367A	Smith Siding (C. & P. R. R.)...		273.5		
1823				31			367C	367C	Potomac Edison Co..............		274.0		
1824				172			367D	367D	Kelly-Springfield Tire Co.......	Allegany	274.7		
1825											275.8		
1826							1003	1003	Yard Limit Board...............		275.9		
									Baker Branch		Engle-Baker Branch Switch		
1974		3			1-WV-36.2	N	272	272	Baker Branch Switch—Engle (1694)...W.Va.	Jefferson	0.0	See Index 1693	
1975							E 0	20000	Main Line Connection...........		0.4		
1976		12					E 2	20002	Bakerton, P. 288—**SW**........		2.3		
1977		56					E 2B	20002B	Standard Lime & Stone Co.....		2.4		
1978									End of Branch.................		2.7		
									Frog Hollow Branch		Martinsburg		
1979					1-WV-36.11	NA			Frog Hollow Branch Switch (1713).....W.Va.		0.0		
1980		4					286	286	**Martinsburg**, P. 15,063 (1714)—**S**.....		0.0		
1981							E400	20100	Team Track....................	Berkeley	0.0		
1982		12					E400A	20100A	Standard Lime & Stone Co.'s Team Track.		0.4		
1983		12					E401B	20101B	Standard Lime&StoneCo.'s StorageTrack.		0.5		
1985		207					E402C	20102C	Standard Lime & Stone Co.....		1.7		
1986							E403	20103	End of Branch.................		2.4		
									Cherry Run & Potomac Branch		Miller		
1987									C. R. & P. Branch Switch (1738)........W.Va.		0.0		
1988						R	302	302	Miller (1759)...................		0.0		
1989		268	17	267			301B	301B	Cherry Run Yard..............		0.0		
									Cherry Run Yard (W. Md. R'y)				
1990					1-WV-36.6		301	301	**Cherry Run** (1735)............		0.8		W.Md.—a.
1991									County Line..................		1.4		
1992		12					E307	20007	Halfway Siding...............		6.8		
1993		398					E309	20009	Cumbo Yard—Yard "A"—**S**...		10.8		
1994						W	292A	292A	West Cumbo Tower (1727)—Main Line Conn.		11.6		
1995		172					E312A	20012A	Cumbo Yard—Yard "C"—**W**...		11.6		
1996		261	65				E312B	20012B	Cumbo Yard—Yard "B".........	Berkeley	11.6		
1997									Beginning of Joint Property....		11.8		
1998				366			E312C	20012C	Cumbo Yard—Yard "E" (P. R. R)		12.0		
1999						BO			**Cumbo** P. 20................		12.6	F. M. Hooge.....G.Y.M	
2000			469		1-WV-36.4		E312	20012	Cumbo Yard—Yard "F" (P. R. R.)		13.0		
A2000				30			E312D	20012D	W. S. Frey....................		14.4		
2001	2			135			E315A	20015A	J. Allen Prather...............		14.6		
2002									End of Joint Property..........		14.7		P.R.R.—a,i.
2003							E315	20015	*Pennsylvania Junction* (Berkeley) on (P.R.R.).		14.9		
									Berkeley Springs Branch		Hancock		
2004					1-WV-36.7	HO	310B	310B	Berkeley Springs Branch Switch—Hancock (1742).........W.Va.		0.0		
2005		27		183			E104A	21004A	Penna. Glass Sand Co..........		3.5		
2006				5			E106B	21006B	A. C. Unger & Sons............		5.8		
									W. J. Hunter..................	Morgan			
2007		42					E106E	21006E	Interwoven Mills...............		6.0		
									Berkeley County Cold Storage Co.......				
A2007		5					E106F	21006F	Victor Products Corp..........		6.0		
2008		20				BG	E106	21006	**Berkeley Springs**, P. 1,141—**CP**...		6.1	F. B. Hansroth........F.	
A2008									End of Branch................		6.1		

215

EASTERN REGION
CUMBERLAND DIVISION

Index Reference	SIDING CAPACITY Cars 45 feet long				Valuation Section	Telegraph Call	STATION NUMBER		STATIONS AND SIDINGS with character references, population and additional index references	County	Miles from	AGENTS, Etc.	Foreign Lines and Track Connections
	Passing	Company	Joint	Private			For Engineering Dept. Use	For Reporting Car Movements					
									Magnolia Cut-Off		Orleans Road Tower		
2009					1-WV	AD	326B	326B	Orleans Road Tower (1756) Main Line Conn.W.Va.		0.0		
2010					—36.1		327	327	Rockwell Run (Water Station)—**W** (1758)... "		0.6		
2011		10					327A	327A	E. B. Backoff Siding... "		1.0		
2012							328	328	Doe Gully (1760)... "		1.8		
2013									Randolph Tunnel {East Portal... "	Morgan	2.8		
					1-WV-36.8				{West Portal... "		3.0		
2014		8					330A	330A	Dump Track... "		4.3		
2015									Main Line Connection... "		4.5		
2016									Stuart Tunnel {East Portal... "		5.0		
									{West Portal... "		5.6		
2017									West Va.-Md. State Line... W.Va.-Md.		6.3		
2018					1-M D				Graham Tunnel {East Portal... Md.	Alle-gany	6.5		
					—40.4				{West Portal... "		6.8		
2019									Md.-West Va. State Line... Md.-W.Va.		6.9		
2020					1-WV				Carothers Tunnel {East Portal... W.Va.	Morgan	8.5		
					—36.8				{West Portal... "		8.7		
2021									*County Line*... "		9.9		
2022		11					344	344	Little Cacapon (1772)... "		11.9		
2023						NO	315	345	Okonoko Tower Main Line Conn. (1773)... "		13.2		
									South Branch		Green Spring Point of Switch		
2024									South Branch Switch (1776)... W.Va.		0.0		
2025		22			1-WV-37.1	GI	351	351	**Green Spring**, P. 300 (1777)—**WY**		0.1	See Index 1777	
2026							E201	22001	Millen, P. 40... "		1.3		
2027							E203	22003	Donaldson, P. 30... "		3.3		
2028							E207	22007	Milleson... "		7.3		
2029		7		1			E208	22008	Springfield, P. 400... "		7.5		
2030	13						E209	22009	Grace, P. 100... "		9.3		
2031							E210	22010	Ritter, P. 20... "		10.0		
2032							E211	22011	Ridgedale, P. 36... "		10.9		
2033							E213	22013	Rocks... "		12.5		
2034							E214	22014	Vance... "	Hampshire	13.3		
2035		21					E215	22015	{Wapacomo... " }		15.2		
									{Fruit Growers Coop. Storage Assn... " }				
2036							E215A	22015A	Romney Junction (2043)... "		15.4		
2037				17			E216A	22016A	J. Natwick Co... "		15.9		
2038		45					E216C	22016C	Team Tracks... "		16.0		
2040		5					E216K	22016K	Company Siding... "		16.1		
2041		10					E216	22016	**Romney**, P. 2,059—**Y**... "		16.1	C. V. Smith	F
2042									End of Branch... "		16.3		
									Moorefield & Virginia Branch				
2043							E215A	22015A	Romney Junction (2036)... W.Va.		15.4		
2044							E216M	22016M	Valley... "		16.2		
2045		20					E217	22017	West Romney, P. 120... "		17.6		
2046							E220	22020	Hampshire Club... "		20.7		
2048		3					E223	22023	Pancake... "		23.7		
2049	★	19					E226	22026	Glebe... "		26.2		
2050							E227	22027	Camp Wickham... "		27.5		
2051							E228	22028	Trough Club... "		28.2		
2052						Operated by Telephone			*County Line*... "		28.6		
2053							E232	22032	Sycamore... "		32.2		
2054	★	14			1-WV-37.2		E233	22033	McNeill... "		33.3		
2056							E235	22035	Mapleton... "		35.2		
2057		18					E236	22036	Cunningham... "		36.6		
2058							E237	22037	Meadow... "		37.4		
2059	★	30					E239A	22039A	{Company Siding... " }		39.0		
									{Baker Feed & Supply Co... " }				
2060		11					E239B	22039B	Company Siding—**L**... "		39.0		
2061							E239	22039	**Moorefield**, P. 1,401... "		39.1	G. S. Patterson	F
2062		10					E239C	22039C	{Wilson Feed Service... " }		39.2		
									{Sunshine Feed Store... " }				
2063		8					E239D	22039D	{Hardy County Cooperative... " }	Hardy	39.2		
									{Baker Feed... " }				
2064				4			E239E	22039E	Moorefield Plywood Corp... "		39.4		
2065		13					E239F	22039F	{M. A. Bean... " }		39.4		
									{Moorefield Plywood Corp... " }				
2066				26			E240A	22040A	J. Natwick Co... "		39.6		
2067				76			E240B	22040B	Moorefield Tanning Co... "		39.9		
A2068				1			E241A	22041A	Rocco Feeds, Inc... "		40.7		
2069							E241	22041	Taylor... "		41.3		
2070							E243	22043	Brook Hill... "		43.5		
2071							E245	22045	Spring Brook... "		45.1		
2072		8					E247	22047	Durgon, P. 25... "		46.8		
2073							E249	22049	Welton... "		48.7		
2074									*County Line*... "		50.3		

★ These sidings also used as passing sidings.

EASTERN REGION
CUMBERLAND DIVISION

Index Reference	SIDING CAPACITY Cars 45 feet long				Valuation Section	Telegraph Call	STATION NUMBER		STATIONS AND SIDINGS with character references, population and additional index references	County	Miles from	AGENTS, Etc.	Foreign Lines and Track Connections
	Passing	Company	Joint	Private			For Engineering Dept. Use	For Reporting Car Movements					
									Moorefield & Virginia Branch—Con.		Green Spring Point of Switch		
									Potomac Feed & Supply Co..........W.Va.				
									Atlantic Refining Co.................. "				
2075		27			1-WV-37.2		E252A	22052A	Grant County Farm Service........... "	Grant	51.7		
									Standard Oil Co...................... "				
									Ours Feed Service.................... "				
									Stock Pens............................ "				
2076		8		10			E252B	22052B	Shawnee Milling Co.................. "		51.7		
									Central Tie & Lumber Co............. "				
2077		16					E252C	22052C	Station Track........................ "		51.8		
									Mathias Grocery Co.................. "				
2078							E252	22052	**Petersburg**, P. 1,751—**Y**......... "		51.9	J. L. Boor.........F.	
2079									End of Branch........................ "		52.0		
2080				20			E252E	22052E	Md. and W. Va. Lumber Co......... "		52.0		
									American Oil Co..................... "				
					1-WV-35.9				**Patterson Creek & Potomac Branch**	Mineral	Patterson Creek Tower		
2081						FN			Patterson Creek Tower (1788)-Main Line Connection..............W.Va.		0.0		
2082									Knobley Tunnel {East Portal / West Portal}		4.6 / 5.4		
2083					1-MD-40.5				West Va.-Md. State Line........W.Va.-Md.		5.5		
2084						CO	1009	1009	McKenzie (1883) Main Line Connection......Md	Allegany	6.3		W.Md.—b,u.

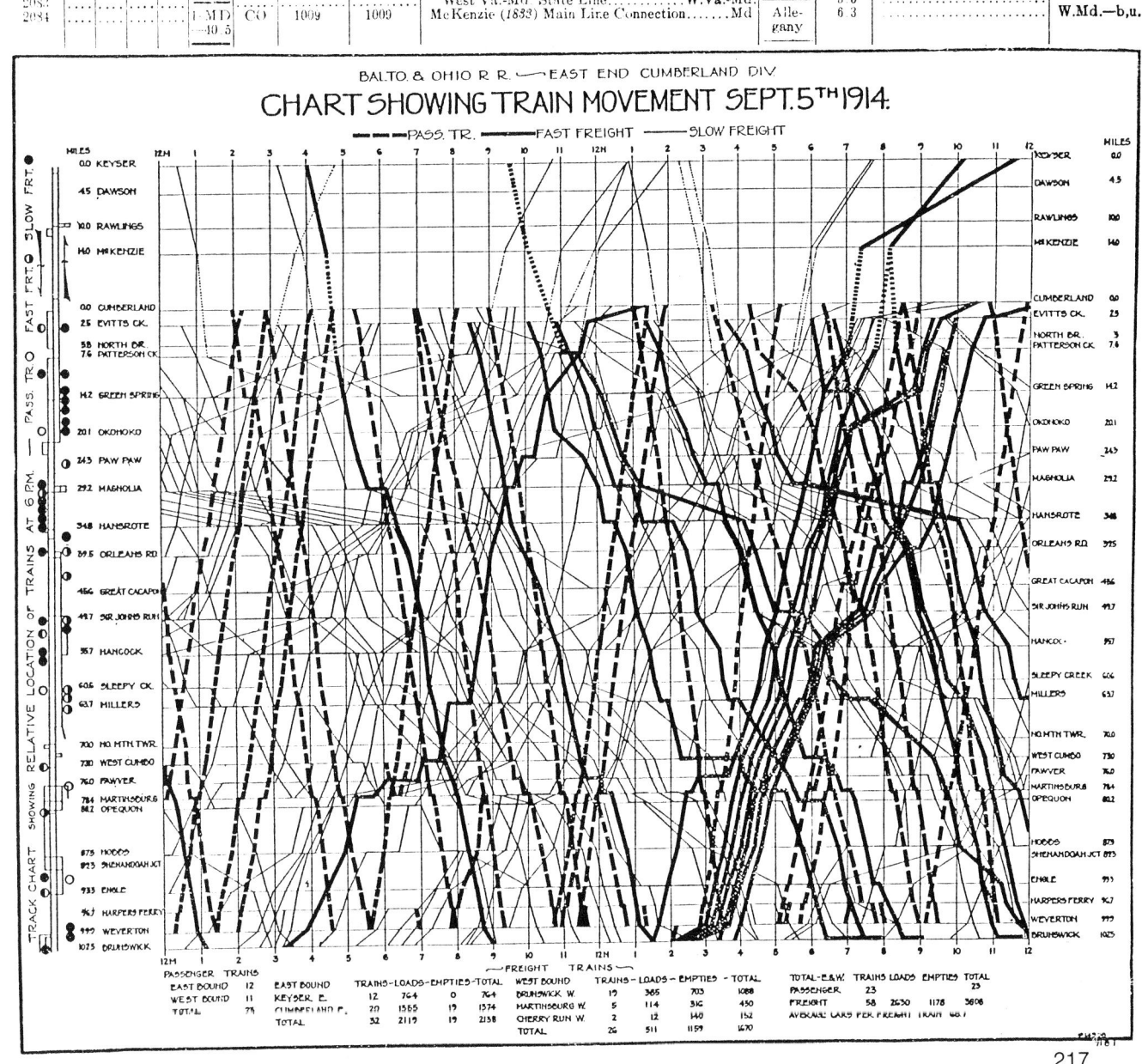

Chapter 13

Reflections

The authors have chosen to create a final "wrap-up" chapter to deal, at least in part, with various issues and hope the reader will be both enlightened and, in some cases, amused.

First of all, we should explain just what is meant by "co-authored." Simply put, Hollis did almost all of the research and Roberts almost all of the writing. Roberts is responsible for all conclusions as well as the theme of the work.

There was a third person involved ... Herbert H. Harwood, Jr., edited *East End* and did so with the professionalism to be expected from such a renowned railroad historian and skillful writer.

Any writer who edits himself has a fool for an editor and the co-authors submitted to this necessary discipline. Harwood's criticisms were many and bouquets few, precisely what is required, and the reader may rest comfortable with the knowledge that he played a major role in the production of *East End*.

American tradition in this regard is quite clear and should be noted. All praise and approbation should accrue to the authors ... all blame to the editor. There are many cases in recorded history when tar was boiled, feathers plucked and rails split ... invariably the subject of such honorable attention is the editor, never the writer, and readers with discomfort should comport themselves accordingly. That is the American Way.

Many other individuals played important, even vital, roles in this work and they will be honored later in this chapter.

All three of the principal players were united on one matter of policy ... footnotes should be avoided and bibliography highly detailed. If a reader wishes to expand or reinterpret the work, then let him go to the original sources, dig it out for himself and come to his own conclusions in the full context of the available material ... in short, do his own homework.

And in this connection an important point must be made quite clear. We are *all* reporters and observers of a series of events *at which we were not present* and about which we have *no knowledge*. We are victims of our sources and our conclusions are consequently flawed.

A few matters of style should be noted. We have chosen to use generic expression ... thus Harpers Ferry, not Harper's Ferry. And we have spelled words appropriate to the time frame being treated ... thus sometimes "Pittsburg" and other times "Pittsburgh."

And now commentary by chapter ...

CHAPTER ONE: As B&O forefathers considered the myriad routes to Cumberland, avoidance of conflict with the C&O Canal was a prime factor in their deliberations. The battle for space along the Potomac between Point of Rocks and the Ferry had consumed the legal energies of both companies as so ably reported in Harwood's *Impossible Challenge*, resulting in delay and expense so that neither side wished for another "War of the Roses."

Thus a good case could be made that B&O made its final selection of route as a choice between peace and war ... speedy completion was essential and B&O could not afford another war. Yet we still feel the chosen path was a good one in any event.

Incidentally, the floods that plagued B&O also savaged the canal ... in the end, the 1924 unpleasantness ruined the canal beyond repair.

As to coal, the reader may be surprised to learn that B&O was not all that eager to handle this traffic in the 1840s and there was vigorous debate for a number of years on the subject. B&O did not warm to the idea of committing precious dollars to buy specialized equipment, more power, heavier rail, extensive branch lines, stronger bridges and additional track to service a mineral that could not command high rates and still be competitive in the marketplace. So B&O was initially a reluctant virgin in hauling what would turn out to be the backbone of B&O revenues.

And speaking of virgins, we must report that the lady on page 18 was included to meet a supposed demand on the part of many readers for sex and violence. Actually, Julian Barnard sent this photo and caption to Roberts years ago in private correspondence and we wish to honor his creativity. For violence, reread the Civil War chapter.

CHAPTER TWO: B&O had a terrible time getting out of Harpers Ferry and your authors and editor wish to report that we shared the same frustrations a century and a half later.

The Winchester and Potomac *et al* has been lightly treated and this was a conscious decision, although not made without some debate. A whole book could be devoted to this subject if the job were to be done properly and the W&P was never really a part of the East End. By the way, "Rock Runner" is a generic CSX expression and the Millville train is one of several. And, on page 40, our editor insists that we point out that any station, no matter how small, served by more than one railroad is a "union" station.

CHAPTER THREE: There was a "little Saluda" grade on the Bakerton Branch . . . the climb ranged from 4.73 to 4.80 percent for almost a half mile.

CHAPTER FOUR: Why "Martinsburg" and not "Stephensburg"? It seems that a Col. Thomas Martin was a good friend of Adam Stephen and the town was named in his honor. There is some belief that Stephen City on the W&P was so named for the same reason in reverse.

The expression "Great Coal Push" really evolved from the history of the CVRR . . . that poor road almost collapsed under the volume.

For mystery on the East End, one will have his fill by studying the Pillar Bridge. It was incongruous and unique. This bridge was definitely built when the B&O first reached Martinsburg . . . the town's *Weekly Gazette* of 26 May 1842 dutifully reported its presence when the first B&O train arrived.

The design itself is without known precedent in American railroad bridge construction and is fundamentally stupid . . . the width-span is so great that one wonders where the builders found timber thick enough to carry the weight. And why round stone pillars with capitals? Where did they come from and how did they get there? Why not a simple trestle in keeping with all other early bridge construction on the East End? Sad to say, we have only questions . . . no answers.

CHAPTER FIVE: With the abundance of fruit along the East End, it would be reasonable to assume that Cherry Run was named accordingly. Apparently not so . . . a very early property owner was a John Cherry.

In the early years, it was the Central States Despatch . . . the "e" became an "i" in this century.

CHAPTER SIX: The sand in the Berkeley Springs area is so fine that it played a role in a B&O yarn reported in the company magazine. In the days when trainmen lived in their cabooses between runs, a young brakeman decided to kiss up to his conductor by preparing a special gravy for the evening meal and used "flour" from a jar on the shelf. The meat dish was tasty but a bit gritty . . . the jar, it seems, contained sand. This tidbit is included at the insistence of Hollis . . . Roberts found it a little hard to chew, let alone swallow.

CHAPTER SEVEN: Why *Kessler* Bridge? Apparently there was a tiny town in this vicinity, hence the name.

When passenger trains began to use the Magnolia Cutoff with regularity, the problem of West Virginia liquor laws was briefly avoided . . . the bar would be open between Magnolia and Kessler's because the train was in Mother Maryland for about a mile. Blessed, brief relief.

CHAPTER EIGHT: After the devastating 1936 flood, B&O engineers were ordered to prepare a plan to raise mainline tracks above the high water mark from Tuscarora (east of Rocks) to Patterson Creek, exclusive of the section from Sir Johns Run to Okonoko because the cutoff could be used for all traffic in an emergency. The price tag was over $15 million, B&O was entering still another financial crisis and the plan was shelved.

CHAPTER NINE: The city of Cumberland went by many names in early history, but acquired its final one from the British Duke of Cumberland.

It is important to note, in regard to the Queen City Hotel, that B&O offered to donate the building to any governmental entity . . . none stepped forward to accept title.

CHAPTER TEN: Napoleon is supposed to have said that the moral is to the physical as three is to one. After three years of bloody convulsion, the Rebels pinned their hopes on the 1864 Federal presidential election and hoped the Northern "Peace Party" would prevail . . . even Lincoln thought he would lose. To us, the most significant thing about that election was not Lincoln's victory . . . it was that the long suffering and badly led line troops in the Union Army of the Potomac voted solidly for him. Soldiers have an absolute right to demand integrity in their highest command and these blueclad infantrymen recognized that they had just that in their Commander-in-Chief.

As to Cameron, historians generally agree that his appointment was the result of a convention deal made without Lincoln's knowledge.

CHAPTER TWELVE: Automatic signaling on the East End was generally in service during the teens of this century. In 1992, active towers total six . . . Martinsburg, Cumbo, Cherry Run, Hancock, Mexico and Viaduct Junction.

The 17th day of February 1912 was an exciting one on the East End. Train 46 struck a buggy at Knoxville (near Brunswick); a broken rail derailed a train at Magnolia with much track damage; an overheated stove in Hedgesville Tower (W) started a fire which destroyed the tower and telegraph wires; a journal burned off on the lowgrade line and a derailment ensued; another vehicle was struck at Knoxville.

IN GRATITUDE: A work of this magnitude is a major undertaking and would have been impossible without the selfless help of many, many individuals. Photo credits and bibliography notes tell only part of the story. As the book was co-authored, each will express their thanks in order.

Roberts bows in homage to Editor Herb Harwood; Gary Schlerf and Andy Holzopfel of B&OHS; Anne Calhoun and Dennis Fulton of the B&O Museum; Harry C. Eck, retired B&O officer; Michael Welsh, devoted B&O historian; Brian Paulus, a comer in railroad history; art director Warren Somerville; typographer Frances Weber; Jan Maxwell and Suzanne Rhodes of Walsworth Publishing as well as those scores of craftsmen we will probably never meet, but without whom no book is possible; those victims of our fragile memory; Jeff Hollis, whose vigor and good humor was always a tonic.

Hollis wishes to extend thanks to . . . my wife Bessie and kids, Jeff, Amanda, Matthew and Sarah for giving me up for lost for nearly a year to this project. Look out, I'm back; my parents Charles and Eleanor Hollis, and grandfather Clarence Beard for taking me to the station every time this kid whined to see the trains; Paul Westhaeffer for inspiring me early in life to want to compile a railroad history, and Charles Roberts for giving me that chance; Jeff Madden and Jim Eells for their scrounging of pictures at unreasonable hours and at the last minutes to supply a needed item; Raymond Litten for use of pictures and for personal recollections which livened up Cherry Run; Wesley Welsh and his family and Mrs. Elwood Hamstead for picture availability and personal recollections of the way it was in Kearneysville; Virginia Walker for calling every time she found a shred of information for consideration; Mr. Elmer Gletner for information offered and pictures considered; Mr. William Rodgers for personal recounts of his experiences in NA Tower as well as photos; the crew at the Martinsburg Model Railroad Club for encouragement, and for guidance to whomever had something of interest that I should know about.

MUSING: In his declining years at age sixty-two, Roberts wishes to present a thought on the human condition that has always puzzled him. Why is it that those men and women who always do the dirtiest, hardest and most dangerous jobs in society, whether rider, brakeman, soldier, trackman, garbageman or cop, always get the lowest pay? It should be the other way around.

BIBLIOGRAPHY

BOOKS

William E. Bain, *B&O in the Civil War*, Sage Books, Denver CO 1966.

Julian and Eileen Wolford Barnard, *Research Workbook: Cars of the B&ORR*, by authors, Shelby OH 1979.

Howard N. Barr, Sr./William A. Barringer, *(B&O) Q*, Barnard, Roberts & Co., Baltimore MD 1978.

Ele Bowen, *Rambles in the Path of the Steam Horse*, Bromwell and Smith, Baltimore MD 1854.

Robert V. Bruce, *1877: The Year of Violence*, Bobbs, New York NY 1959.

George H. Burgess and Miles C. Kennedy, *Centennial History of The Pennsylvania Railroad*, by the railroad, Philadelphia PA 1949.

William D. Edson, *B&O All-Time Roster Steam Locomotives*, by author, Potomac MD 1992.

Virginia Geiger, *Maryland Our Maryland*, (Maryland at the Crossroads), John Hankey, University Press of America 1987.

David Gilbert, *Where Industry Failed*, Pictorial Histories Publishing Co., Charleston WV 1984.

G. P. Grimsley, *West Virginia Geological Survey County Reports*, (Berkeley, Jefferson and Morgan Counties), Wheeling News Litho, Wheeling WV 1916.

Herbert H. Harwood, Jr., *Impossible Challenge*, Barnard, Roberts & Co., Baltimore, MD 1979.

Edward Hungerford, *The Story of the B&O Railroad*, (2 vols.), G.P. Putnam, New York NY 1928.

A. J. Johnston II, *Virginia Railroads in the Civil War*, University North Carolina Press, Chapel Hill NC 1961.

V. C. Jones, *Ranger Mosby*, University North Carolina Press, Chapel Hill NC 1944.

B. F. G. Kline, Jr., *Tall Pines and Winding Rivers*, by author, Lancaster PA 1976.

Diane Newell, *Queen City Hotel and Station*, Preservation Press, Washington DC 1975.

Milton Reizenstein, *Economic History of B&ORR 1827-1853*, Johns Hopkins Press, Baltimore MD 1897.

Charles S. Roberts, *West End*, Barnard, Roberts & Co., Baltimore MD 1991.

Charles S. Roberts, *B&O Great Photos (Series)*, Book 1 (H. N. Barr, Sr.) 1977; Book 2 (H. H. Harwood, Jr.) 1977; Book 3 (J. C. Kelly) 1977; Book 4 (E. L. Thompson) 1977; Book 5 (Bob Lorenz) 1979, Barnard, Roberts & Co., Baltimore, MD

Lawrence W. Sagle, *B&O Power*, Staufer, Medina OH 1964.

William Prescott Smith, *History and Description of the B&O RR*, John Murphy and Co., Baltimore MD 1853.

William Prescott Smith, *Great Railway Celebrations of 1857*, D. Appleton and Co., New York 1858.

John F. Stover, *History of the B&O RR*, Purdue University Press, West Lafayette IN 1987.

E. F. Striplin, *The N&W: A History*, N&W Railway Co., Roanoke, VA 1981.

Festus P. Summers, *The B&ORR: A Study in the Civil War*, dissertation, Morgantown WV 1933.

Kevin H. Supel, *Rebel: the Life and Times of John Singleton Mosby*, St. Martins Press, New York NY 1983.

A. W. Thompson, *The Magnolia Cutoff Improvement on the B&ORR*, The Engineers Society of Western Pennsylvania, Proceedings of, presented at Pittsburgh PA 24 Nov 1914.

George E. Turner, *Victory Rode the Rails*, Bobbs-Merrill, New York NY 1953.

Thomas Weber, *The Northern Railroads in the Civil War*, King's Crown Press, (Columbia University) New York NY 1952.

Paul J. Westhaeffer, *History of the Cumberland Valley Railroad*, National Railway Historical Society, Washington DC Chapter 1979.

(unknown), *Photographic Views of the B&ORR and its Branches from the Lakes to the Sea*, first series, Cushings & Bailey/Hagadorn Bros., Baltimore, MD 1872.

PERIODICALS

Baltimore and Ohio (Employees) Magazine, various issues, October 1912 to February 1962, B&ORR, Baltimore MD.

B&O Railroader, various issues, January/February 1972 to March 1978, Neilson Wood, Jr., Levittown PA.

Engine 5304, Run Extra, various issues, January 1979 to September 1982, B&ORR Historical Society, Baltimore MD.

Martinsburg Gazette, 26 May 1842 . . . *Herald* 17 Feb 1912 . . . *Journal* 10 Mar 1949, 2 Jan 1957, 2 Mar 1988, 5 May 1992 . . . *News* 22 Jan 1943 (article by Fred Voegele).

Maryland Magazine, Winter 1991.

Nat'l Model RR Ass'n, Bulletin April 1979.

Nat'l Railway Historical Society, Bulletin Vol. 54 #6 1989 (article by Bert Pennypacker).

Passenger Train Journal, Feb 1986.

Railway Age, 11 Jun 1927 . . . *Railway Age Gazette*, 20 Jun 1913, 17 Oct 1923, 19 Dec 1913 . . . *Railway Review*, 18 Oct 1919.

Sentinel, various issues, December 1983 to May/June 1992, B&OHS.

B&ORR PUBLICATIONS AND RECORDS

Annual Reports: 1836 to 1977.

B&O Coals: mid-1940s.

Carroll Bateman, *The B&O Railroad*, by the railroad 1951.

CSX News, Jun/Jul 1989.

Dispatchers Record of Movement of Trains: East End Cumberland Division 30 Jan 1952, 9 Feb 1956, 10 Jul 1992.

Employee Timetables Cumberland Division, thirty-six issues on various dates from 23 Apr 1855 through 1987.

Form 6 (Official List), 1 Sep 1889, twenty-three issues from 1904 to 1954.

General Orders Cumberland Division, various dates from 12 Aug 1933 to 1 Dec 1961.

Improvements, Folders A, 3-5, 7, 10-12 May 1915; Magnolia Cutoff Mar 1916.

Maps, c. 1870 Martinsburg.

Summary of Equipment, all issues 1 Jul 1912 to 1 Jan 1960.

Track Charts Cumberland Division East End, c. 1930, 1948, 1964.

A. W. Thompson, *Cherry Run and Potomac Valley*, by the railroad 1918.

Various correspondence files, reports and memos.

MISCELLANEOUS

Berkeley County Court House, various deed and corporation records; Berkeley County Historical Society, various files and memos; *Green Ridge Railroad of Maryland*, undated, by Bob Zimmerman and Mason Cooper; U.S. Army Topographic Command Maps 1969; U.S. Geological Survey Maps 1959; West Virginia Geological Survey Maps, various issues; Authors' interviews and analytical notes.

INDEX

Albany 11
Amtrak 47, 105, 158
Antietam 11, 79
Apples 17, 18
Arsenal (Harpers Ferry) 12, 20, 24, 27-29, 42, 43, 177
Articles of Confederation 10

Back Creek 79
Baird 16, 112
Bath 100
Baltimore 9, 13, 14, 16, 17, 72, 93
Baker, N. P. (Hospital) 41, 49
Bakerton Br 44, 67, 219
Baldwin E. F. 40
Berkeley 54, 73, 74
Berkeley Hotel 60-62, 66
Berkeley Springs et al 18, 94, 96-100, 198, 210
Berkeley Springs & Potomac RR 100
Big Pool 86, 90
Blairton 42
Blockhouses 182, 183
Blockhouse Hill 79
Bollman, Wendel (Bridges) 22-29, 33, 43, 148
Boonsboro 10, 11
Brick House Curve 6
Brossius 96
Brown, John 180
Brown, George 8
Brown, Revell 67
Brunswick 17, 152, 172
Bulleye Bridge 42, 53
Byrnes Isl 43

Cameron, Simon 178, 179, 220
Capitol Limited 63, 202, 204
Carothers Tunnel 109, 131, 202
Carroll, Charles of Carrollton 100
Central States Dispatch (CSD) 73, 74, 79, 90
Charlestown 37
Cherry Run 13, 16, 73, 78-93, 197
Cherry Run & Potomac Valley RR 16, 17, 54, 74, 80
Chesapeake & Ohio Canal 10-12, 19, 22, 24, 43, 93, 101, 105, 139, 148, 151, 153, 179, 218
Chesapeake Western 35
Chessie System 15
Chicago 93, 209
Cincinnati 16
Civil War 6, 9, 20, 23, 35, 41, 55, 79, 146, 175-183
Clark, E.W. & Co 42
Coal 14, 15, 218
Coal Pen Hill 82, 83
Concrete Wall 109, 126-130, 200, 201
Conrail 47
CSX 47
Cumberland 6, 9-17, 139, 151-174, 205, 206, 208, 209, 211

Cumberland Valley RR 16, 38, 40, 46, 83-87
Cumbo 16, 53-79, 81, 90, 196

Deep South Route 11, 35, 36, 46
Deshler 16
Doe Gully 6, 13, 92-94, 105, 109, 115-117
Dry Run Creek 6, 65
Duffields 42, 45

Elk Run 11, 41, 45
Employee Timetables 184-192
Engle 16, 17, 42, 44, 45, 67
Erie Canal 10, 11
Erie RR 176, 178
Evitts Creek 16, 17, 138, 139, 150, 174

Fawver 16, 59
Fifteen Mile Creek 11
Fink, Albert (Bridges) 22, 25
Flagg's Crossing 42, 52
Form 6 213-217
Frederick 9, 12
French & Indian War 10
Frog Hollow Branch 57-62, 66

Garrett, John W. 35, 40, 46, 65, 72, 155, 177, 178
Georgetown 10
Georges Creek Valley 153
Gould, George 73, 80
Grafton 14, 209
Graham Tunnel 109, 121-125
Grant, U. S. 179
Grasshopper Hollow 6, 101
Graveyard Curve 53
Great Cacapon 16, 94, 104
Great Valley Line 46
Green Ridge RR 108
Green Spring et al 14, 16, 32, 138-144, 203

Hagerstown 10-12, 35, 42, 46, 73, 78, 79, 82, 89, 90
Halltown 12, 19
Hancock 11, 13, 16-18, 92-94, 96-99, 197, 210
Hansrote 16, 92, 93, 105, 106, 109, 112, 114, 119
Harpers Ferry 6, 8, 9, 11-14, 16, 17, 19-40, 42, 177, 181, 193, 194
Hampshire Sou RR 145
Harrisburg 14, 90, 99, 178, 179
Harrisonburg 35, 40
Hedgesville 16, 73, 77, 220
Heskett, T. J. 155
Hillside Cut 113, 114
Hobbs 16, 17, 42, 47, 52, 62
Hopkins, Barbara Jean (introduction) 105

Illinois 10
Indiana 10
Island Park 43

Jackson, T. J. (Stonewall) 53, 56, 57, 60, 67, 177-179, 181
Jefferson, Thomas 19

Kearneysville 18, 42, 45, 48, 118, 182
Kees, D. N. 18
Kelly Island 42
Kesslers et al 114, 123-125, 128, 200, 201, 219
Keyser 18, 152, 209
Kimball, Fred. 46
Koppers Co (Industries) 143
Kroeson 60, 62, 64

Latrobe, B. F. 22
Lee, Robert E. 35, 175-181
Lexington 35, 36
Lincoln, Abraham 175-179, 220
Little Cacapon 94, 108
Little Catoctin Crk 11
Locust Pt 16
Long Girls Curve 6
Lovers' Leap 101

Magnolia et al 6, 16, 48, 92, 99, 104, 106, 109-137, 217
Martinsburg 9, 11-14, 16-18, 41, 42, 45-47, 52, 53-77, 178, 181, 194, 195, 209, 210, 219
Maryland 10
Maryland Hgts 24, 27, 32, 43
McAdams, John 10
McKenzie 17, 147
Meadow Branch Coalfields 92
Meads Bridge 53
Mexico (Farm) 6, 138, 139, 150, 204
Middletown Valley 11
Miller 80, 82, 84, 88, 90, 210
Miller, Wm S 17
Millville 37
Moorefield 138, 145
Moorefield & Virginia RR 145
Morgan, House of 99
Mosby, John 180, 182
Mt. Dallas 99
Murray's Cut 105, 119

Narrows 151
Nat'l Road 10-12, 15, 94, 154
Nemacolin Indian Path 10
New Orleans 35
New York 10, 11
New York Central lines 99, 176, 178
Nine Mile Grade 9, 42, 47, 49, 52, 58
Norfolk & Western Rlwy 16, 35, 40, 42, 46, 47
Norfolk Southern 46, 47
North Branch 16, 17, 138, 139, 148, 149

North Mtn 9, 11-13, 16-18, 54, 55, 78, 79, 81, 83, 196
Northern Central Rlwy 176, 178, 179

Ohio 10
Ohio River 8, 12, 14, 79
Okonoko 16-18, 92, 93, 108, 132, 133, 209
Old Bird Shit Hollow 6
Old House Curve 6
Oldtown 11, 139
Opequon 16, 41, 42, 47, 52
Orleans road 16, 17, 92, 93, 104, 105, 109, 210

Parkersburg 14
Patterson Creek et al 16, 17, 138, 139, 146-148, 204, 209
Pattenall, Frank 16
Paw Paw 6, 9, 13, 16, 18, 92-94, 107, 109, 131, 133, 202
Peachers Mill 41, 43
Pear Orchard Curve 6
Pennsylvania 10, 14, 79
PRR 14, 38, 40, 46, 72, 73, 80, 90, 99, 176, 178
Pennsylvania Turnpike 99
Petersburg 138, 145
Philadelphia 10, 14, 79, 90, 178
Phila & Columbia RR 79
PW&BRR 176, 178
Piedmont 17, 93, 209
Pillar Bridge 55-58, 219
Pittsburg(h) 10, 11, 14, 79, 99
Pleasant Valley 11
Point of Rocks 16, 22, 133
Port Perry 99
Potomac & Allegheny RR 99
Potomac Canal 10
Potomac RR 111
Potomac River 8, 9, 11, 12, 20, 21, 78, 79
Potomac Tunnel 34, 41, 43

Queen City Hotel 155-159, 207, 211, 219
Queen Street Crossing 65

Rail Mill 152, 160
Randolph Tunnel 105, 109, 117-119, 133, 199

Rattling Bridge 6, 42
Reading RR 14, 73, 90
Red Rock 6
Reedson 45
Revere House Hotel 154
Retarders 173
Revolution 10
River Wall 132
Roanoke 35, 42
Rockwell Run 109, 112-114, 199
Romney 18, 138, 140, 145
Round Top 93, 94, 101
Rumsey, James 95, 102

St. Louis 93, 209
Savery, T. E. 27
Schenectady 11
Scott, Thomas A. 46, 178, 179
Sheridan, P. 179
Sherman, Wm 176
Shenandoah et al 6, 9, 16, 17, 19, 33, 35-37, 42, 46
Shippensburg 90
Shoop 42
Sinclair, Sir John 102
Sir Johns Run 16, 17, 83, 93, 100, 102-104, 211
Skeetersville 6
Sleepy Crk 6, 94-96, 210
South Branch et al 138, 140, 145, 203, 210
South Mtn 11
South Penna RR 99
Southern Rlwy 35
Springfield 148
Springhouse Curve 6
Stanton, Edwin A. 179
Staunton 35, 40, 178
Stevens, John 11
Stevens, Thaddeus 79
Stephens, Adam 56, 57, 219
Stephens City 39, 219
Stephens, Peter 20
Stockton & Darlington 13
Strasburg 35, 39
Strike 1877 72
Stuart, F. L. 99, 110, 133
Stuart Tunnel 109, 119, 120
Sycamore 146

"Tapeworm" 79
Tennessee 35
Tie Plant 141-144
Tonnage Ratings 212
Town Hill/Crk 11, 94, 108
Train Robbery 55, 56, 220
Tulisses Crk 11
Turbo Train 63, 195
Turkey Foot Curve 6
Tuscarora Crk 11, 41, 55, 71

U.S. Silica 100, 198

Valley RR 35, 46
Vanclevesville 49
Vandalia 10
Viaduct Jct 174, 208
Virginia 9-13, 175, 176
Virginia Lane/Ave 16, 163

Wager Family 20, 22
Warm Spring Run 94, 100
Washington DC 10, 16, 93
Washington, George 20, 100, 102
Washington Jct 16, 133
Wernwag, Lewis 22
West End 6, 14, 16, 138
West Virginia 176
WVC&PRR 73, 80
Western Maryland Rlwy 16, 73, 78-80, 83-87, 89, 90, 92, 109, 112, 138, 149
Wet Rock 6
Weverton 11, 17
Wheeling 10-12, 14-16, 93, 99
White, R. B. 107
Willard, Daniel 94, 99, 110, 162
Wilsons 77
Williamsport 12
Winchester & Potomac RR 9, 11, 12, 17, 19, 21, 22, 27-29, 32, 35-40, 46, 178
Winchester & Strasburg RR 35
Wreck 1 Jan 1957 91
Wreck 12 Feb 1980 105

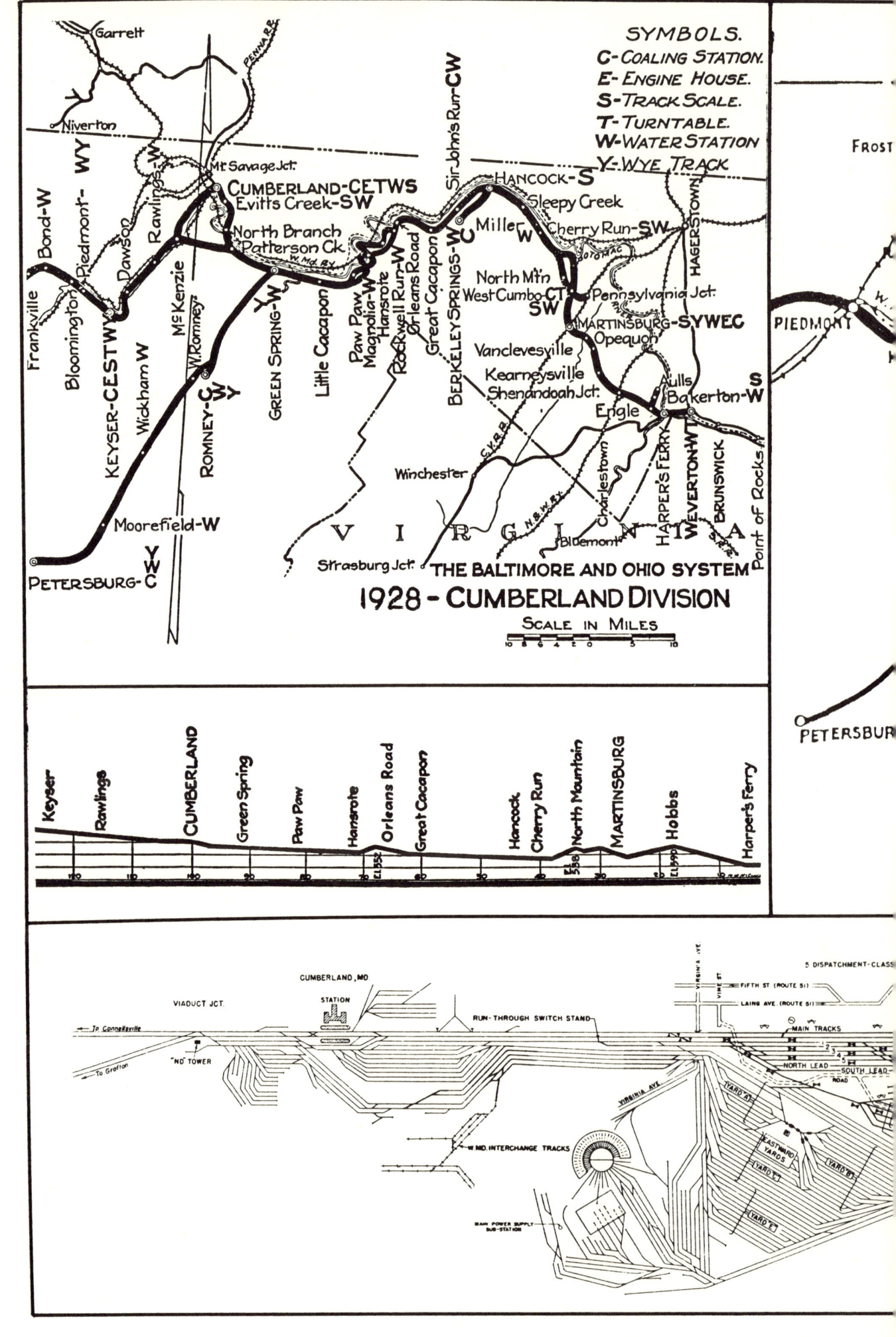